Interculturality and the English Language Classroom

Mabel Victoria · Chittima Sangiamchit
Editors

Interculturality and the English Language Classroom

Editors
Mabel Victoria
The Business School
Edinburgh Napier University
Edinburgh, UK

Chittima Sangiamchit
Department of English
University of the Thai Chamber of
Commerce
Bangkok, Thailand

ISBN 978-3-030-76759-4   ISBN 978-3-030-76757-0   (eBook)
https://doi.org/10.1007/978-3-030-76757-0

This Palgrave Macmillan imprint is published by the registered company Springer Nature Switzerland AG
The registered company address is: Gewerbestrasse 11, 6330 Cham, Switzerland

Preface

We are both teachers and researchers of English as a foreign language. In the last few years, we have become aware of our students' growing needs to be able to communicate with people from different linguistic and cultural backgrounds. Increased mobility and high interconnectivity have made communication across cultures an important part of their daily lives. Thus, we felt that it is no longer viable to teach English without, at the same time, equipping the learners with the knowledge and skills that will help them navigate intercultural encounters effectively. This challenge has inspired us to put this volume together.

In this collection, we have collected enthusiastic voices and experiences of English language teachers and researchers from around the world. The contributions in this volume have been written *for* English language teachers *by* English language teachers and practitioners from Brazil, Czech Republic, Iran, Denmark, Germany, Norway, Poland, Tunisia, Thailand, the United States and the United Kingdom. The chapters reflect a wide diversity of perspectives from local contexts with global relevance and applicability. The readers will be able to compare their own local contexts and adapt/adopt what other practitioners have reported in their chapters.

We envisage the collection to be useful in teacher training/education programmes. The strong pedagogical component is reflected in the 'Engagement Priorities' and 'Recommended Texts' of the core chapters. We hope that English teachers and practitioners will find ideas in this volume that will challenge and inspire them to incorporate interculturality in their classrooms and in their research.

Edinburgh, UK   Mabel Victoria
Bangkok, Thailand   Chittima Sangiamchit

Acknowledgements

Our sincerest thanks to the people who have been part of this book.

We are very grateful to Prof. Fiona Copland and Dr. Sue Garton for drawing our attention to the possibility of publishing a collection on interculturality in ELT. We are very thankful for their valuable feedback in the initial stages of this collection.

We would also like to thank Ananda Kumar Mariappan for coordinating the production of this volume. His prompt responses to all our queries and active monitoring of each step of the publication process are much appreciated. Our gratitude also goes to Cathy Scott, our Commissioning Editor, for her guidance and support.

Our heartfelt thanks go to the contributors of this volume. Despite the gut-wrenching challenges and real fears brought on by the covid-19 pandemic during the writing, re-writing and review process, they never wavered in their commitment to forge ahead. Besides working on their own chapters, the contributors also participated in the (blind) peer-review system, giving each other helpful feedback. This means that every chapter in this collection has been reviewed at least two times by different authors. Our appreciation also goes to Palgrave Macmillan's reviewers whose valuable input enabled us to make improvements to the collection.

Finally, we would like to thank our families for their understanding, patience and support throughout the project. To you, we dedicate this work.

Mabel Victoria
Chittima Sangiamchit

Contents

Notes on Contributors

Nadia Abid is an Assistant Professor at the English department of the Faculty of Letters and Human Sciences of Sfax, Tunisia. She received a Ph.D. in Applied Linguistics from the University of Lorraine in France and the University of Sfax, Tunisia. She teaches TEFL, TEYL, ESP, theories of learning and teaching pedagogy. She is currently doing research on the analysis of the intercultural and global dimensions of EFL textbooks, and the development of intercultural communicative competence in virtual exchanges and study abroad programmes with focus on issues such as attitudes and identity construction in those contexts.

Minoo Alemi is Associate Professor of Applied Linguistics at Islamic Azad University, West Tehran Branch, and a research associate at Sharif University of Technology, Iran. She has published papers in journals such as *Journal of Intercultural Communication Research, The Asia-Pacific Education Researcher, Language and Intercultural Communication, International Journal of Science and Engineering Ethics, TESL-EJ, TESL Canada Journal, International Journal of Social Robotics* and *Language Learning and Technology*, and two book chapters in *Lessons from Good Language Teachers* (Cambridge University Press, 2020). She is also the co-editor (with Zia Tajeddin) of *Pragmatics Pedagogy in English as an International Language* (Routledge, 2020).

Anna Czura is an Assistant Professor at the Department of Second Language Learning and Teaching at the University of Wroclaw, Poland and a Marie Curie (MSCA-IF) post-doctoral researcher at the Autonomous University of Barcelona. In her research, she focuses mainly on learning mobility (face-to-face and virtual), European language policy, intercultural competence, teacher training, language assessment, learner autonomy and CLIL. In the years 2012–2018, she has been a team member of two projects funded by the European Centre for Modern Languages in Graz: 'PluriMobil: Plurilingual and intercultural learning through mobility' and 'A Quality Assurance Matrix for CEFR Use'. She is the Polish Ministry of Education expert responsible for certifying published teaching materials for school usage.

Christian Kramer holds a master's degree in language sciences and currently works as a Lecturer/Research Assistant in the TEFL/English Didactics department of the Institute of English and American Studies at the University of Oldenburg, Germany. In this capacity, he co-operates with in-service EFL teachers and supervises student internships at schools as well as empirical projects dealing with classroom research. His research focus includes plurilingualism in EFL contexts, classroom research and teacher training. His (research) interests extend to gender/queer/diversity teacher education. He is currently working on his Ph.D. project on strategic plurilingual interactional language use in advanced EFL speakers.

Helen Margaret Murray works at the Institute for Teacher Training at the Norwegian University of Science and Technology in Trondheim (NTNU), Norway. She works in the English Section and is also the leader of the interdisciplinary research group Indigenous Topics in Education. Her research interests include curriculum analysis and representations of indigenous peoples in textbooks. She is also engaged in creating teaching materials about indigenous peoples and in holding courses for teachers. Before starting work at NTNU, Helen worked for seventeen years as a teacher at lower and upper secondary schools in Norway.

Joanna Pfingsthorn is a researcher at the Department of English Language Education at the University of Bremen. She holds a Ph.D. in TEFL from the University of Oldenburg and is a trained cognitive scientist (M.Sc. from the University of Amsterdam) and psychologist (B.A. from Jacobs University Bremen). Her research focuses on student teachers' cognition and competences, inclusive education and learner diversity, language awareness as well as interlanguage pragmatics and linguistic judgement of appropriateness. She has taught a number of B.A. and M.Ed./M.A. courses in university teacher education dealing with a range of topics (e.g. Teaching Communicative Competence, Teaching Plurilingualism/pluriculturalism, CLIL, Dealing with Learner Errors, Teaching Pragmatics, Testing and Assessment, Research Methods in EFL, The Use of Corpora in FL Education) and supervised more than 100 student research projects and theses.

Nick Pilcher is a Lecturer in The Business School at Edinburgh Napier University. He teaches a range of areas including supporting students with their academic work. His research interests centre around education, language and qualitative research methods. He has published and contributed to work published in journals such as *Qualitative Research, Psychology of Music*, the *International Journal of Qualitative Studies in Education* and *the International Journal of Shipping and Transport Logistics*.

Kendall Richards is a Lecturer with the role of academic support adviser in the school of Computing supporting the schools of Engineering and the Built Environment and Creative Industries at Edinburgh Napier University (UK). Dr. Richards' research interests include pedagogy, academic support, education as social justice and Neoliberalism's impact on Higher Education. He has presented globally and has contributed to a number of journals and books including the *International Journal of Qualitative Studies in Education, Researching Intercultural Learning (Edited by Martin Cortazzi and Lixian Jin); Higher Education Research and Development, Teaching in Higher Education, Maritime Business Review* and *Power and Education*.

Chittima Sangiamchit is a Lecturer at the University of the Thai Chamber of Commerce. She has published and presented internationally on English as a Lingua Franca (ELF), Online Intercultural Communication, English language teaching and English as a medium instruction. Her recent work is the publication: 'Transcultural communication: language, communication and culture through English as a lingua franca in a social network community', in Language and Intercultural Communication, 2019.

Rob Sheppard is a Teacher and Curriculum Designer focused on adult ESOL and intensive English programmes. His interests include programme development, materials design, assessment and advocacy in English language teaching. Rob is assistant director for curriculum and instruction at Temple University Center for American Language and Culture (TCALC) and the founder of Ginseng English. He serves as sociopolitical concerns chair on the board of PennTESOL East and past chair of TESOL International's Adult Education Interest Section.

Sávio Siqueira is an Associate Professor of English and Applied Linguistics at Bahia Federal University in Salvador, Brazil, with many years of experience in ELT and teacher education. He has conducted postdoctoral studies at the University of Hawai'i at Mānoa, Honolulu, HI, USA, and among his research interests are English as a Lingua Franca, Critical Language Pedagogy, Decolonial studies, CLIL and Bilingual Education, Translanguaging and Intercultural Education.

Martin Štefl received his Ph.D. from the Department of Anglophone Literatures & Cultures at Charles University in Prague in 2014, where he studied English philology and Philosophy. Currently, he works at the School of Business, University of Chemistry and Technology in Prague where he teaches courses in English and German, focusing on skills training, in particular using telecollaborative practices. He has experience in designing e-learning educational content for non-profit educational institutions. Besides ELT, Martin is professionally interested in philosophy of business, ethics and philosophy of technology, and researches into critical thinking and its applications in ELT.

Lone Krogsgaard Svarstad is Associate Professor, Ph.D., in English language teaching at the Department of Education, University College Copenhagen, Denmark.

Svarstad's research focuses on Cultural Studies, critical intercultural communication and critical media literacy as key components in the cultural dimension of English language teaching. In collaboration with Professor Emerita, Karen Risager, she has written the book *Verdensborgeren og den interkulturelle læring* (The Global Citizen and Intercultural Learning) (Risager & Svarstad 2020). This work is an introduction to intercultural learning in foreign languages and all subjects teaching culture and society. Svarstad is also the author of several articles and chapters in Danish and international journals and books. Svarstad is co-editor of *Sprogforum Journal of language and culture pedagogy*, Roskilde University, Denmark.

Zia Tajeddin is Professor of Applied Linguistics at Tarbiat Modares University, Iran. His main areas of research include L2 pragmatics, teacher education and EIL/ELF. He is co-editor of *Applied Pragmatics* (John Benjamins). He has published his studies in *Journal of Language, Identity, and Education, International Journal of Applied Linguistics, The Language Learning Journal, Language and Intercultural Communication,* and *Journal of Intercultural Communication Research,* among others. He is the co-editor (with Carol Griffiths) of *Lessons from Good Language Teachers* (Cambridge University Press, 2020) and the co-editor (with Minoo Alemi) of *Pragmatics Pedagogy in English as an International Language* (Routledge, 2020).

Pimsiri Taylor, EdD is a faculty member at the Language Institute, Thammasat University where she currently works as the Vice Director for Planning and Organisational Development. She teaches English for Specific Purposes courses to undergraduate and postgraduate students, and supervises research projects on English-medium instruction, teacher professional development, and identity of English language learners. She is also involved in teacher training programmes, focusing especially on English-medium instruction. Her research interests include English-medium instruction, English as a lingua franca, English for specific purposes, internationalisation of higher education, interculturality and sociocultural aspects of education.

Mabel Victoria is a border crosser. She was born in the Philippines, lived in Canada and Switzerland, completed her masters and doctoral studies in the UK, worked in Thailand, and has, since 2014, been teaching at Edinburgh Napier University. She teaches Sociolinguistics, Communication in International Management, Intercultural Business Communication and Intercultural Organisational Management. Her research interests are interdisciplinary and wide-ranging from *latrinalia* or toilet graffiti to linguistic landscapes to dark tourism, to humour, to intercultural communication and the use of English as a lingua franca.

List of Figures

List of Tables

1

Introduction: Interculturality and the English Language Classroom

Mabel Victoria and Chittima Sangiamchit

Introduction

This volume has been primarily written for teachers of the English language. It explores how teachers and researchers from around the world have engaged with the notion of interculturality in teaching English as a foreign/second language. In the last three decades, we have witnessed the advent of an increasingly globalised and interconnected world. This has contributed to the growth of English as a global lingua franca and the preferred contact language between multilinguals who do not share the same first language (Galloway & Rose, 2015; Jenkins et al., 2018). Indeed, individuals and groups from highly diverse linguistic and

M. Victoria (✉)
The Business School, Edinburgh Napier University, Edinburgh, UK
e-mail: M.Victoria@napier.ac.uk

C. Sangiamchit
University of the Thai Chamber of Commerse (UTC), Bangkok, Thailand
e-mail: chittima_san@utc.ac.th

cultural backgrounds are more interconnected than ever using English as the most common medium of intercultural communication (ICC) whether virtual or face to face. This presents challenges for the English language teacher whose pedagogical training and background privilege the teaching of vocabulary and syntax using accepted methods. What about culture? Whose culture?

The teaching of culture has always been an integral part of ELT. Arguably, with globalisation and advances in digital technology, there have been increased contacts between multicultural individuals. Fluency in English between interlocutors from different mother tongues can make it more difficult to detect potential misunderstanding due to 'cultural' differences. We would argue therefore that in order to facilitate the learners' development as interculturally aware/competent communicators, educators need the practical skills and knowledge of how to integrate 'culture' and 'interculturality' into the teaching of English (Kramsch & Hua, 2016; Reid, 2015). The chapters in this series are for English language teachers who are faced with the challenge of helping students develop their intercultural communicative competence (Reid, 2015; Snodin, 2016) so that they are able "to think and act critically, and to negotiate the complexities of today's world" (Byram & Wagner, 2018, p. 141).

It is widely accepted by ELT teachers and practitioners that L2 learners need both linguistic competence in a foreign language as well as intercultural competence (Byram & Wagner, 2018). Yet, despite the sustained body of work on the 'intercultural' and its centrality in language teaching and learning (Young & Sachdev, 2011), there seems to be a lack of agreement amongst scholars and little practical guidance from language pedagogy experts regarding how interculturality can be effectively and systematically incorporated into the language classroom (Baker, 2015). Furthermore, given that most English as a lingua franca encounters are intercultural, "there has been so little uptake of ELF research in intercultural communication literature, and that where it has been discussed it has often been marginalised and misrepresented" (Baker, 2018, p. 26).

Why is there a lack of uptake of interculturality in ELT classrooms? As both ELT researchers and teachers, we see two major factors that contribute to why interculturality has not been widely accommodated by English teachers around the world. First, the vastness and contradictions in the literature have made navigation through it a very confusing and demanding task for language teachers (Perry & Southwell, 2011). The very notion of culture itself is problematic. Which culture or whose culture should be taught—American, British, Australian (in which case English is tied to the large culture nation-based approach)? Second, with few notable exceptions, there is still a glaring scarcity of studies investigating the actual take-up and applicability of theoretical concepts on the intercultural into the ELT classroom (Baker, 2015; Young & Sachdev, 2011). This is despite extensive literature and professional learning opportunities for enhancing the development of intercultural capability in language teaching (Biebricher et al., 2019). Reid (2015) notes that "teachers find it difficult to identify themselves with and apply intercultural aspects of the target language" (p. 939). For one, there is a lack of specific guidance on how to teach intercultural knowledge and skills alongside the target language. As a result, teachers are "often confused and the question of content, materials and techniques often arises" (Reid, ibid.). In spite of numerous publications presenting conceptual models of interculturality and intercultural competence, they do not often come with relevant theories of learning that classroom teachers can readily implement (Byram & Wagner, 2018). It does not help that within the field of intercultural studies, there is disagreement about the notoriously polysemous nature of 'culture'. Consequently, this has made pinning down 'interculturality' a huge task. Nonetheless, ELT practitioners have continued to argue for the importance of the intercultural dimension in ELT and indeed, this movement is starting to be reflected in newer ELT materials and language policy frameworks (Baker, 2015).

The aim of this volume therefore is to present a diversity of perspectives from ELT and intercultural communication scholars from around the world. While the empirical investigations were conducted in local contexts, the practical applications are of global relevance, with implications that transcend geographic borders. The chapters in this collection, written by practitioners for practitioners, explore aspects of interculturality identified by the contributors as important in their work.

English Language Teaching and Culture

The prefix 'inter' in interculturality immediately evokes a sense of being in-between two or more entities. Thus, INTERculturality can be interpreted to mean being between two CULTURES. So far so good. However, the complexity arises when we try to unpack the term 'culture'. Its multifaceted nature defies straightforward answers and yet one's notion of what culture is has a direct bearing on the conceptualisation of what is taken to be 'intercultural'.

It is important to establish at the outset that culture is always implicated in the teaching of English (Baker, 2018; Kramsch, 1993). For example, aspects of culture manifest in the classroom every time teachers make decisions about which specific pronunciation, grammar, or vocabulary to teach. The reading and listening contents can also reveal culture and ideologies. Even the teacher's choice of instructional methods, textbooks, and materials is permeated with implicit cultural beliefs and values (Nault, 2006).

Essentialism and Non-essentialism

There are two major paradigms deployed in the conceptualisation of culture: the essentialist and the non-essentialist view (also known as anti-essentialist view). There is another perspective—neo-essentialism—which will be discussed at the end of this section after contrasting the two general paradigms. The essentialist view derives from a macro-level perspective whereby individuals are seen as passive bearers of a stable set of characteristics and identities that they share with a group of people. This view is associated with a large culture, nation-based perspective favouring geographic borders as a way of conceptualising culture. For example, Japanese people belong to the Japanese culture, Thais belong to the Thai culture and so on. On the other hand, the non-essentialist approach takes a constructivist perspective. It considers culture as a process, always dynamic and in flux (Angouri, 2010); it is not something one has, but what one does (Drummond, 2018). A non-essentialist view recognises that individuals can simultaneously belong to different small cultures (Holliday, 1999b) such as a sports club, a volunteer organisation, and an occupational membership. Furthermore, there is the recognition that an individual's identity is not about "some fundamental essence of character" but rather "a continuous process, accomplished through actions and words" (Baxter, 2016, p. 38). Put another way, individuals perpetually construct fluid, multiple and non-unitary identities (ibid.). National culture is arguably one of the multiple identities that seem to be evoked or become salient in ELT classrooms. Nation-based culture is not rejected but is considered as just one aspect of a person's identity repertoire.

Studies in cross-cultural disciplines, and organisational management tend to employ essentialist notions of culture in the Hofstedian tradition (Nathan, 2015) whereby culture is seen as homogenous, static and bounded. In language teaching, the essentialist paradigm tends to be deployed using the country of the target language as content and context. This might include teaching and learning the customs, traditions, food and festivals of English-speaking countries such as the UK and US. Materials usually include geography, history and other pertinent facts or body of knowledge about the particular country (Fernández-Agüero & Chancay-Cedeño, 2018; Liddicoat & Scarino, 2013). Therefore, interculturality comes to be viewed as the level of knowledge about the target culture. Consequently, the learners' competence is often measured against how closely they can reproduce the native speakers' variety of English. Pronunciation, grammar, and lexical items taught in the classroom are derived from the predominantly American and British variety.

The culture-as-nation approach has been criticised for not addressing the global use of English. English learners cannot be assumed to be motivated by the need to communicate with British or American native speakers. Indeed, with the widespread use of English as a global lingua franca, learners may only require the language to communicate with other lingua franca speakers both locally, regionally and internationally (Nault, 2006). For example, in a country like the Philippines with more than 170 languages, English is used as the common language of communication between multilingual Filipinos. On the other hand, given the economic and political influence of the US, English learners might benefit from familiarity with features of American English (Nault, 2006). Indeed, learners who might have long-term goals of working in western English-speaking countries might find it useful to learn relevant facts about these countries.

Also, somewhat essentialist in perspective is the treatment of culture as norms where being interculturally competent involves "knowing about what people from a given cultural group are likely to do and understanding the cultural values placed upon certain ways of acting or upon certain beliefs" (Liddicoat & Scarino, 2013, p. 19). The inherent difficulty for the learners though is the challenge of having to "interpret the words and actions of an interlocutor from another cultural paradigm using their own cultural paradigm" (ibid.). Liddicoat and Scarino (2013) add that just like the nation-based approach to culture, the culture as norm approach tends to see norms as fixed and homogeneous which could lead to generalisations and stereotyping about the target culture. English language teachers who do not have exposure and familiarity with the target culture might also lack confidence in adopting this approach. Depending on how culture as norm is mediated by the English teacher, this approach could encourage either self-reflection or exoticisation. If learners are encouraged to be critical of the Other's behaviour and beliefs and compare them to their own, this could lead to self-awareness.

According to Liddicoat and Scarino (2013), another approach to culture in language teaching is to treat it as a system of symbols that enable people to construct meanings. In this view, culture can be seen as a lens "through which people mutually create and interpret meanings and the frame that allows the communication of meanings that go beyond the literal denotations of the words being used" (p. 20). This notion of culture extends beyond culture as nation-based (body of knowledge about the target country) and culture as norms (values as expressed in behaviour and beliefs). Within this culture-as-symbol approach, intercultural competence equates to the development of interpretative resources to be able to decipher the meaning of symbols in a specific context.

From a non-essentialist (also anti-essentialist) perspective, culture is viewed as liquid, heterogenous, complex, dynamic and not bound by geography (Dervin, 2011; Nathan, 2015). This perspective recognises intersectionality and the fluidity of multiple identities of each individual (Jameson, 2007). Drawing from their ethnographic studies, Heath and Street (2008), argue for the conceptualisation of culture as a verb and not a noun which is a fixed thing. They point out that culture is always in flux and dynamic, unbounded, kaleidoscopic and is always under construction (p. 7). Put another way, culture is not 'what is' but 'what one does'. In this non-essentialist view, culture can be seen as cohesive practices that are constituted through interaction (Holliday, 1999b). In language teaching contexts, Liddicoat and Scarino (2013) refer to this approach as culture as practice where culture is conceived as being created in social interaction. If we accept language to be social practice, then we can say that culture emerges through the linguistic practices of individuals. This resonates with the small culture view of Holliday that posits that culture is the "composite of cohesive behaviour within any social grouping" (Holliday, 1999b, p. 247). Intercultural competence may thus entail on the part of the learner, not only awareness of potentially useful practices in achieving particular goals, but also a keen sense of observation and reflection to notice culture as being created in interaction.

Also from a non-essentialist perspective and arguably of relevance to ELT is the discursive approach that has its roots in intercultural communication research (Kramsch & Hua, 2016). This is similar to the culture as practice approach described above. The discourse perspective focuses on the co-constructive aspects of interactions by interlocutors from diverse groups or discourse systems including professional memberships in organisations, gender, age and so on. Based on this notion, an intercultural approach considers irrelevant aspects of cultural, group and social differences that are not directly implicated in specific interactions between individuals who are from different groups. Thus, the focus will involve getting learners to notice and analyse social interactions and then encouraging reflection on how culture is produced (Scollon & Scollon, 2001) and how salient the plural identities are.

Neo-essentialism

It is acknowledged that the binary dichotomy between essentialism and non-essentialism is artificial. As Holliday (2011) notes, there are positions that can be cross-overs and positions located between the two general paradigms. He employs the term 'neo-essentialism' to refer to a "dominant approach within the subdiscipline of intercultural communication studies which follows the essentialist and highly influential work of theorists such as Hofstede, while claiming a more liberal, non-essentialist vision" (Holliday, 2011, p. 6). In other words, it is argued that despite engagement with "diversity of cultural behaviour which contradicts and recognises the problems with essentialism", the "basic cultural models […] are often implicitly maintained so that diversity continues to be the exception to the essentialist rule rather than being recognised as the norm" (Holliday, 2010, p. 261).

While the neo/essentialist and non/anti-essentialist paradigms of conceptualising culture seem to be in opposition and mutually exclusive, the chapters in this volume demonstrate that this is not the case. Empirical research from the contributors shows that culture can be deployed as a multidimensional resource. Indeed, the issue is more of emphasis rather than of content, that it is in the intersections between the different conceptualisations of culture that the intercultural can be most effectively mined in the teaching and learning of languages (Liddicoat & Scarino, 2013). We therefore argue that a dynamic approach to the teaching of culture in ELT should necessarily be able to incorporate "a range of different understandings" (Liddicoat & Scarino, 2013, p. 21).

In many intercultural communication studies, the word 'essentialist' is almost treated as a slur, a bad thing (Phillips, 2010). Consequently, scholars who support the non-essentialist/anti-essentialist paradigm have continued to critique studies that even remotely hint at neo/essentialism. However, versions of neo/essentialism have continued to be employed in cross-cultural and organisational management studies. So, perhaps there is not much point rubbishing it. As Phillips (2010, p. 20) points out, "essentialism is a way of thinking not always so easily distinguished from more innocent forms of generalisation, and what is wrong with it is often a matter of degree rather than categorical embargo". Zhou and Pilcher

(2018) proposed that rather than an outright rejection of essentialism, it can be deployed as a simplistic 'starting point' and "should be recognised as existing symbiotically with non-essentialist notions and could be used critically throughout intercultural learning" (Zhou & Pilcher, 2018, p. 125).

In their study, Zhou and Pilcher (2018) note that the students who participated in the investigation used essentialist notions of culture as a resource in that their reflection of cultural complexity tended to be facilitated by a "reflective dialectic between non- essentialism and essentialism" (p. 141). It is further proposed by the authors that "essentialist conceptualisations be acknowledged in intercultural education [...] "because they are conceptualisations people will inevitably and often ineluctably be drawn towards and can be purposeful reflectors providing a complex and ever-present alter ego for learners" (ibid.).

As posited by Widdowson (2004, p. 385), given that English "serves the communicative and communal needs of different communities, it follows logically that it must be diverse". Along the same lines, Warschauer (2000, p. 514) argues for a multifaceted approach to the teaching of culture to account for the diversity of English speakers' cultures around the world. He further emphasises, "There is no single formula for how to handle issues of culture in teaching. Teachers will need to vary their approach depending on the particular audiences being taught and their purposes in learning English" (ibid.). The use of Anglophone contexts in ELT is thus not rejected. But what is more important is for educators to question the relevance of these contexts given the diverse settings where English interactions take place (Baker, 2015, p. 26).

From the above review of how culture and ELT are intertwined, we can see how the essentialist view of culture as nation or culture as a body of knowledge about the target English-speaking country has continued to exert an influence in ELT.

Teaching culture from a non-essentialist perspective, on the other hand, is more abstract and would require more teacher involvement in mediating between the teaching materials and the students' knowledge. There are legitimate queries such as how can teachers encourage learners to "transcend cultural boundaries when they have not yet developed a strong confidence in their 'native culture' and local identities – national, ethnic, regional, religious, etc.?" (Zheng & Gao, 2019, p. 203). In other words, there are instances when invoking nation-based conceptualisation of culture might be important for the learners. For various reasons, they might even say that they prefer to learn English the way that people from X culture speak/write it, rather than how people from Y culture use it. It gives teachers a starting point from which to begin awareness-raising.

Based on the above review of the different approaches to teaching culture in language classes, we therefore posit that ELT educators need to recognise that culture, even with nation-based social constructions, can be used as resource by learners. Therefore, to be interculturally competent means having the knowledge and ability to treat culture as a powerhouse of "facts, artifacts, information, and social practices as well as an understanding of culture as the lens through which people mutually interpret and communicate meaning" (Liddicoat & Scarino, 2013, p. 46).

Defining Interculturality

Our attempt to delineate our use of interculturality in this collection is tempered by the knowledge that dealing with definitions and theories has the potential to "trigger a certain amount of violence against those cultures that do not accord the centrality to that definition" and that we "might slip into a theoretical project based on a mono-cultural background, which will be far from recognition of and respect for cultural diversity" (Svetelj, 2018, p. 398). We acknowledge the existing 'plurality of perspectives' in existing literature (Jin, 2017, p. 309) as well as in practices in ELT classrooms around the world. As Taylor (this volume) notes, the 'intercultural' has been used to refer to intercultural competence, intercultural communicative competence, intercultural awareness, and so on. Following Jin (2017), the suffix '-ality' suggests a more dynamic, and critical reading (p. 310).

Given the high interconnectivity and mobility in today's world, teachers and students of English and other foreign languages already have some perspective on interculturality even before they enter the L2 classroom. Indeed, as Dervin (2017, p. 101) observes, "they have already, in some cases, a long experience of interculturality and, most importantly, have reflected and been critical towards certain misconceptions about it". With the ubiquitous presence of social media platforms, films, television, and other online resources, L2 students of today are constantly exposed to a rich, if confusing, ecology of multiple languages and cultures. The challenge for the educator then is to create a space for learners to make sense of their observations and experiences to help them further develop their interculturality.

Interculturality can be viewed as a *paradigm* that privileges the 'inter' in interactions and does not take cultural differences as given. The main focus is to "interpret how participants make (aspects of) cultural identities relevant or irrelevant to interactions through the interplay of language and social relationship" (Hua, 2015, p. 10). Thus, if a Filipino and a Thai are in an interaction, their differences based on nationality may or may not be salient because both speakers belong to different 'small' culture memberships such as being a tourist, customer service clerk, Buddhist, heterosexual, chess player, movie fan, etc. This paradigm does not necessarily exclude the essentialist culture-as-nation approach as the interactants might make their nationalities salient in the encounter. This is along the lines of Parry's (2003) view that interculturality is a way of being in the world, defining the term as "transcending barriers of communication based on different ways of seeing, feeling, and understanding the world, and as these differences are articulated in language" (Parry, 2003, pp. 101–102). For Parry, if critical self-awareness is paramount, it is argued that it is not possible to have empathy with others unless one understands oneself.

Another way to view interculturality is as a dynamic *process* "by which people draw on and use the resources and processes of cultures with which they are familiar but also those they may not typically be associated with in their interactions with others" (Young & Sercombe, 2010, p. 181). Some scholars argue that 'interculturality' enables researchers to focus on the processual aspect of the phenomenon under study; 'intercultural' on the other hand, when used as an adjective, is "based on the idea of an encounter with otherness or a meeting of different cultures, themselves considered islands or distinct entities with clearly defined borders" (Lavanchy et al., 2011, p. 12). Nonetheless, it can be argued that despite pressure from post-structuralist researchers to disregard the essentialising effect of nation-based culture, many English learners still find differences based on nationalities, alongside educational background, and social interests, to be relevant (Taylor, this volume). Along the same lines, Murray (this volume) sees interculturality as a reflexive relationship between the learners' culture and that of the others. As Holliday points out, interculturality is a "seamless process whereby we employ our existing cultural experience to engage with new cultural domains within which we can also find ourselves, and we make new sense of the existing cultural identities of ourselves and others" (Holliday, 2017, p. 214).

Most of the contributors to this volume use interculturality as a *heuristic device* or a *set of lenses* to analyse their own local contexts. As such, there is a recognition that its definition does not have to be watertight and can integrate both the process and paradigm perspective of interculturality. For example, Svarstad (this volume) uses the term in the field of Cultural Studies to refer to a non-essentialist way of integrating different aspects of cultural life in society and in the world with all its diversity and complexity, identities, and subjectivities including different types of everyday intercultural encounters and discourses. In the Cultural Studies tradition of interculturality, it is posited that individuals' multiple identity repertoires including factors such as class, race, ethnicity, nationality, gender, sexuality, language, religion, and age always intersect. Abid (this volume) foregrounds the view of interculturality as the site for the interaction of diversities and variabilities. Siqueira (this volume), on the other hand, focuses on what it means to be intercultural. He suggests that interculturality is characterised by developing a critical attitude towards accepted norms and values, enhancing empathy towards the Other, reflexivity and having the ability to transform intercultural analysis into action. Sheppard (this volume) situates interculturality in the specific context of immigrants in the US. Thus, he adds 'critical' to 'critical interculturality' to refer to an attitude of being open to 'perspectives, frames of reference, and ways of knowing that may be different from one's own' combined with critical stance towards power imbalances and unjust status quo. Pilcher and Richards's (this volume) entry point into interculturality is unique. They focus on the culture of ELT as a process and how this process can be deployed by teachers within the disciplinary culture of EAP (English for Academic Purposes).

In this section, we have offered different conceptualisations of interculturality as a paradigm, a process, and a heuristic device. We have also proposed that the concept is way too important for language learning and teaching to pin it down to one definition. Consonant with the stance of other intercultural/ity scholars, this collection has been put together as 'advocacy' for interculturality given that "intercultural contact and interchange are greater than ever, necessitating approaches to understanding and brokering difference through effective communication" (Young & Sachdev, 2011, p. 82). The English language classroom presents an ideal vantage point from which to observe the interplay between language and culture.

Indeed, "While the goal of English language teaching has undergone changes from imitating 'native speakers' to becoming an intercultural communicator, pedagogical implementations have not been fully realized in classrooms, especially the ones that enable students to communicate globally while at the same time help them maintaining their native/traditional languages and cultures" (Zheng & Gao, 2019, p. 199). Arguably, while many English teachers seem to accept the importance of interculturality in L2 teaching, they seem reluctant to put it in practice. The stated reasons, according to Young and Sachdev (2011) were: "perceived lack of interest by the learners, a lack of curricular support, a lack of suitable textbook material, a lack of ICC testing, and concern about engaging with controversy" (ibid., p. 95).

The chapters in this volume have been written for both experienced and pre-service teachers to enrich their practice in making interculturality an integral part of the English learning experience.

What the Volume Is About?

The contributions are drawn from a wide range of educational contexts involving researchers from different parts of the world. In this multi-voiced collection, the primary target readers will benefit from being able to compare diverse approaches to teaching/researching interculturality in ELT; they will be able to learn from the practical experiences of educators from various educational settings including countries where English is learnt as a foreign language and countries where it is the 'native' language.

This proposed volume fills a much-needed gap in language pedagogy. Indeed, while English has become the undisputed global lingua franca and the most taught foreign language in the world, the focus on the teaching of its linguistic aspects has far overshadowed the intercultural dimension which is of equally great importance. Advances in digital technology have enabled learners to communicate with other multilingual speakers from highly diverse backgrounds highlighting the need for intercultural communication skills.

In this collection, we create a space where English teachers can find a toolkit of practical recommendations that can help them find their own answers to questions such as—which/whose culture should I teach? Should it be the culture of countries where English is spoken as a native language or the local culture? What about the occupational, academic, or social media culture?

Intended to be used on teacher education programmes, this collection features contributions from teacher-researchers who deploy a variety of approaches such as ethnography, content analysis, cultural studies, discourse analysis, self-assessment survey, and documentary analysis in their investigations. The diverse research contexts take the form of virtual intercultural tandem/collaboration, international study abroad programmes, face-to-face classroom situations, and textbook analysis.

Structure of This Volume

In this section, we show how interculturality has been conceptualised and operationalised by the contributors in this volume in their particular contexts. Part I, *Teachers' voices: exploring ways to research interculturality in ELT*, focuses on exploring the perspectives of teachers, both pre-service and in-service, and their views on interculturality. Part II, *Integrating interculturality in ELT textbooks*, takes a critical look at how some of the more popular teaching materials used by English teachers in different parts of the world reflect (or not) interculturality. Part III, *The role of the English language in the learning and teaching of interculturality*, examines the English language as a complex site where interculturality, and ethnocentrism/ethnorelativism can be enacted. This section also invites the readers to consider ELT as in itself a culture and its implications in the field of EAP.

Chapter 2, by Lone Krogsgaard Svarstad, explores the potentials of a Cultural Studies approach to interculturality in ELT in pre-service teacher education, Copenhagen, Denmark. This chapter unpacks three key interrelated concepts: intersectionality, othering, and subtextuality. Using examples taken from an ELT module in intercultural competence, the chapter sheds light on the perspective of pre-service/student-teachers regarding the use of popular culture, gender, social class, equity, globalisation, identity, and fashion in designing and analysing ELT material. It is posited that popular culture can be deployed as an empowering resource for engaging in intercultural encounters whereby English language students also benefit from developing a 'critical' reading of the world. This chapter provokes the target readers into reflecting on the interrelatedness between Cultural Studies, critical intercultural communication, and critical media literacy to encourage the questioning of concepts such as essentialism and culturalism, and promoting diversity and the global citizenship.

Chapter 3, by Sávio Siqueira, discusses and problematises the (dis)connection between ELT and interculturality in theory and practice. It takes inspiration from a study with pre-service student-teachers, all non-native speakers of English, from an English language extension programme in a Brazilian university. The analysis of data, generated through open-ended questionnaires and classroom observations, suggests that the concept of interculturality is ambiguous for most participants. The study finds that the intercultural dimension is underexplored in the teaching of English in this specific context, and that the research participants are only vaguely aware of the notion of interculturality and therefore were only partially able to incorporate it into their pedagogy. Practical recommendations are made on how ELT practitioners and pre-service teachers can effectively integrate interculturality into their teaching of English.

Chapter 4, by Joanna Pfingsthorn, Anna Czura, Christian Kramer, and Martin Štefl, explores the perspectives of student-teachers from three European countries—Germany, Poland, and the Czech Republic—regarding their views on the potential of telecollaboration as a tool for enhancing interculturality and professional development. Data, in the form of self-reported quantitative assessment and open-ended statements were collected to explore the student-teachers' professional identity as language teachers and how this connects with their view on telecollaborative learning as a way to enhance the students' interculturality. The study finds that student-teachers failed to fully embrace the intercultural dimension of telecollaborative exchanges although they do seem to see the link between interculturality and professional identity. The researchers present recommendations for increasing the potential of telecollaborative exchanges as a valuable tool for developing ICC in teacher education programmes.

Chapter 5, by Nadia Abid, examines the potential of an ELT textbook, "Skills for Life", in the promotion of intercultural citizenship through exposure to global issues. The author points out that orientation to intercultural citizenship in a foreign language classroom necessitates focusing less on 'national' citizenship bounded by a country; rather a move towards being a 'global' citizen of the world community. Citizenship is conceptualised not as a single identity but membership of multiple and overlapping communities. Thus, it is argued that in order to be global citizens, foreign language learners need to develop knowledge of cultures, human rights (including issues such as racism, gender and children's rights), and democratic citizenship, alongside an attitude of respect and openness to other cultures, and the development of intercultural skills. Using Content analysis to evaluate the textbook's representation of cultures and global issues and employing an eclectic framework, the results obtained show that: global issues are underrepresented; the distribution of culture is imbalanced; and tasks are limited in number and have a low potential for teaching culture. The findings of the study will be useful to researchers and EFL practitioners not only in Tunisia but in wider contexts where English is taught to speakers of other languages. The chapter provides insights for ELT teachers on how they can effectively mediate the limitations of textbooks in order to extend the learners' understanding of intercultural citizenship and global issues.

Chapter 6, by Helen Margaret Murray, also focuses on a selection of EFL textbooks used in Norwegian secondary schools to unpack the relation between curriculum requirements and textbook interpretations of curriculum goals within the context of interculturality. It presents analyses of how theories of intercultural competence are reflected in the texts and tasks of curriculum for 13–18 secondary school students. The results of the study highlight the importance of the teacher's role in mediating between the textbooks (which sometimes contain stereotypical representations of countries and people) and the learners' knowledge. Indeed, textbooks can also tend towards stereotypical representations of countries and people, which hinder real cultural understanding. It is recommended that teachers take on the challenge of finding good teaching materials to work with the intercultural so that pupils will be exposed to a variety of perspectives. While drawing from the Norwegian context, the chapter also shows how the insights can be applied to similar endeavours in different parts of the world. Simply put, this chapter highlights the lessons and 'cautions' that can be learnt from the Norwegian experience.

Chapter 7, by Rob Sheppard, reviews some of the most widely used textbooks used in adult ESOL programmes for immigrants in the US. The textbooks were analysed to determine the extent to which they are likely to foster 'critical interculturality'. In the context of the study, Sheppard takes *interculturality* to mean a 'stance of openness to perspectives, frames of reference, and ways of knowing that may be different from one's own'. This openness, however, needs to be tempered with *criticality* or scepticism towards power imbalances and the status quo. It is argued that this critical interculturality will help immigrants prepare for self-advocacy, leadership and transformation in the community should they choose to do so.

The study finds that the representation of culture in the textbooks privileges the American culture and the implicit, uncritical stance towards it. Based on the findings, it is argued that a shift from acculturation towards critical interculturality is necessary in adult education. While a focus on American culture may remain necessary in most ESOL programmes in the US, the author proposes that employing a critical-intercultural stance will help immigrants to approach the nation-based culture as empowered agents rather than passive recipients. The chapter ends with recommendations for cultivating a critical-intercultural stance in classroom instruction, not only in education, but also in contexts where culture is often taught as 'content'.

Chapter 8, by Pimsiri Taylor, investigates international Higher Education programmes in Thailand and Malaysia to explore how interculturality is constructed and enacted in English as a lingua franca encounters. The chapter examines different concepts pertaining to the 'intercultural' such as 'intercultural encounters', 'intercultural communication', 'intercultural competence', and 'intercultural awareness'. Analysis of interview data suggests that English was deployed by research participants not only as a 'lingua' franca but also as a type of 'cultural' franca'. Simply put, English in intercultural interactions evolves into a complex site for the enactment of nationality, language, and identity. This chapter concludes by engaging with the question: *how can English language teachers embed interculturality in their teaching?*

Chapter 9, by Zia Tajeddin and Minoo Alemi, locates the English language as the focal point in examining intercultural sensitivity, ethnocentrism, and ethnorelativism amongst EFL and non-EFL students in an Iranian university. It deals with the question that most L2 teachers ask: does learning English help develop the learners' intercultural knowledge and ability? Using a mixed-methods approach, this study compared EFL and non-EFL Iranian students to tease out the impact of English learning experiences in the development of intercultural sensitivity. The results suggest that English language competence is not necessarily associated with intercultural competence. After interrogating the complex relationship between language proficiency and the intercultural, the chapter presents recommendations for ELT practitioners in both intercultural education and language education contexts.

Chapter 10, by Nick Pilcher and Kendall Richards, is not one particular empirical research project. Rather, it is drawn from various studies conducted by the authors in the field of EAP in the UK. The chapter reframes the practice and approach to ELT as an academic culture in its own right. It explores the important role that interculturality plays in how this ELT culture, with emphasis on EAP, can be adapted and modified to increase its perceived value in academic contexts. The culture of EAP is argued to be grounded exclusively in written text analysis and production techniques such as Systemic Functional Linguistics, Genre Analysis, and Corpus Linguistics. However, the subject degrees that students follow arc often approached through a different practice and process (culture) involving not only written text but also non-text based media such as visual or mathematical language. The chapter then presents an 'interculturality' framework, based on a robust model of intercultural competence, to help teachers and students navigate the sometimes confusing waters of EAP.

Chapter 11, by Chittima Sangiamchit, gives a hindsight view of all the chapters in the volume. It aims to re-examine major issues and practical approaches to interculturality in ELT. Implications emerged from a range of chapters are presented as a useful guidance for relevant sectors of ELT, policymakers and practitioners. These implications would be beneficial for making a necessary adjustment in ELT curriculum and a syllabus and supporting an integration of interculturality into the ELT classroom. ELT teachers can develop their professional intercultural skills and offer learners opportunities to engage in interesting intercultural contents and activities on both local and global scales. In this way, the learners can be supported in developing their intercultural knowledge and effectively preparing themselves for intercultural communication as global citizens.

References

Angouri, J. (2010). 'If we know about culture it will be easier to work with one another': Developing skills for handling corporate meetings with multinational participation. *Language and Intercultural Communication, 10*(3), 206–224. https://doi.org/10.1080/14708470903348549.

Baker, W. (2015). Research into Practice: Cultural and intercultural awareness. *Language Teaching, 48*(1), 130–141. https://doi.org/10.1017/S0261444814000287.

Baker, W. (2018). English as a lingua franca and intercultural communication. In J. Jenkins, W. Baker, & M. Dewey (Eds.), *The Routledge handbook of English as a lingua franca* (pp. 25–36). Routledge.

Baxter, J. (2016). Positioning language and identity: Poststructuralist perspectives. In S. Preece (Ed.), *The Routledge Handbook of Language and Identity* (pp. 34–49). Routledge. https://doi.org/10.4324/9781315669816.ch2.

Biebricher, C., East, M., Howard, J., & Tolosa, C. (2019). Navigating intercultural language teaching in New Zealand classrooms. *Cambridge Journal of Education, 49*(5), 605–621. https://doi.org/10.1080/0305764X.2019.1581137.

Byram, M., & Wagner, M. (2018). Making a difference: Language teaching for intercultural and international dialogue. *Foreign Language Annals, 51*(1), 140–151. https://doi.org/10.1111/flan.12319.

Dervin, F. (2011). A plea for change in research on intercultural discourses: A "liquid" approach to the study of the acculturation of Chinese students. *Journal of Multicultural Discourses, 6*(1), 37–52.

Dervin, F. (2017). "I find it odd that people have to highlight other people's differences—Even when there are none": Experiential learning and interculturality in teacher education. *International Review of Education, 63*(1), 87–102. https://doi.org/10.1007/s11159-017-9620-y.

Drummond, R. (2018). Maybe it's a grime [t]ing: Th-stopping among urban British youth. *Language in Society, 47*(2), 171–196. https://doi.org/10.1017/S0047404517000999.

Fernández-Agüero, M., & Chancay-Cedeño, C. (2018). Interculturality in the language class—Teachers' intercultural practices in Ecuador. *RELC Journal*. https://doi.org/10.1177/0033688218755847.

Galloway, N., & Rose, H. (2015). *Introducing global Englishes*. Routledge.

Heath, S. B., & Street, B. (2008). *On Ethnography: Approaches to Language and Literacy Research*. Language & Literacy. Teachers College Press.

Holliday, A. (1999a). Culture as constraint or resource: Essentialist versus non-essentialist views. *IATEFL Language and Cultural Studies SIG Newsletter Issue, 18,* 38–40.

Holliday, A. (1999b). Small cultures. *Applied Linguistics, 20*(2), 237–264. https://doi.org/10.1093/applin/20.2.237.

Holliday, A. (2010). Cultural descriptions as political cultural acts: an exploration. *Language and Intercultural Communication, 10*(3), 259–272. https://doi.org/10.1080/14708470903348572.

Holliday, A. (2011). *Intercultural communication and ideology.* Sage.

Holliday, A. (2017). PhD students, interculturality, reflexivity, community and internationalisation. *Journal of Multilingual and Multicultural Development, 38*(3), 206–218. https://doi.org/10.1080/01434632.2015.1134554.

Hua, Z. (2015). Negotiation as the rule of engagement in intercultural and lingua franca communication: Meaning, frame of references and interculturality. *Journal of English as Lingua Franca, 4*(1), 63–90.

Jameson, D. A. (2007). Reconceptualizing cultural identity and its role in intercultural business communication. *Journal of Business Communication, 44*(3), 199–235. https://doi.org/10.1177/0021943607301346.

Jenkins, J., Baker, W., & Dewey, M. (Eds.). (2018). The future or English as a lingua franca? In *The Routledge handbook of English as a lingua franca.* Routlledge.

Jin, T. (2017). Moving beyond 'intercultural competence': Interculturality in the learning of Mandarin in UK universities. *Language and Intercultural Communication, 17*(3), 306–322. https://doi.org/10.1080/14708477.2016.1259320.

Kramsch, C. (1993). *Context and culture in language teaching.* Oxford University Press.

Kramsch, C., & Hua, Z. (2016). Language and culture in ELT. In G. Hall (Ed.), *Routledge handbook of English Language Teaching.* Routledge.

Lavanchy, A., Gajardo, A., & Dervin, F. (2011). Interculturality at stake. In F. Dervin, A. Gajardo, & A. Lavanchy (Eds.), *Politics of interculturality.* Cambridge Scholars Publishing.

Liddiocoat, A., & Scarino, A. (2013). *Intercultural language teaching and learning* (1st ed.). Blackwell. https://doi.org/10.1002/9781118482070.ch3.

Nathan, G. (2015). A non-essentialist model of culture: Implications of identity, agency and structure within multinational/multicultural organizations. *International Journal of Cross Cultural Management, 15*(1), 101–124. https://doi.org/10.1177/1470595815572171.

Nault, D. (2006). Going global: Rethinking culture teaching in ELT contexts. *Language, Culture and Curriculum, 19*(3), 314–328. https://doi.org/10.1080/07908310608668770.

Parry, M. (2003). Transcultured selves under scrutiny: W(h)ither languages? *Language and Intercultural Communication, 3*(2), 101–107. https://doi.org/10.1080/14708470308668093.

Perry, L. B., & Southwell, L. (2011). Developing intercultural understanding and skills: Models and approaches. *Intercultural Education, 22*(6), 453–466. https://doi.org/10.1080/14675986.2011.644948.

Phillips, A. (2010). *What's wrong with essentialism? Distinktion, 11*(1), 47–60. https://doi.org/10.1080/1600910X.2010.9672755.

Reid, E. (2015). Techniques developing intercultural communicative competences in English language lessons. *Procedia—Social and Behavioral Sciences, 186,* 939–943. https://doi.org/10.1016/j.sbspro.2015.04.011.

Scollon, R., & Scollon, S. W. (2001). *Intercultural communication: A discourse approach* (2nd ed.). Blackwell. http://books.google.com/books?id=Sy81ZI4n214C&pgis=1.

Snodin, N. S. (2016). Rethinking culture teaching in English language programmes in Thailand. *RELC Journal, 47*(3), 387–398. https://doi.org/10.1177/0033688215609231.

Svetelj, T. (2018). Philosophy of interculturality: Philosophy of humanism for our time. *Social Identities, 24*(3), 395–402. https://doi.org/10.1080/13504630.2017.1387040.

Warschauer, M. (2000). The changing global economy and the future of English teaching. *TESOL Quarterly, 34*(3), 511–535.

Widdowson, H. G. (2004). *Text, context, pretext.* Blackwell.

Young, T. J., & Sachdev, I. (2011). Intercultural communicative competence: Exploring English language teachers' beliefs and practices. *Language Awareness, 20*(2), 81–98. https://doi.org/10.1080/09658416.2010.540328.

Young, T., & Sercombe, P. (2010). Communication, discourses and interculturality. *Language and Intercultural Communication, 10*(3), 181–188. https://doi.org/10.1080/14708470903348523.

Zheng, X., & Gao, Y. (2019, December). Promoting intercultural competence in Englilsh language teaching: A productive bilingualism perspective. In M. Sato (Ed.), *Second handbook of English Language Teaching* (pp. 199–218). https://doi.org/10.1007/978-3-319-58542-0.

Zhou, V. X., & Pilcher, N. (2018). 'Intercultural competence' as an inter-subjective process: A reply to 'essentialism.' *Language and Intercultural Communication, 18*(1), 125–143. https://doi.org/10.1080/14708477.2017.1400510.

Part I

Teacher's Voices: Exploring Ways to Research Interculturality in ELT

2

A Cultural Studies Approach to Interculturality in ELT

Lone Krogsgaard Svarstad

Introduction

The chapter unfolds and discusses the potentials of a Cultural Studies approach to interculturality in ELT in teacher education. It is one of many responses to the shift in foreign language teaching towards broader understandings of intercultural competence and interculturality with 'the inclusion of other analytical elements such as equity, social justice, human rights and democracy but also a mix of foci (gender, religion, social class etc.)' (Dervin, 2019). The current chapter explores how Danish student teachers training for children grades 1–10 worked with a Cultural Studies Approach to Interculturality as part of an intercultural module to become teachers of English. The Cultural Studies approach presented here draws on the research findings from an action research study in lower secondary school that explored the potentials of a Cultural

L. K. Svarstad (✉)
University College Copenhagen, Copenhagen, Denmark
e-mail: losv@kp.dk

© The Author(s), under exclusive license to Springer Nature Switzerland AG 2021
M. Victoria and C. Sangiamchit (eds.), *Interculturality and the English Language Classroom*, https://doi.org/10.1007/978-3-030-76757-0_2

Studies approach to interculturality (Svarstad, 2016, 2020). Three key concepts: intersectionality, othering and subtextuality emerged from the action research and the subsequent analysis. Thus, these concepts will be explored in the transformation of research findings to curriculum development in teacher education.

In Denmark, an increasing orientation towards intercultural competence in foreign language teaching made its mark on curriculum development in teacher education and in school in 2012–2014. The new curriculum guidelines explicitly define culture as complex and dynamic, highlighting that culture is not something static that is ascribed to an individual or to groups of people, but is rather defined by what you do or what people in different social contexts do (Danish Ministry of Education, Guidelines for English, 2019). These guidelines state that there is national curriculum orientation towards 'culture' perceived as processes, identity and agency. Thus, previous perceptions of 'culture' in language education based on banal nationalism (Billig, 1995) with stereotypical and touristic representations in language textbooks as the German notion of *Landeskunde* sometimes is interpreted (Kabel & Svarstad, 2019; Svarstad, 2018) is given much less attention. A term that is increasingly used to explain a complex and diverse approach to intercultural learning is 'interculturality'.

The notion of interculturality in this chapter draws on Cultural Studies. In a Cultural Studies tradition 'culture' is not seen as something that exits out there and can be described as norms and values, products and practices (an essentialist view) because Cultural Studies accentuates process and agency—constructed in discourse (a non-essentialist view) (Risager, 2018, p. 130). Thus, in a Cultural Studies tradition 'culture' consists of many different identities that intersect; class, race, ethnicity, nationality, gender, sexuality, language, religion and age. Cultural processes, individual identities and agency are explored in a historical and discursive perspective (Risager & Svarstad, 2020, p. 130). The notion of interculturality in this chapter therefore refers to a non-essentialist umbrella concept that integrates different aspects of cultural life in society and in the world: diversity and complexity, identities and subjectivities, the many different kinds of intercultural encounters and discourses about all these things in everyday life, in the media, in education and in politics (Risager & Svarstad, 2020, p. 144). Intercultural learning based on such a notion of interculturality draws on Cultural Studies as an interdisciplinary and politically engaged field, which covers multiple topics, including the relationship between language and culture, politics and cultural analysis, agency and structure, identity, gender and power (Grossberg, 2010; Hall et al., 2013).

Thus, Cultural Studies offers a discursive approach to intercultural learning providing analytical tools for teachers, students and researchers to engage in many different aspects of interculturality. Adopting Cultural Studies analyses as resources for student engagement in broader intercultural issues has the potential to empower students to take a critical stance and to develop language skills to support this stance. In this chapter, I argue that a Cultural Studies Approach to Interculturality is one response (among many) to the changing curriculum demands in ELT towards broader issues of interculturality.

Teacher Perceptions and Practices of Interculturality

Introducing a Cultural Studies Approach to Interculturality in ELT calls for research on teacher perceptions and practices of the notion of interculturality presented in this chapter. What challenges do teachers and student teachers face working with broader understandings of interculturality in ELT? Recent research reveals that language teachers' views on interculturality as well as their personal intercultural experiences significantly affect how intercultural learning takes place in classroom interaction.

Kohler's (2015) study examined teachers' perceptions of language and culture and the relationship between them through interviews and classroom observation. Her study revealed that teacher mediation in intercultural language teaching draws upon a teacher's orientation towards his/her own language and culture, understanding of language and culture (and the relationship between them), and overall stance towards language teaching and learning (Kohler, 2015, p. 193). The study also revealed

that teachers who viewed language as structure and culture as information gave factual, often generalised, information, asking display questions
and providing explanations about the target culture. However, teachers
who viewed language and culture as social semiotics (language is a
resource for making meaning: text as a process of making meaning in
context (Halliday & Matthiessen, 2014) used exploratory discussion,
open-ended questioning, interpretation, personalisation, comparison and
reflection. These teachers would also challenge student assumptions
about the target language and culture, encouraging them to view their
own language and culture more critically and to normalise linguistic and
cultural diversity and variability (Kohler, 2015, p. 194).

Kearney's (2016) study investigated the practical issues in translating a
social semiotic view of intercultural learning into teaching practice that
engages in meaning-making activity. In semiotics meaning making is an
investigation into how meaning is created and communicated through
the study of signs and symbols. Kearney observed that the lecturer in
the study equipped students with a metalanguage of social semiotics and
a general analytical approach to dealing with cultural texts and representations. This expanded the students' perceptual and meaning-making
capacities. According to Kearney, one of the many challenges of using
culture in language teaching is getting beyond cultural 'facts' to acknowledge complexity and contradiction in cultural knowledge and experience
(Kearney, 2016, p. 19). Engaging in meaning-making activities is one
response to this challenge.

The challenge of getting beyond cultural 'facts' and exploring complex
understandings of culture was also a main concern in my study (Svarstad,
2016). It explored teacher perceptions and practices of interculturality as
well as student perceptions and engagement in interculturality drawing
on Cultural Studies. Classroom observations revealed much creativity in
terms of variation in types of activities, but very little focus on meaning-
making between activities. Interviews with teachers showed that they
mainly based their culture teaching on intuition and assumptions
showing a limited metalanguage of culture concepts and intercultural
learning. Teachers found it challenging, but rewarding, to conceptualise
and teach broader aspects of interculturality based on Cultural Studies
and issues of popular culture, representation and identity. The study's

interventions demonstrated that knowledge about Cultural Studies with focus on three key concepts; intersectionality, othering and subtextuality helped the teachers to develop a common metalanguage of culture learning. This qualified their decisions on learning objectives, selection criteria for text and media, and furthermore, it made room for analysis and interpretation in classroom dialogue.

To overcome the challenges teachers and student teachers face in teaching broader issues of interculturality, the findings of the three studies above point at the importance of equipping student teachers with a metalanguage of 'culture' perceived as processes, identity and agency and Cultural Studies offers just that. In addition, to expand students' analytical capabilities of text and media that they select for their teaching can be supported by a view of language as social semiotics. Cultural Studies and a social semiotic approach to language learning support discursive approaches to culture learning and engagement in broader issues of interculturality.

A Cultural Studies Approach to Interculturality

The current chapter reveals how the research findings from the Danish study mentioned above (Svarstad, 2016) were transformed into teacher education, exploring how Danish student teachers worked with a Cultural Studies Approach to Interculturality. The Danish study's interventions demonstrated that knowledge about Cultural Studies with focus on three key concepts; intersectionality, othering and subtextuality supported the teachers' development of a common metalanguage to talk about 'culture' and intercultural learning. The outline below will explain the relationship between Cultural Studies, intersectionality, othering and subtextuality and how intercultural learning can be scaffolded using a model of interactions processes of intercultural learning (Liddicoat & Scarino, 2013).

Cultural Studies is an interdisciplinary and political field engaged in cultural analysis. It was initially developed by the Birmingham Centre for Cultural Studies in Britain, founded in 1964 by Richard Hoggart and Stuart Hall. The main concern was to change the prevailing way of thinking about culture, identity and mass media. Research within the field investigates how cultural practices relate to wider systems of power such as ideology, class structure and gender with an accentuation of process and agency, historicity and subjectivity and different kinds of identity (Risager, 2018). Today the field covers multiple topics, including the relationship between language and culture, politics and cultural analysis, identity, agency and structure, gender and power, queer theory, diaspora and hybridity, and consumer culture and lifestyle (Barker, 2002). In a Cultural Studies tradition as explained earlier in this chapter:

> 'culture' is not seen as something that exists out there and can be described as norms and values, products and practices (an essentialist view). As a Cultural Studies tradition accentuates process and agency, it favours a view of culture that presupposes that it is constructed in discourse (a non-essentialist view). (Risager, 2018, p. 130)

A discursive approach implies a critique of essentialism; a view of culture as something that can be used to explain people's actions and beliefs. Cultural Studies explores diverse forms of power and includes analyses of representation of gender, race, class and colonialism (Barker, 2002). These analyses are also concerned with intersectionality and how the study of inequality intersects in terms of race, class, gender, sexuality and other dimensions of identity (Dervin, 2016, p. 83).

Cultural Studies consists of several sub-fields, among them critical intercultural communication, which focuses on the complex connections between language, culture, identity, agency, power and context. Another subfield is postcolonial studies which has been interested in the study of *the Other* from the very beginning in the 1970s. Edward Said is renowned for his work *Orientalism* (1978) in which he writes about an imagined geography in which the 'West' constructs the 'Orient' as *Other* in a reductionist and distancing way.

The concept of *the Other* is an advance of that of the stereotype as it 'heightens attention both to the subjugation of the stereotypical *Other*, and to those who produce the stereotypical object and thereby by implication define themselves as subjects' (Pickering, 2001, p. 71). *Othering* is a concept dealing with the process by which some social categories are constructed leading to 'stereotypical misrepresentation more firmly on the structures and relations of power which give them their building power' (Pickering, 2001, p. 69). Dervin (2014) emphasises the 'us' and 'them' dichotomy as a key aspect of critical intercultural communication. He suggests that analysing processes of *othering*, social interaction, power relations, and the intersection of different identities (such as nationality, race, language, religion and gender) is central to interculturality. As such, the way in which representations are presented to and described by teachers and students becomes central to culture teaching in foreign languages (Dervin, 2014, p. 189).

Another Cultural Studies sub-field is Critical Media Literacy, which focuses on the analysis of social media, multimodality and popular culture. Allan Luke and Julian Sefton-Green (2017) argue for:

> giving young people renewed and powerful tools for weighing, analyzing and engaging with truths and lies, representations and misrepresentations, narratives and fictions, residual and emergent traditions, competing cultural epistemologies and world views. (Luke & Sefton-Green, 2017)

Kellner and Share (2009, 2019) also argue that society calls for the development of critical media literacy in order to empower students to successfully produce and interpret media messages for them to be active participants in a democratic society. Critical media literacy also draws on an understanding of *subtextuality* (Svarstad, 2016) which means that students can read between the lines and pose critical questions to potential cultural subtexts such as hidden messages and values encoded in cultural artefacts, text and media. The current chapter explains how student teachers were scaffolded to engage in broader issues of interculturality, including issues of celebrity, identity, gender and sexuality.

Teacher Education: Module in Intercultural Competence

The local example in this chapter is taken from a B.A. teacher-training programme at University College Copenhagen in Denmark. In the autumn 2017, I explored a Cultural Studies approach to interculturality with a class of 18 students who were studying to become English teachers in primary and lower secondary school (grades 1–10). The students formed a homogenous group of Danish students aged 22–30 with equal gender division. One of the Danish students had an immigrant background. The data in this chapter comprise 18 student portfolios (wix.webpages with student artefacts such as reflections on academic texts, analyses of teaching material and design of teaching plans, etc.) and 16 exam synopses from this class (4 pages with theoretical and practical reflections on teaching plans, views of language and culture learning). The students were in their second year of the B.A. programme. To qualify as an English teacher, students must study three modules of 10 ECTS each. Module 1 is called Language and Language Use (including a view of language as socio semiotics), Module 2 is entitled Processes in Language Learning and Communicative Skills and Module 3 is called Intercultural Competence. The classroom language is English and the literature for the module is primarily in English. During the B.A. programme, students also study other fields such as general pedagogy, psychology and two other teaching subjects.

At the beginning of the English course, the students were presented with teacher and student statements about intercultural language learning and concrete cases from my doctoral work in lower secondary school (Svarstad, 2016, pp. 79–113). Teacher participants' perceptions and practices of interculturality prior to the explorative interventions showed examples of essentialism and culturalism and of banal nationalism. However, the teachers perceived the purpose of intercultural learning to evolve around the students' personal development and preparing the students for a globalised world. The participating students stated in focus group interviews that they did not think of popular culture used in class as part of their intercultural learning, but only to learn the language. The study accentuated the challenges of combining language learning with intercultural learning in a Danish ELF context.

The students were asked to reflect on the challenges the teachers and students faced in terms of perceptions and practices of language and culture teaching. The concrete cases show how English language teaching took place in two schools in the Greater Copenhagen area. The participating teachers were experienced teachers, but they were not educated in intercultural learning. Like the teachers in Kohler's study (2015), the participating teachers primarily based their culture teaching on intuition and assumptions and had limited metalanguage for cultural concepts and cultural learning (Svarstad, 2016). Furthermore, the teaching material used in the schools did not address intercultural learning but instead favoured communicative competences and language skills. These findings were an eye-opener to the student teachers and many of the students recognised the English classes from their own schooling.

Following the analysis of the teacher and student perceptions and practices in the action research study, the student teachers were introduced to the historical development in the field of intercultural communicative competence (Byram, 1997, 2009; Risager, 2012, Svarstad, 2018), intercultural citizenship (Porto et al., 2017) and intercultural language teaching and learning (Liddicoat & Scarino, 2013). The class worked with texts about Cultural Studies and representation (Hall et al., 2013), processes of othering (Dervin, 2014), essentialism and non-essentialism (Holliday et al., 2010) and Cultural Studies chapters on identity, lifestyle and subculture, consumer culture and fashion studies, media studies, visual culture, audience, performance and celebrity, transnationality, globalisation and postcoloniality (Ryan, 2010).

A Cultural Studies Case: An Open Letter on Facebook

A Facebook dispute between the American country-pop singer Miley Cyrus and the Irish pop-folk singer Sinead O'Connor is used as a Cultural Studies case to illustrate how student teachers were scaffolded to engage in broader issues of interculturality drawing on Cultural Studies including issues of celebrity, identity, gender and sexuality.

In the 2013 MTV Video Music Awards show, Miley Cyrus made the headlines because of her controversial twerking performance and the music video '*Wrecking Ball*'. These performances could be said to be examples of 'Miley feminism' where a young woman is rejecting the rules that tell us that girls need to be quiet and good (Apolloni, 2014). Miley later stated in an interview in October 2016 that 'I didn't understand my own gender and my own sexuality' and continued to say that she is pansexual and always has felt involved in the LGBTQ community (Oppenheim, 2016; Svarstad, 2020). The case is still relevant as former Oasis frontman Noel Gallagher, has called out that 'US is responsible for the sexualisation of female pop stars' referring to Miley Cyrus performance at the MTV Video Music Awards in 2020, where she sat on top of a giant, 'wrecking ball'-inspired disco ball (Lewis, 2020).

However, in the aftermath of the MTV Video Awards show in 2013, a dispute on Facebook evolved. Sinéad O'Connor responded to Miley Cyrus in an open letter on Facebook after Miley Cyrus claimed in an interview in Rolling Stone that the music video for '*Wrecking Ball*' was inspired by Sinéad O'Connor's megahit '*Nothing Compares to You*' from 1990. A series of tweets followed this letter and, when Miley Cyrus alluded to O'Connor's mental health problems, the Irish singer instructed her to 'remove her tweets immediately' (BBC News Entertainment, 2013; Svarstad, 2020).

Principles for Intercultural Language Learning

The student teachers' engagement in the Facebook dispute was scaffolded around Liddicoat and Scarino's model for interacting processes of intercultural learning (Liddicoat & Scarino, 2013, p. 60) with a focus on the three key concepts: intersectionality, othering and subtextuality (Fig. 2.1).

The model is based on five principles for intercultural learning: active construction, making connections, social interaction, reflection and responsibility. The principles are not in themselves intercultural

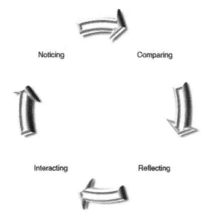

Noticing   Comparing

Interacting   Reflecting

Fig. 2.1 Interaction processes of intercultural learning (Liddicoat & Scarino, 2013, p. 60) (*Source* Scarino, A., & Liddicoat, A. J. [2009]. *Language Teaching and Learning: A Guide*. Melbourne: Curriculum Corporation)

but are a prerequisite for an intercultural perspective: Liddicoat and Scarino (ibid.). The model demonstrates how the above principles can be put into practice by structuring them in the four phases *noticing*, *comparing*, *reflecting* and *interacting*. The model is a cycle of interconnected processes in which students engage in experiences of languages, cultures, and their relationship. The processes are interrelated and do not have a necessary beginning point.

In the teaching sequence of the Cultural Studies case about the Facebook dispute, the four phases looked like this:

Noticing

In this phase, student teachers may become aware of things that challenge their current assumptions, spark interest, raise questions or provide points of connection (Liddicoat & Scarino, 2013, p. 60). The student teachers watched the music video to Sinead O'Connor's song *Nothing Compares to you* from 1990 and to Miley Cyrus' song *Wrecking Ball* from 2013. They discussed how Miley Cyrus and Sinead O'Connor were represented in the music videos. This was followed up by a short search on the internet for relevant representations of the two singers: images, stories and language use. The student teachers were also presented with the article from Rolling Stone in which Miley Cyrus gave the interview that set off the dispute. Following this, the student teachers were asked to consider the importance of representation and misrepresentation considering intersectional perspectives on identity markers—was Miley Cyrus valued for more than her sex appeal? And what about Sinead O'Connor—how was she represented in 1990 and was that provocative at the time?

Comparing

The process of comparison is about inviting student teachers to engage in the identification of similarities and differences between the learner's background culture and the target culture. The comparison process is a way of entering opportunities for developing greater complexity of thinking. This involves understanding an experience from multiple perspectives (Liddicoat & Scarino, 2013, p. 60). The student teachers compared their own analyses of Miley Cyrus' music video *Wrecking Ball* with data from the action research project mentioned earlier in this chapter (Svarstad, 2016). The data was a brainstorming exercise on Miley Cyrus that took place in the classes (15-year-olds) that also worked on the Facebook dispute. The brainstorming exercise portrays opposite and diverging opinions on Miley Cyrus in the music video *Wrecking Ball*. She is described by the 15-year-old students as a *slut, a whore, disgusting, normal, getting mature*, and as *showing a new part of herself*. The student teachers discussed the grade eight students' potential gender bias, but most importantly, they became aware of these 15-year-old students' judgemental language use and discussed pedagogical ideas to overcome this and educate students about the role of language use in interaction. In this phase, student teachers discussed processes of othering and how the grade 8 students' language use displayed these processes and multiple perspectives on Miley Cyrus (Fig. 2.2).

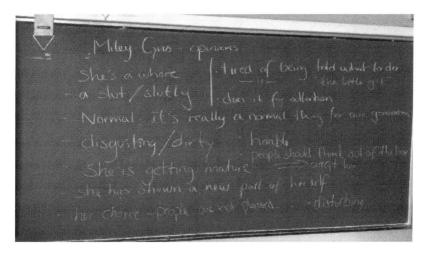

Fig. 2.2 Brainstorming exercise on the popular cultural phenomenon Miley Cyrus in a grade 8 class (Svarstad, 2016, p. 174)

Reflecting

In the act of reflection, the student teachers think about the signifi-cance of what has been observed, of their reactions to this. This phase involves inquiry and connecting new knowledge with old knowledge. In this process, the student teachers reflect on their own experience of linguistic and cultural diversity (Liddicoat & Scarino, 2013, p. 61). The inquiry took place when the student teachers analysed the Face-book dispute using a social semiotics approach, inspired by Derewianka (2015). The student teachers examined the 'interpersonal' function of language, 'how language is used to foster social interaction, to create and maintain relationships, to develop and project a personal identity, to express opinions and engage with views of other' (Derewianka, 2015, p. 109). The student teachers analysed how Sinead O'Conner used atti-tudinal language to express her feelings, emotions and opinions on Miley Cyrus e.g. *in any way "cool" to be naked and licking sledgehammers in your videos', 'you will obscure your talent by allowing yourself to be pimped', 'from allowing yourself to be exploited, and it is absolutely NOT in ANY way an empowerment of yourself or any other young women, for you to send across the message that you are to be valued (even by you) more for your sexual appeal than your obvious talent'.*

The student teachers analysed the letter as an example of evaluative and judgemental language use that convey issues of othering and intersecting identities—is Miley Cyrus to be valued for more than her sex appeal? The analysis is also an example of how student teachers can work with subtextuality reading between the lines and posing critical questions to potential cultural subtexts such as hidden messages and values encoded in cultural artefacts, text and media (Fig. 2.3).

Dear Miley,

I wasn't going to write this letter, but today I've been dodging phone calls from various newspapers who wished me to remark upon your having said in Rolling Stone your "Wrecking Ball" video was designed to be similar to the one for "Nothing Compares" ... So this is what I need to say ... And it is said in the spirit of motherliness and with love.

I am extremely concerned for you that those around you have led you to believe, or encouraged you in your own belief, that it is in any way "cool" to be naked and licking sledgehammers in your videos. It is in fact the case that you will obscure your talent by allowing yourself to be pimped, whether it's the music business or yourself doing the pimping.

Nothing but harm will come in the long run, from allowing yourself to be exploited, and it is absolutely NOT in ANY way an empowerment of yourself or any other young women, for you to send across the message that you are to be valued (even by you) more for your sexual appeal than your obvious talent.

I am happy to hear I am somewhat of a role model for you and I hope that because of that you will pay close attention to what I am telling you. The music business doesn't give a sh– about you, or any of us. They will prostitute you for all you are worth, and cleverly make you think it's what YOU wanted... and when you end up in rehab as a result of being prostituted, "they" will be sunning themselves on their yachts in Antigua, which they bought by selling your body and you will find yourself very alone

---

Fig. 2.3 Extract from Sinéad O'Connor's letter on Facebook (Svarstad, 2016, p. 165)

The letter reveals processes of othering; the 'us' and 'them' dichotomy, because Miley Cyrus is represented by Sinead O'Connor as one of 'them', *a prostitute*, who will ultimately require rehab. Some critics say that Miley Cyrus' position, her whiteness and her wealth, allow her to do this with relatively few consequences. She has also been criticised for drawing on musical traditions from communities of colour to facilitate her transgressions (Apolloni, 2014). This critique is also concerned with intersectionality and identity issues.

Interacting

Interculturality is not a passive knowing of aspects of diversity, but an active engagement with diversity. Student teachers, thus, need to be engaged in interacting based on their learning and experiences of diversity in order to create personal meanings and to communicate about them (Liddicoat & Scarino, 2013, p. 61). Interaction can be understood as a process in which student teachers actively use their newly acquired knowledge and language. This can take many different forms such as writing a blog, producing a podcast, re-writing a story, making an interview, etc.

The interacting dimension in the intercultural module evolved around an analysis and redesign of existing ELT material on subjects such as friendship, love, music, MeToo, BlackLivesMatter, gay pride, voices of Africa, etc. that address broader issues of interculturality drawing on Cultural Studies, representation, intersectionality, othering and subtextuality. The student teachers were encouraged to use their analyses and redesign for the final exam.

Exam Synopsis: A Cultural Studies Approach to Work with Representation and Gender in the EFL Classroom

The following example illustrates how one student used her newly acquired knowledge from the intercultural module at the final exam in her second year of her B.A. studies. The English exam introduced with the 2012 Teacher Education Reform (mentioned above) requires that students submit four synopses within the different fields they have studied. The students draw one of the synopses at random, which forms the basis for an individual oral exam (45 min). Students must include both theoretical and practical elements in the synopses. The following example is from one of the student's synopses in Intercultural Competence from the summer exam in 2018, entitled: *A Cultural Studies Approach to Work with Representation and Gender in EFL Classroom*. The student's research questions (Fig. 2.4) indicate that the student is developing a metalanguage to address representation both theoretically and in practice. The research questions first consider theoretical perceptions of representation, the next question relates the theoretical perceptions to analyses of teaching material, and finally, the student presents her own development of teaching activities that support awareness raising in terms of representation and gender.

Research Questions:

• What is Representations and what is the theoretical background for this?

• Why is it important to consider representations when working with teaching materials?

• How can you work with representations in a teaching material in the EFL-classroom?

Fig. 2.4 Synopsis exam, research question (student 15)

The student demonstrates the beginnings of a metalanguage to discuss theoretical perspectives on representation with reference to relevant theories. Figure 2.5 is an extract from the theoretical section in the synopsis.

Since the Danish School Reform in 2014, the Ministry of Education economically supported the development of digital learning portals for all school subjects age 7–19. There are three dominant publishers, one of which is Clio Danmark. Municipalities buy access for their schools to one or more of the teaching portals. At Copenhagen University College, students have access to all the portals. The practice example the student chose for her synopsis is taken from the portal www.Clio.dk. The material is called *Friendship between boys and girls* (Figs. 2.6 and 2.7) and is designed for 11-year-old students in grades 5–6.

In the synopsis, the student analyses the material from an intercultural perspective with focus on representation. Figure 2.8 is an extract from the student's analysis of the practice element from Clio.

The student highlights the simplistic and categorising view of gender in the material and states that the text omits individuals who do not

---

The Cultural Studies approach views representation as a product of a constructive subjective process that work as an essential part of creating and exchanging meaning of culture (Hall 2013). Representation is the way we present the world through language, signs and imagery (Hall 2013). Risager (2014) presents us with three types of analyses for working with representations in teaching material: *Thematic analysis, intercultural analysis* and *power and empowerment analysis.* I have chosen to work with representation by an intercultural analysis and power and empowerment analysis. The intercultural analysis focus on sociocultural identities and has traditionally been used for a national culture aspect, but can be used for other social purposes like religion, lifestyles etc. In this particular case, the focus is on gender representation.

Fig. 2.5 Extract from theoretical section in exam synopsis (student 15)

Fig. 2.6 Friendship between boys and girls © Clio, 2019. *The text is not an expression of Clio's attitude toward the relationship between boys and girls, or between children in general. The text is randomly generated for the purposes of training oral proficiency and vocabulary skills* (*Photo* Monkey Business Images/Shutterstock.com)

Fig. 2.7 Boys have a lot fun playing sports together © Clio, 2019. *The text is not an expression of Clio's attitude toward the relationship between boys and girls, or between children in general. The text is randomly generated for the purposes of training oral proficiency and vocabulary skills* (*Photo* Colourbox.dk)

In this practice element, I have chosen to analyse and work with a teaching material from Clio Online for 5-6th grade called: 'Friendship between boys and girls' (APPENDIX 1).

The text from the teaching material, is about mixed friendships between boys and girls and why this can be a positive thing. The text concludes that *"a mixed friendship is beneficial because it's like having a brother or a sister, it is a perfect way to find out how the female and male mind works and that they could even help you get the number on that cute boy or girl that you have been wanting."*

If we look at the text with an intercultural analysis, we see a factual text where the author has an anonymous authoritative voice. The characterization gives us a quite unvaried picture of what it means to be a boy or a girl. There is no room for assertive approaches to gender.

The statement in the text about cons of mixed friendships, is characterized by a male-female binary view on sexuality as a self-evident discourse. The text also leaves out individuals who do not fit into these binary categories. In the choice of words, we see a clear imbalance in the power relations, but also in the imagery. The words chosen to describe boys and girls are very different. The girls are represented as mysterious, scheming individuals, the boys on the other hand are descripted like less dramatic, and in a way too superior to converse about emotions, which is rooted in a patriarchal discourse were men is portrayed as the dominant sex.

Fig. 2.8 Practice element in exam synopsis: analysis of teaching material (student 15)

fit into these binary categories. Furthermore, she states that the vocabulary and imagery emphasise the patriarchal discourse in which men are portrayed as the dominant sex. Although the student does not refer directly to essentialism or intersectionality, her analysis acknowledges gender as an aspect of interculturality. By identifying the patriarchal discourse on gender in the material, one could argue that the student is aware of processes of othering, although she does not refer to othering explicitly. The student engages in subtextuality, because she substantiates her analysis with analyses of vocabulary and imagery; however, she is not explicit about a socio semiotic approach to the analysis of the language use in the material. She could have drawn on the 'interpersonal' aspects of socio semiotics (Derewianka, 2015, p. 109) that the students worked with in module 1 of the B.A. programme.

The final step in the student's synopsis is how she would work with the material from the portal in class (Fig. 2.9). She states that she would make the students reflect critically on the representations of gender and sexuality. One way of doing this, she argues, is to deconstruct the representations in the material and to engage students in defining their own interests that might intersect and draw on many aspects of the students' identities. This is an example of how the student uses a critical discourse analysis to discover which potential subtexts are at play and how she can encourage the students to reflect on them. Again, she does not explicitly refer to a critical discourse analysis, but I would like to argue that she makes one.

The student's exam synopsis demonstrates that a Cultural Studies Approach to Interculturality provided her with a beginning metalanguage for language and culture analyses as well as pedagogical ideas to qualify existing material on the English language learning portal.

Teaching Interculturality in ELT

The new curriculum guidelines in Denmark for intercultural language learning explicitly define culture as complex and dynamic, highlighting that culture is not something static that is ascribed to an individual or to groups of people. Thus, these new guidelines for culture teaching in foreign language education implicitly form a critique of the German notion of *Landeskunde* (Svarstad, 2016, p. 20), sometimes interpreted as banal nationalism with stereotypical and touristic representations in language textbooks.

Words: 6.895 without references.

> If I were to work with this teaching material, I would use the text to make the students reflect critically on these representations of gender sexuality. I would also work with deconstructing the student's own ideas of gender and sexuality by making the students relate to the text and work with their own ideas of gender and sexuality.
>
> I would not use any of the activities from Clio but create an activity where the students are given statements that they have they write down in one of the two categories: *Boy* or *Girl.* such as "like playing football" "like getting new clothes" Then make an exercise where the students have to stand in a circle. The teacher read the definitions out loud and the students who thinks the definition fits on their personality, switch places with another student.
>
> This way we can work with the definitions again and see if they are somewhat constructed. Then I would have a plenary discussion about the exercise to further develop the students' critical awareness about the representations of gender, where I would also talk about other options that we have not spoken about, that doesn't fit into the binary and heterosexual category.

Words without references: 7.152

Words: 7809 with references

Fig. 2.9 Practice element in exam synopsis: implications for intercultural language teaching (student 15)

The new guidelines may place newly educated teachers in a difficult position in which they will have to collaborate with experienced teachers, who have not been educated in Cultural Studies and broader issues of interculturality nor social semiotics. Thus, there might be a clash of perspectives on intercultural learning and the view of language learning. As Kohler (2015) states in her study mentioned above, teachers who view language as structure and culture as information tend to give factual, often generalised, information and ask display questions. This is in alignment with Kearney's study, which claims that one of the many challenges of using culture in language teaching is getting beyond cultural 'facts' to acknowledge complexity and contradiction in cultural knowledge and experience (Kearney, 2016, p. 19). In addition to this language, teachers might be reluctant to teach controversial issues and to address diversity explicitly. A possible explanation for this is that some language teachers base their culture teaching on personal experiences, drawing upon their orientation towards their own language and culture, intuition and assumptions about what was good for the students to know (Kohler, 2015, p. 193; Svarstad, 2016, p. 114). Thus, there is a strong need for professional development in the field of teaching interculturality in foreign language education.

Implications for Teacher Education

The shift in foreign language education towards broader understandings of interculturality has global implications for teacher education in terms of curriculum, syllabus and intercultural language pedagogy. First of all, the curriculum must explicitly address non-essentialist approaches to culture learning and draw on discursive understandings of culture learning that equip student teachers with a metalanguage of key concepts from among others Cultural Studies that support a general analytical approach to dealing with cultural texts and representation. In addition, the curriculum must acknowledge a functional view of language education in which language is understood as social semiotics. Curriculum demands such as these have the potential to support discursive approaches to culture learning and engagement in broader issues of interculturality. Exam requirements must also include broader understandings of interculturality in student teachers' analyses of language textbooks and learning portals as well as in student design of teaching sequences and teaching plans. Kohler's study (2015) revealed that teachers who understand language and culture as social semiotics use exploratory discussion, open-ended questioning, interpretation, personalisation, comparison and reflection.

Secondly, the syllabus design must also include broader understandings of interculturality. In my study (Svarstad, 2016), I argue that a syllabus drawing on Cultural Studies and representation (intersectionality) with the sub-fields critical intercultural communication (othering) and critical media literacy (subtextuality) has the potential to foster engagement in complex understandings of representation and power and to meet the new curriculum demands.

In the process of syllabus development, it is worth considering to invite students to engage in the syllabus design; what aspects do they find relevant; identity politics, celebrities, blackfacing, Brexit, the American Election, Nigerian women's rights or the UN Sustainable Development Goals? Reaching out to the students and involving them in syllabus decisions may bridge different perspectives and interests in intercultural learning.

Thirdly, the shift towards broader understandings of interculturality calls for further research into intercultural language pedagogy as well as teachers' and students' perceptions of and engagement in interculturality. Intercultural language learning can take many forms and the current chapter draws on research findings based on Liddicoat and Scarino's model of interacting processes of intercultural learning (Fig. 2.1) (Liddicoat & Scarino, 2013, p. 60; Svarstad, 2016). The model provided the student teachers with a tool for redesigning teaching material based on Cultural Studies and broader aspects of interculturality.

Conclusion: A Cultural Studies Approach to Interculturality and Language Learning and Teaching

The current study is concerned with teacher education and how student teachers worked with a Cultural Studies Approach to Interculturality. However, to succeed with broader understandings of interculturality in language teaching, new teaching material must be developed. In Denmark, there was a unique opportunity for this in the period 2014–2019, because the Ministry of Education funded the development of new digital portals for all school subjects from grades 1–10 (ages 7–19). The digital portals developed for English teaching in Denmark are concerned with diversity and a non-essentialist view of culture learning to meet the new curriculum demands for primary and lower secondary school in Denmark. New topics such as METOO, Black Lives Matter, Brexit, Scottish independence, Climate change, indigenous people in Canada or Australia, religion, terrorism, subcultures, gay pride, voices of Africa and hip hop open up for Cultural Studies and discursive approaches to teach cultural texts and representation. Despite that, some of the teaching material is still essentialist and based on stereotypical notions about people and the world such as the teaching sequence *Friendship between boys and girls* analysed by the teacher student in this chapter.

From a trainer's-eye-view perspective, I recommend a combination of Cultural Studies and Liddicoat and Scarino's model of intercultural learning processes. Below is a list of central reflection questions developed by Risager (2018, p. 138) and Risager and Svarstad (2020, p. 158) to use in Cultural Studies analyses of textbook material, digital portal material or in design of teaching plans:

1. What cultural identities are represented, and how? (dealt with, or just mentioned) (class, gender, sexuality, race, ethnicity, religion, education, language, etc.).
2. What social identities are represented (dealt with, or just mentioned)? (celebrities, refugees, businesspeople, engineers, school children, homeless, journalists, etc.)
3. How are the people/identities represented, and what do they do? (work, spare time, consumption).
4. What kind of intercultural encounters are represented? Is there a power relation?
5. How are culture and identity viewed in the textbook/digital portal? (essentialist/non-essentialist? Static/dynamic?).

Recommended Texts

Kellner, D. & Share, J. (2019) *The Critical Media Literacy Guide: Engaging Media and Transforming Education*. Leiden: BrillSense. This book provides a theoretical framework and practical applications for educators and teacher education programmes who wish to engage in critical media literacy.

Liddicoat, A. J., & Scarino, A. (2013). *Intercultural Language Teaching and Learning*. Malden: Wiley-Blackwell. Students can find inspiration in a research-based survey of teaching and learning practice in intercultural language education. The model referred to in this chapter is elaborated on in Chapter 4.

Risager, K. (2018) *Representations of the World in Language Textbooks*. Bristol: Multilingual Matters. Risager's latest work presents a new and comprehensive framework for the analysis of representations of culture, society and the world in textbooks for foreign and second language learning.

Ryan, M. (2010). *Cultural Studies. A Practical Introduction*. Malden: Wiley-Blackwell. Ryan introduces students to Cultural Studies in short chapters that are very useful to spark an interest and discussion in class.

Engagement Priorities

1. How does a Cultural Studies Approach to Interculturality in ELT presented in this chapter align with your national curriculum and teaching context?
2. What opportunities do the language textbooks you have access to offer students in terms of engagement in broader issues of interculturality? In what ways could you qualify the material to address broader issues of interculturality?
3. I suggest further research into teacher and student perceptions and practices of interculturality.

4. I suggest further research into intercultural language learning processes drawing on cross-curricular collaboration between languages and social studies, geography, science, history, arts etc.

References

Books

Barker, C. (2002). *Making sense of Cultural Studies: Central problems and critical debates*. Sage.

Billig, M. (1995). *Banal nationalism*. Sage.

Byram, M. (1997). *Teaching and assessing intercultural communicative competence*. Multilingual Matters.

Derewianka, B. (2015). *A new grammar companion for teachers* (4th ed.). PETAA.

Dervin, F. (2016). *Interculturality in education: A theoretical and methodological toolbox*. Palgrave Macmillan.

Grossberg, L. (2010). *Cultural Studies in the future sense*. Duke University Press.

Hall, S., Evans, J., & Nixon, S. (2013). *Representation* (2nd ed.). Sage.

Halliday, M. A. K., & Christian, M. I. M. M. (2014). *Halliday' introduction to functional grammar* (4 udgave). Routledge.

Holliday, A., Hyde, M., & Kullman, J. (2010). *Intercultural communication: An advanced resource book for students*. Routledge.

Kearney, E. (2016). *Intercultural learning in modern language education: Expanding meaning-making potentials*. Multilingual Matters.

Kellner, D., & Share, J. (2019). *The critical media literacy guide: Engaging media and transforming education*. BrillSense

Kohler, M. (2015). *Teachers as mediators in the foreign language classroom*. Multilingual Matters.

Liddicoat, A. J., & Scarino, A. (2013). *Intercultural language teaching and learning*. Wiley-Blackwell.

Pickering, M. (2001). *Stereotyping. The politics of representation*. Palgrave Macmillan.

Risager, K. (2018). *Representations of the world in language textbooks*. Multilingual Matters.

Risager, K., & Svarstad, L. K. (2020). *Verdensborgeren og den interkulturelle læring* [The global citizen and intercultural learning]. Samfundslitteratur.

Ryan, M. (2010). *Cultural Studies: A practical introduction.* Wiley-Blackwell.

Said, E. (1978). *Orientalism.* Penguin.

Articles in Books

Byram, M. (2009). Intercultural competence in foreign languages: The intercultural speaker and the pedagogy of foreign language education. In D. K. Deardorff (Ed.), *The Sage handbook of intercultural competence* (pp. 321–332). Sage.

Dervin, F. (2014). Cultural identity, representation and othering. In J. Jackson (Ed.), *The Routledge handbook of language and intercultural communication* (pp. 181–194). Routledge.

Kabel, K., & Svarstad, L. K. (2019). Refleksiv literacy og interkulturalitet I L1 og L2. In *Sprogfag i forandring* (3. edt.). Samfundslitteratur.

Kellner, D., & Share, J. (2009). Critical media literacy, democracy and the reconstruction of education. In D. Macedo & S. R. Steinberg (Eds.), *Media literacy: A reader* (pp. 3–23). Peter Lang.

Porto, M., Daryai-Hansen, P., Arcuri, M. E., & Schifler, K. (2017). Green kidz: Young learners engage in intercultural environmental citizenship in an English language classroom in Argentina and Denmark. In M. Byram, I. Golubeva, H. Hui, & M. Wagner (Eds.), *From principles to practice in education for intercultural citizenship.* Multilingual Matters.

Risager, K. (2012). Intercultural learning: Raising cultural awareness. In M. Eisenmann & T. Summer (Eds.), *Basic issues in EFL teaching and learning.* Universitätsverlag Winter Heidelberg.

Svarstad, L. K. (2018). A Cultural Studies approach to intercultural encounters and interculturality. In P. Daryai-Hansen, A. Søndergaard Gregersen, S. K. Jacobsen, J. von Holst-Pedersen, L. K. Svarstad, & C. Watson, *Foreign language education: Between topic and educational theory.* Hans Reitzel Publishers (e-book).

Articles in Journals

Apolloni, A. (2014). "The biggest feminist in the world": on Miley Cyrus, feminism, and intersectionality. *American Music Review, XLIII* (2).

Luke, A., & Sefton-Green, J. (2017). The case for critical media literacy and digital ethics. *Sprogforum, Journal of Language and Culture Pedagogy, 65,* 1–7.

Svarstad, L. K. (2020) Cultural Studies and intersectionality in English language education: Exploring students' engagement in issues of celebrity, identity, gender and sexuality. *The Language Learning Journal*.

Web Sources

BBC News Entertainment. (2013). *Miley Cyrus and Sinead O'Connor row escalates.* https://www.bbc.co.uk/news/entertainment-arts-24395755.

Dervin, F. (2019). Open Call: *Interculturality in Teacher Education.* Retrieved January 3, 2019, from https://www.kau.se/interculturality-teacher-education-and-training.

Lewis, I. (2020). Noel Gallagher calls Miley Cyrus 'god awful woman' and claims British culture would 'never' sexualise female popstars. *The Independent.* Retrieved September 23, 2020, from https://www.independent.co.uk/arts-entertainment/music/news/noel-gallagher-miley-cyrus-mtv-vmas-midnight-sky-joe-rogan-b512638.html.

Ministry of Education. (2019). *Undervisningsministeriet, Vejledning for faget engelsk.* Retrieved December 18, 2019, from https://emu.dk/grundskole/engelsk/laeseplan-og-vejledning.

Oppenheim, M. (2016). Miley Cyrus: 'I didn't understand my own gender and own sexuality', Independent Retrieved from https://www.independent.co.uk/news/people/miley-cyrus-sexualitypansexual-variety-parents-lgbt-a7357871.html.

Teaching material: *Friendship between boys and girls.* (2018). Retrieved January 3, 2019, from https://www.clio.dk/engelskfaget/udskoling/.

Theses

Svarstad, L. K. (2016). *Teaching interculturality: Developing and engaging in pluralistic discourses in English language teaching.* Ph.D Thesis, Århus University Press.

3

ELT and Interculturality: Approaching Such a (Dis)Connection Through the Voices of Future Brazilian Teachers of English

Sávio Siqueira

Culture does not make people. People make culture.
Chimamanda Ngozi Adichie (2014)

Abbreviations Used in the Text

EFL   English as a Foreign Language.
ELF   English as a Lingua Franca.
ELT   English Language Teaching.
ESL   English as a Second Language.
ESP   English for Specific Purposes.
FL   Foreign Language.
SL   Second Language.
IC   Intercultural Competence.
TEFL   Teaching of English as a Foreign Language.

S. Siqueira (✉)
Bahia Federal University, Salvador, Brazil

© The Author(s), under exclusive license to Springer Nature
Switzerland AG 2021
M. Victoria and C. Sangiamchit (eds.), *Interculturality and the English Language Classroom*, https://doi.org/10.1007/978-3-030-76757-0_3

Introduction

The current phenomenon of globalization, directly derived from the post-war scenario, has transformed the world into "a tremendously complex web of villages, towns, neighbourhoods, settlements connected by material and symbolic ties in often unpredictable ways" (Blommaert, 2010, p. 1). As a result of such a phenomenon, international relations have increased exponentially, and naturally made intercultural communication a sine qua non element for people from all linguistic and cultural backgrounds to engage in all types of global interactions.

Kimura and Canagarajah (2018, p. 296) argue that postmodern social conditions, especially due to the increasingly immense mobility of different groups of people across geographical and digital spaces, have led researchers to "view communication as involving mobile semiotic resources that can be put together for particular contexts, audiences, and purposes". This means that, according to the authors, drawing on Blommaert (2010), we are to move from a *sociolinguistics of community* to a *sociolinguistics of mobility*, being the latter an emerging paradigm which focuses "not on language-in-place but on language-in-motion, with various spatiotemporal frames interacting with one another" (Blommaert, 2010, p. 5).

With this mind, Blommaert (2010, p. 19) goes on to assert that "the bits of language that are globalized are equally bits of culture and society, [so] in order to understand language globalization, we need to look at larger semiotic and cultural packages". Such panorama illustrates the complexities of today's superdiverse world (Vertovec, 2007) in which more and more communities, cultural backgrounds, and sociolinguistic resources are intensifying their contacts through encounters that are essentially intercultural. In other words, intercultural communication in our current reality has become crucial for people to be able to express their "culturality of ideas, theories, attitudes, values, and ways of life" (Estermann, 2010, p. 35).

According to Kumaravadivelu (2006, p. 131), "the most distinctive feature of the current phase of globalization is the global electronic communication, the Internet", which has unquestionably become "the major engine, [...] a unique source that instantly connects millions of individuals with other individuals". So far, the language of overall global communication is English, regarded by de Swaan (2001) as the only "hypercentral language" within the so-called *global language system*. English has been turned into a global merchandise to be acquired practically at all costs if we do not want to be excluded from the supposed benefits of globalization. It became synonymous of big business, marketed as "the language of development, modernity, and scientific and technological advance" (Phillipson, 1992, p. 11), and if we do not speak it, we are to feel like creatures of another planet.

In the background of the dominance of English as an international language is English Language Teaching (ELT), which has decisively contributed to such enduring hegemony. As Phillipson (1992) would contend, with all the paraphernalia of an established profession, ELT became a billion-pound industry. In his words, "the spread of English has not been left to chance, and language pedagogy has played a part in this process" (p. 6). Along the years, ELT has been carried out under different perspectives, following ideological constructs, which have generated great scholarship and massive scrutiny of its practices, principles, premises, and consequences.

For Phillipson (1992, p. 8), ELT has seldom pursued "connections between the English language and political, economic, and military power". On the contrary, its focus has predominantly been "on what goes on in the classroom, and related organizational and methodological matters" (p. 8). In fact, due to the strong emphasis on the "methodization" of pedagogical practices, where linguistic aspects have prevailed over others of even greater importance, several gaps have surfaced along the way. The intercultural dimension is one of these neglected aspects, although it has always been there in the background, especially when we take into consideration the condition of English as a global lingua franca. Despite the fact that English as a lingua franca (ELF) is deeply intercultural and "is presently likely to be the most common medium of intercultural communication" (Baker, 2018, p. 25), interculturality in these studies is still an under-researched issue (Holmes & Dervin, 2016). Actually, as Baker (2018, p. 25) argues, "it is a concern that there has been so little uptake of ELF research in intercultural communication literature, and that where it has been discussed it has often been marginalised and misrepresented".

Bearing this in mind, it is my contention that in order for ELT to live up to the demands of current potential global users of English as a lingua franca, we need ELT educators who are essentially aware of the importance of their intercultural competence (IC), defined by Spitzberg and Changon (2009, p. 7) as "the appropriate and effective management of interaction between people who, to some degree or another, represent different or divergent affective, cognitive, and behavioral orientations to the world". Thus, we need teachers prepared to teach interculturally sensitive classes as they envision paving the way for the development of their learners' intercultural competence so as to become active world citizens.

The reality described above, its implications, consequences, and outcomes, certainly offers itself as a prime site of investigation, and that is exactly what this chapter proposes. Drawing on a small scale study with non-native student-teachers from an English language extension programme of a Brazilian university whose purpose was to investigate the (dis)connection between ELT and interculturality both in theory and practice, my objective here is to discuss and problematize such aspects in light of the study's results in this specific context. Among other issues, the study has shown that interculturality is still a somewhat vague concept to these participants. Due to this, the intercultural dimension needs to be overtly explored in class once the future teachers come to realize that "an intercultural perspective emphasizes the learners' own cultures as a fundamental part of engaging with a new culture" (Liddicoat & Scarino, 2013, p. 29). But before I go deeper into such issues, I provide a brief overview of ELT in Brazil.

The ELT Scenario in Brazil

Brazil and South America are some of the most promising and desired markets by the global ELT industry (Kamhi-Stein et al., 2017). As a country from the so-called "expanding circle" (Kachru, 1985), English here is taught and spoken as a foreign language (EFL), and, of course, taken as a cultural product of great value. According to Rajagopalan (2003, p. 92), "the overwhelming presence of English in Brazil is no news to anyone, [and] over the past several years, the language has been making steady inroads into the nation's cultural scenario, dominating practically all walks of life and making its presence felt in every nook and corner of the country". But despite different policies and initiatives to stimulate and create opportunities for students to learn foreign languages in regular schools in the country, this intent as whole has not so far reached greater levels of success. A fairly recent report released by the *British Council* in São Paulo (2014) has shown that only 5.1% of the Brazilian population aged over 16 has some knowledge of the English language. Results of that study revealed that there are important differences between generations, and just as an example of this disparity, among younger people aged 18–24, the percentage of those stating they speak English just doubles, reaching 10%. This picture shows that in terms of English and foreign language education, Brazil is still very far from a democratization of the access to additional languages, especially when we take into consideration the socioeconomic underprivileged, overtly the greatest majority of the Brazilian population (Cogo & Siqueira, 2017).

This not so optimistic reality has in many ways planted in the Brazilian society a general belief that learning a foreign language in regular schools is a very challenging, if not an impossible, endeavour. English is a compulsory subject in both public and private schools, but as the official educational system has proved incapable of offering quality FL courses and programmes, compensatory education has promptly flourished with the objective of responding to a huge and profitable national market (Bohn, 2003).

The perfect illustration of this disturbing discrepancy in FL education in Brazil is the case of the myriad of private language institutes which have proliferated at an enormous pace, selling foreign languages, especially English, as a powerful and attractive product, even when they are commercialized at the most utilitarian level. In other words, the failure of one segment (regular public/private schools) has meant the success of another (private language institutes). And this is especially true in Brazil and in several other countries in South America, as Bohn (2003, p. 160) precisely remarks, since neither the private nor the public school systems in Brazil offer adequate English education in the regular elementary and secondary curriculum, wealthier families send their children to special private language courses where they can develop the necessary linguistic skills for immediate academic as well future professional needs.

As a regular discipline, English is part of all curricula at different levels, including in its instrumental modality, English for Specific Purposes (ESP), and the development of reading skills in university programmes. In the contexts where English is thought to be taught and learned successfully (language schools), the ELT industry exercises a very strong influence in local institutional policies which basically respond to the demands of an elite who is deeply affiliated to an enduring EFL tradition.

The global demand for English has broad implications for ELT, and no matter through which lenses we see and approach this expansion, the fact is that "ELT practices that have for long been in place need to be reviewed drastically with a view to addressing the new set of challenges being thrown at us by [the phenomenon]" Rajagopalan (2004, p. 113). Critiques towards the Anglocentric positioning of much ELT are not new. As English assumes the role of connecting people from very different linguacultural backgrounds, routinely (re)constructed in intercultural interactions, it is about time we go for a "dynamic and fluid approach that recognizes the nature of intercultural communication, particularly in [lingua franca] scenarios, as well as the situated, emergent relationship between language and culture" (Holmes & Dervin, 2016, pp. 17–18).

Although such aspects are fairly well-understood by teachers and teacher educators in Brazil, the traditional EFL orientation still seems to prevail, endorsing classroom practices that take place disconnected from social, historical, cultural, and political issues. That is, despite the fact that the celebrated globality of English and its consequent de-nationalization have "[called] into question the linguistic and pragmatic norms of English that have traditionally been taken for granted and conceptually pluralize [its] forms and uses" (Kubota, 2015, p. 23), significant changes in ELT in the country are still to fully reach practitioners, as they inevitably start moving into a post-native modelled TEFL era (Fay et al., 2016).

The Culture(s) of a Global Language

As well-known, culture is perhaps the most complex term to define in social sciences, and no language is ever culturally neutral. Even when we are discussing English in its role of a global lingua franca, my contention is that in this specific function English is a non-neutral intercultural zone of power, an arena of different struggles (Siqueira, 2018a). In this condition, "language (with its linguaculture) can be disconnected from one cultural context and reconnected to another as a consequence of linguistic flow, i.e. language users moving about in the world" (Risager, 2016, p. 39).

This overall picture is extremely relevant for ELT in today's world as we are to leave behind traditions like the unrivaled submission to the native speaker model, and engage with the development of the *intercultural speaker*, this interpreter, intermediary, catalyst, whose role is "more oriented towards social, cultural and linguistic complexity, involving the person relating to the identities of different people or groups and their conceptions of each other" (Risager, 2007, p. 234).

Along this line of thought, Nault (2006) reminds us that the "world of English" is much more complex than we generally acknowledge, as "English speakers in the Outer and Expanding Circles are not merely absorbing and parroting the English spoken in traditional centres of influence; they are actively reinterpreting, reshaping and redefining English in oral and written form" (p. 316). So, because English is now being used across diverse cultures at a pace never seen before, "English educators will not only need to be more culturally and linguistically aware but also able to design curriculums with an international and multicultural focus" (Nault, 2006, p. 320), posing, among other things, new challenges for EFL/ESL culture teaching.

Although regularly approached unsystematically and stereotypically, the cultural has always been part of ELT. According to Liddicoat and Scarino (2013, p. 21), "a solid approach to culture in language education should integrate a range of different understandings of culture". Due to its intrinsic complexity, the term is better thought of in the plural, i.e., "cultures". So, when it comes to language teaching and learning, we can see cultures as national attributes, societal norms, symbolic systems, practices, among others (Liddicoat & Scarino, 2013).

According to Widdowson (1994, p. 385), once a language "serves the communicative and communal needs of different communities, it follows logically that it must be diverse". Diversity and variety that are to be praised and explored at all levels, and when it comes to ELT, this certainly raises different questions, including those related to which culture(s) to teach and how to approach the issue related to the (in)separability of language and culture in such multilingual and multicultural contexts. In this sense, As Warschauer (2000, p. 514) highlights, "culture remains an integral part of language learning, but the approach toward culture must become multifaceted, taking into account the diverse cultures of the many people who speak English around the world".

The language and culture connection, for sure, poses immense implications for FL/SL education, ELT included. For Kumaravadivelu (2008, p. 22), based on all the studies the theme has generated for decades, "it is safe to assume that language and culture are linked, but they are not linked inextricably". Considering this reasoning, we can overtly defend that the cultures of a transnational language like English are many and as rich. They mix, they hybridize, and new ones are to blossom every single day in the endless ELF interactions that take place all around the world.

More than ever ELT has been called upon to respond to such a scenario of complexities and challenges involving language and culture. As Risager (2007, p. 3) adds, "a transnational language and culture pedagogy must see itself as being interdisciplinary and thereby be interested in language, culture, society and the individual (the subject)". Once it deals with the multilingual and multicultural subject as a world citizen, "the transnational paradigm[1] ought to be the new anchorage for language and culture pedagogy" (Risager, 2007, p. 190). Since English is currently the *par excellence* global means of intercultural communication in this context of massive transnational connections, and because "language education inevitably [privileges] language as the entry point to cultures" (Liddicoat & Scarino, 2013, p. 24), interculturality emerges as a core concept to this whole process. It is this relationship between interculturality and ELT that I will discuss in the next section.

Interculturality and ELT

As Liddicoat and Scarino (2013, p. 1) suggest, with the current process of globalization, increased mobility, and technological development, "there has been a growing recognition of the fundamental importance of integrating intercultural capabilities into language teaching and learning". A denationalized language like English, which in its function of a global lingua franca massively mediates contacts in "our transnational world of cultural flows of people, products, and ideas" (Risager, 2016, p. 58), embraces the complexities within the world of its global users, as much as it poses many challenges to ELT and its traditional tenets.

Bearing a much greater number of non-native than native speakers, ELF brings to surface several of its intrinsic characteristics such as high levels of hybridity, great diversity of users, and, above all, it makes possible for global speakers to engage in more and more meaningful intercultural interactions. With that in mind, as Risager (2016, p. 47) points out, "language teaching that aims at preparing and training students to take part in lingua franca communication is not necessarily required to focus primarily on national institutions and discourses on national identity", especially when one of the most important goals in this process is the development of the intercultural competence of the global citizen.

Contemporarily, it may sound weird and outdated to discuss the process of teaching and learning languages, especially English, without connecting certain fundaments to the concept of interculturality. Guilherme (2002, p. 297) defines interculturality as "the ability to interact effectively with people from cultures we recognize as being different from our own". Or, as she points out more recently, "the capacity of living with the unknown" (Guilherme, 2019, w/p). For Estermann (2010, p. 33), "interculturality describes symmetric and horizontal relations between two or more cultures, with the objective of mutually enriching one another and contributing to greater human plenitude". Young and Sercombe (2010, p. 181) refer to interculturality as "a dynamic process by which people draw on and use the resources and processes of cultures with which they are familiar but also those they may not typically be associated with in their interactions with others". Parry (2003), in turn, considers interculturality as a way of being in the world. For her, it is crucial that we retain a sense of self throughout the experience of encountering a new language or a new culture, as it is impossible to have empathy with others unless we understand ourselves.

As for this initial discussion on the term, I see also of crucial importance to understand what it means to be intercultural in this almost totally connected world we now live in. For Alred et al. (2006, p. 1), being intercultural involves:

- questioning the conventions and values we have unquestionably acquired as if they were natural;
- experiencing the Otherness of Others of different social groups, moving from one of the many in-groups to which we belong to one of the many out-groups that contrast with them;
- reflecting on the relationships among groups and the experience of those relationships;
- analysing our intercultural experience and acting upon the analysis.

Liddicoat and Scarino (2013, p. 29) contend that an intercultural perspective to language teaching "implies the transformational engagement of the learner in the act of learning", and "the goal of learning is to decenter learners from their preexisting assumptions and practices and to develop an intercultural identity through engagement with an additional culture". For such a perspective to materialize, we do need to struggle to have teachers prepared under the design, premises, orientations, and instruments typical of intercultural curricula. For this reason, as language teachers (especially English teachers), in my view, are in the centre of the discussions related to the intricacies of global interactions among people from all walks of life, it is a fact that we are in need of intercultural language educators for a world that is naturally becoming astoundingly intercultural (Siqueira, 2018b).

Founded on my experience as a teacher educator in Brazil, I conceive intercultural language educators as those professionals who assume and implement their everyday practice under an interculturally sensitive perspective; an orientation which invests in building bridges and long-standing connections. These are teachers who have developed, among other aspects, a clear understanding of practices and pedagogies intrinsically associated with an orientation that has the intercultural speaker as the target for second/additional/foreign language teaching.

Based on this, it is intrinsic to an intercultural curriculum to carry the potential to foster and develop teachers' intercultural competence, so as for them to be able to privilege the same process when engaged in their classroom work with their learners. Along these lines, Liddicoat and Scarino (2013, pp. 23–24) postulate that intercultural competence involves at least the following:

- accepting that one's practices are influenced by the cultures in which one participates and so are those of one's interlocutors;
- accepting that there is no one right way to do things;
- valuing one's own culture and other cultures;
- using language to explore culture;
- finding personal ways of engaging in intercultural interaction;
- using one's existing knowledge of cultures as a resource for learning about new cultures;
- finding a personal intercultural style and identity.

As we know, any type of educational process cannot be constructed without the individual's presence and his/her active participation. So, it does not make sense to learn from materials and situations which bring and discuss contents that have nothing to do with students' lives and contexts. In other words, teaching and learning processes guided by curricula, theoretical approaches, methods, procedures, and techniques will be fully effective when we decidedly unveil what is usually invisible or hidden by the (false) premise that the language classroom is to be taken as a neutral instructional venue detached from what happens in real life. It is then imbued with these assumptions that we shall embrace (language) pedagogical practices which feed on principles and premises of interculturality.

With this picture in mind, and conceiving language as much more than an object of teaching, but the mediating dimension between cultural subjects/worlds [whose] focus lies within the dialogical relationships and the place of interaction (Mendes, 2012), I believe that, as aforementioned, different aspects are to change in today's English language classroom. In many ways, we shall need to seriously think about new ways of decolonizing SL/FL education, including methodologies, curricula, assessment systems, materials, etc., which are still extensively used in ELT classes. The adoption of these more realistic and localized perspectives is in line with what Kumaravadivelu (2012) would call an "epistemic break", that is, a thorough re-conceptualization and re-organization of knowledge systems, "the episteme which basically symbolizes West-oriented, Center-based knowledge systems that practitioners in the periphery countries almost totally depend on" (Kumaravadivelu, 2012, p. 15).

For this to become a reality, it is crucial that we involve all ELT professionals, especially future teachers, as they are part of a new generation of practitioners who will have to work with a totally different student, today much better equipped to engage in global intercultural encounters. In an attempt to mirror this scenario, I shall then proceed to the next section which explores and discusses what some pre-service teachers and their classroom practice tell us concerning the (dis)connection between ELT and interculturality in an instructional context of a Brazilian university's language extension programme.

ELT and Interculturality: The Voice of Brazilian Teachers

To openly understand and discuss the (dis)connection between ELT and interculturality based on a local experience, I conducted a study with teachers from the English language extension programme of a Brazilian public university located in Salvador, Bahia. In this programme, pre-service and novice teachers are engaged in a practicum of four semesters at the most, and are supervised by teacher educators from the same university. The language courses are offered to the community at a reasonable cost in order to maintain the infrastructure and cover for students' monthly scholarships. These practitioners are all enrolled in both undergraduate (pre-service) and graduate (novice) programmes, but once they come to the extension programme, they are all considered "student-teachers".[2] Although limited in scope and number of participants, it is my expectation that the insights and results from this short investigation can be turned into practical implications in terms of awareness to the importance of systematically inserting issues of interculturality in ELT classrooms in different contexts.

As for the research design, participants were all non-native pre-service teachers of English and the data were generated through a small open-ended questionnaire and a few classroom observation sessions. The questionnaire comprised 5 (five) open questions sent to the group by e-mail and concerning the observations I basically registered ethnographically what happened in class. Of the 10 (ten) student-teachers I sent the questionnaire to, I received 7 (seven) responses back (5 females and 2 males), which makes a significant return for the cohort chosen. In terms of class visits, previously agreed with teachers, I could be present also in 7 (seven) of them, basically as a non-participant observer, totalling around 12 h of general English class observation. So, in order to have the participants reflect on what they would know about the topic, I decided to address the following questions:

1. *How would you, in your own words, define the term "interculturality"?*
2. *In your view, what is the relationship between English Language Teaching (ELT) and interculturality?*
3. *How intercultural do you think your English classes are? Justify.*
4. *How can teachers contribute to the development of students' intercultural competence?*
5. *What do you normally do in order to approach the ELT materials you use in a more interculturally sensitive way? One example would be interesting.*

As for *Question 1*, respondents did not come up with an articulated definition of what they believed interculturality was, but the associations they made showed that they are relatively aware of at least what interculturality implies:

- "It has to do with social diversity, the facility of being in contact with different cultures, experience new perspectives of life" (ST1);

- "The mix of cultures, different cultural perspectives, the exchange of many kinds of information among cultures, their customs and traditions" (ST2);
- "The coexistence and interaction among different cultures and nations" (ST3);
- "The coexistence and exchange between groups from different cultures" (ST4);
- "The continuous human interaction" (ST5);
- "An approach to improving ourselves and becoming better human beings by understanding other people, other cultures, other beliefs and ways to see life" (ST6);
- "The process and product of mixing different cultures; sometimes, this mixing can end up in a power game in which the dominant culture dominates and leaves the dominated culture in a really bad situation" (ST7).

In the classes observed, none of them addressed the topic directly, but there were moments when they could call their students' attention to cultural differences within topics like "values" (ST2), "attitudes to local/global problems like climate change, corruption, drink and drive" (ST3), "African culture as they talked about the movie *Black Panther*" (ST5), and "wedding celebrations in different countries" (ST6).

As for *Question 2*, student-teachers have depicted a somewhat clear view of what teaching and learning a new language encompasses, especially when it comes to the cultural component. However, by looking at their responses, it seems that there is still a prevalent posture of placing emphasis on the target culture of English-speaking countries:

- "Studying English or another language is not only to study the grammar and/or put the speaking part in action, but it is also knowing its culture to have a huge knowledge of what you are learning and why the language works in this way" (ST1);
- "Culture has an important connection with language, so for students to have a better knowledge and really know what they are studying, they need to go deep into the culture of the country of the language" (ST2);

- "When one decides to learn a language, one also decides to learn the culture associated with that language; when one decides to become a teacher, that responsibility increases immensely since you are responsible for accurately sharing information, so language and culture are two inextricable things, they are impossible to break apart" (ST6).

Within the same question, respondents explored the relationship between ELT and interculturality more directly, and, in some cases, they even considered interculturality as part of ELT:

- "Teaching any language involves a process of learning cultural aspects and translating some cultural notions that are tied intrinsically to the language, so it makes sense to point out that interculturality is a part of ELT" (ST3);
- "Most people use English words in their own vocabulary, for example, zipper, cooler, print, etc.; this is one of the ways to use interculturality in ELT, that is, to show the language use in real situations" (ST4);
- "Interculturality is absolutely necessary when teaching English because it makes students aware of how multifaceted that language is" (ST5);
- "ELT is directly linked to interculturality because in an English class there is always the clash between two (or more) cultures" (ST6);
- "ELT is closely related to interculturality because English is definitely the language that represents the dominant culture of today; by teaching English, liking or not, we are spreading this culture that ends up influencing and changing ours" (ST7).

By observing these teachers' lessons, although in the position of novice teachers, I could realize that they do spend class time discussing cultural information, especially in a comparative way. However, it is clear to me that they do need to understand better what interculturality encompasses in theory, and how to be able to plan and teach interculturally sensitive classes in a way that students realize that any action mediated by language is intrinsically intercultural. So, interculturality is not exactly part of ELT, but ELT is to be carried out embedded in interculturality.

Responding to *Question 3*, the teachers demonstrated an interesting sense of maturity once they had the opportunity to reflect on their practice. Their answers took different paths, some more aligned with the condition of English as a lingua franca (ELF) and all the implications to ELT in terms of change in perspective, and some still very much influenced by the tradition of the EFL perspective, especially when it comes to cultural references, for the latter directly connected to hegemonic English-speaking countries like the US and UK:

- "I think my English lessons are intercultural, but not as much as they could be; the material we work with doesn't provide us with many opportunities to explore interculturality as it seems to focus on the American Standard English; but I look for extra materials to introduce interculturality in class regardless of what I have at hand" (ST2);
- "My classes are not always intercultural because it depends on each group; sometimes students are too focused on grammar and most of them don't worry about this" (ST3);
- "It's hard to measure such an abstract concept, but given that we're teaching and learning a multicultural language in a country where English isn't the first or the national language, the classes are intercultural per se; I try to include as many countries as possible when I teach about English, especially because English is spoken in so many places" (ST4);
- "The language itself shows its cultural aspects, but for every class, I try to bring more things (songs, stories, videos, life experiences with foreigners) related to the language to discuss and make the relation with it even more approachable and intercultural as possible" (ST5);
- "I try my best to do so by bringing music, literature, culture and arts in general to the mix, especially among those students who are still constructing a vocabulary; I promote debates about cultural and behavioural themes when students are expanding and scaffolding the knowledge they already have, so interculturality is always present" (ST6);
- "I always try to bring curiosities, songs, series from countries that speak English to help my students understand better the 'English world'; they learn new slang and new words that Americans and British people use daily" (ST1);

- "Because of my appreciation for the American culture, I usually put a lot of information about it in my classes" (ST7).

By analysing my personal notes of the classroom observations, I could pinpoint several strategies the student-teachers make use of without necessarily approaching interculturality overtly, such as expanding the topic and localizing the discussion, so all students would be able to voice their opinions about different issues in a more secure way. Thinking of both perspectives, ELF and EFL, even intuitively, most participants while teaching depicted strong awareness of the condition of English as global language and that materials are to be critically assessed as they do not respond to the new and complex realities that students will encounter in their everyday life as global users of English.

It appeared to me that although these practitioners are practically compelled to take the native speaker model as a reference, both linguistically and culturally, they already developed a certain autonomy and security to point out that native speakers of English comprise today just a small portion of a huge global community of speakers that, at different levels of proficiency, use the language, engage in translingual practices throughout different world contact zones on a daily basis. And this is to be credited to their intercultural competence. In many ways, we can associate this sort of default orientation towards the affiliation to the native speaker model, especially when it comes to culture, to what Gramsci (1971) called "ideological hegemony". This involves reinforcing power structures and societal ideas and behaviours that sustain statuses of dominance normally reached by coercion and consensus. As any language is by nature a vehicle of culture, Gramsci (1971) asserts that there is always a powerful and prestigious dialect, Standard language, which serves as the language of a "great culture" (see also Baik, 1994). It is this supposed "great culture" that especially under an EFL perspective is expected to be imitated and valued as the passport to enter a world of power, knowledge, and prestige.

As an illustration of the aforementioned autonomy, ST2 brought a video clip by Canadian singer Justin Bieber (*If I was your boyfriend*) and another one by Beyoncé (*If I were a boy*) to practice the second conditional. She initially explored the formal elements and the lyrics to both songs and then proposed a very rich debate among students on genre differences in Brazil clearly under an intercultural perspective. All the other teachers normally complemented the textbook content, and even at elementary levels, a disposition to localize learning was carried out, as it happened in a class by ST5 when students were supposed to practice the verb "there to be". Referring basically to students' local realities (they come from or were born in different cities in the state of Bahia), she explored questions like "Is there any traditional festival in your city?"; "Are there carnival parties all over Brazil?"; "Is there any famous cultural event in your hometown?", etc. Upon answering the questions, the teacher would ask them to share any personal experience (good or bad) they had related to the topic.

Question 4 was designed as an attempt to have the participants reflect on how they could stimulate the development of their students' intercultural competence. For sure, it has probably crossed their mind that for them to foster such a competence in their learners, they themselves would at least need to have an awareness of what that meant and how they would see themselves in the whole process of helping people understand people. The answers, as expected, varied throughout different points of view:

- "Immersing students in the culture, bringing songs, movies, series, books, curiosities, news; doing everything that can help students feel a little how American life is" (ST1);
- "Choosing different ways to contribute to the development of the learners, applying some subjects to our reality" (ST2);
- "Introducing them to other variations of English, such as Jamaican English, Indian English, etc., through music, TV shows, and important cultural dates in these countries; encouraging students to talk about these intercultural aspects more, and really try and engage them in this topic" (ST3);
- "Teaching the language not simply as a tool, but as a way to understand the thinking and the perspective of the native speakers" (ST4);
- "Trying to share the experiences acquired in the continuous cultural development" (ST5);

- "Exposing learners to cultural differences in a respectful manner" (ST6);
- "Encouraging students to know about different cultures and, most importantly, to respect them" (ST7).

It was interesting to notice that all the respondents had at least some idea of what intercultural competence would encompass, as illustrated above. They clearly articulated it with what they would do in class in order to have students deal with the cultural component that normally, as already mentioned, would still be overshadowed by the linguistic component in textbooks and other materials. In the observation sessions, although there were not specific moments when they would explicitly talk about IC, it was not difficult to capture attempts that in a way contributed to expand their students' knowledge of other cultures. ST7, for instance, conducted a whole activity which proposed to compare how people in different parts of the world celebrate birthdays. He asked students to take their mobile phones and "google" the topic. The discussion was very interesting as they started comparing the way people celebrated birthdays in Brazil with other countries. Another one, ST6, approached the topic "happiness" using an extra video about the life story of a man from Thailand which ended up in a very rich discussion on differences in ways of seeing life.

Question 5 inquired what they usually do with materials in order to make their classes more interculturally sensitive.

- "I usually talk about 'Brazilian English' and give students a sense of our importance in the English-speaking community" (ST1);
- "Showing new curiosities or other materials to them" (ST2);
- "I use websites that focus on experiences written by different people around the world like *People in Levels*[3]" (ST3);
- "I try to offer different experiences without dissociating them from the context. If I'm going to show a video on how African people cook different dishes with rice in some countries, I must talk about the importance of their history while showing it" (ST4);

- "Art in general, literature, cinema... so, in class, after content exposition, there is always students' desire to talk about foreign customs and compare them with ours" (ST5);
- "I always try to compare with local examples – Brazilian situations, not only American or British examples and habits, but also examples from Nigeria, New Zealand, Australia, South Africa, and other English-speaking countries" (ST6);
- "I bring materials that deal with popular music and popular culture in general" (ST7).

As for the observations, this was probably the easiest aspect to identify in class. All teachers expanded the textbook's non-linguistic topics interculturally, and normally through extra materials. From a more critical stance, we can see that a lot of what was expanded is based on a more or less essentialist view of culture, especially because it addresses facts and information generally (and many times, stereotypically) linked to the lives of prestigious groups of a given society. But at least they went beyond what was dictated by the syllabus. ST5, for instance, used pictures of famous people from non-English-speaking countries to talk about appearances and share information about their lives. ST3 stimulated learners to write reviews of Brazilian and foreign movies/series hosted on Netflix (India, Cuba, France, Argentina, Germany, US, UK, etc.). ST6 invited learners to share their views of happiness based on the story of a Thai man presented on a video segment. In other words, it was clear to me that awareness towards the importance of making interculturality more and more explicit in ELT classrooms today is gaining ground, and potentially helping teachers understand that interculturally sensitive classes prepare students not to parrot language, but to place themselves in the world as global citizens able to interact in equal conditions with people from any linguacultural background. This behaviour then, in my view, opens important avenues towards conducting language education under a clear intercultural perspective.

Despite the fact that the experience narrated here takes place in a supposedly "monocultural" and "monolingual" part of Brazil, since all students and student-teachers share the same L1 (Brazilian Portuguese), the presence of the intercultural in their classes easily projects them beyond the idea of acquiring English as a mere utilitarian tool. Their intercultural experience, on the contrary, is to help them incorporate English as part of their linguistic and cultural repertoires, so as to empower them to actively participate in this new and complex global sociolinguistic landscape.

Concluding Remarks

Whenever we engage in any social interaction, we are to act interculturally. The spread of English as today's global lingua franca has unveiled, among other aspects, its powerful intercultural nature as a means of communication which puts in contact speakers from all corners of the planet. Taking into consideration the reality and an educational experience in Brazil, this chapter sought to discuss and problematize the (dis)connection between interculturality and ELT, expecting such reflections to lead into important practical implications to the regular English classroom. Through the voices of Brazilian pre-service teachers, it was possible to illustrate that no matter how impregnated they are with traditional EFL orientations that still privilege teaching and learning the language from a national paradigm, it was possible to see that a transnational perspective is (intuitively or not) solidly gaining ground both in theory and practice (Risager, 2007).

The world we live in today is open to all kinds of contacts. English is this line that weaves through the global societal fabric and turns every single person in the world into a potential intercultural speaker. Because of this, it makes all sense to invest in teacher education, course, programmes, curricula (re)formulations at all levels in order to guarantee that ELT is solely decolonized, reinvented, and finally carried out under a broad and democratic intercultural perspective. As Estermann (2010, p. 44) argues, "one of the objectives of interculturality is to foster peaceful relations among human beings, different groups, nations, civilizations, and religions". To respond to this and several other features which involve interculturality, we shall engage in an English language education that is to opt for the premise of teaching language for life, and in a more pragmatic sense, providing students with the proper resources, strategies, and skills for them to be able to develop their competence as world citizens.

I would like to end alluding to Mexican–American scholar Gloria Anzaldúa, author of a remarkable intercultural book called *Borderlands/La Frontera—The New Mestiza* (1987). In her writing, she explains carefully, many times painfully, what it means to live routinely in different worlds, especially if you come from an oppressed culture to survive and fight for your rights in a hegemonic culture. For many people experiencing such conditions, among many other aspects, developing their intercultural competence is sine qua non in order to be able to "survive" through cultures and languages.

In my very personal view, it is this feeling towards English as a global lingua franca that we shall stimulate in our students in ELT classes nowadays for the simple fact that we are teaching a language that respects no borders/*fronteras*, and, thus, in its fluidic dynamics, belongs to no one. Until we can take pride in the English we speak, with all the local traits, the distortions, and identity marks, not worrying about mimicking someone else's linguaculture, this language will never be ours, will never be twin skin to our identities. Engrossed in the endeavour of decolonizing ELT and its outdated pillars and orientations, I am absolutely sure that it is through the permanent presence of the intercultural in the whole pedagogical process that the spirit of change can at last prevail. And taking into consideration how the world functions today in terms of people's contact and interaction, we are to reach a point of no return. We just need to look beyond our own little and limited reality and act.

Recommended Texts

*Baker, W. (2015). *Culture and Identity through English as a Lingua Franca: Rethinking concepts and goals in intercultural communication.* Berlin: De Grutyer Mouton.

Taking into consideration the dynamic nature of intercultural encounters in ELF today, the author discusses the need for new approaches to understanding the relationship between language, culture, and identity.

*Ennis, J. M. & Riley, C. E. (Eds.) (2017). *Practices in Intercultural Language Teaching and Learning*. Newcastle upon Tyne, UK: Cambridge Scholars Publishing.

Aiming to respond to the growing need for intercultural approaches to teaching and learning languages, the book brings a collection of successful experiences rooted in praxis. It shares the activities, methods, models, and approaches which have been developed within specific contexts, highlighting how an "intercultural perspective" can be adopted in language pedagogy.

*Garret-Rucks, P. (2016). *Intercultural Competence in Instructed Language Learning: Bridging Theory and Practice*. Charlotte, NC: Information Age Publishing, Inc.

The book provides a framework to foster learners' deep cultural reflection, bridging CLT pedagogies to intercultural communicative competence (ICC) literacy-based approaches. It challenges language educators to prepare learners with twenty-first-century skills to meet the demands of an increasingly interconnected globalized world.

Engagement Priorities

- Among other aspects, the chapter calls special attention to the importance of the intercultural dimension in ELT classes. What are some of the arguments used to defend this point of view? Do you agree? Disagree? Why?
- How do you describe the Brazilian ELT scenario? How different or similar is it from your context? Was there any aspect of the context described that surprised you? Why? Why not?
- How do you see the definitions of interculturality brought in the text? Do they make sense to you? Is it worth emphasizing the importance of the concept for language teacher education? Why? Why not? What do you understand by interculturally sensitive classes? How would you define an intercultural speaker?
- How do you view the responses of the Brazilian teachers surveyed concerning ELT and interculturality? How similar or different would

they be from the voices of teachers in your context? What practical implications for the ELT classroom could you identify as you read participants' responses?

- Towards the conclusion, the text refers to the importance of decolonizing ELT by challenging its outdated pillars and orientations. Out of your experience, how feasible do you find this proposal? Agree? Disagree? Would you be willing to engage in such endeavour? Why? Why not?

Notes

1. Elaborating her thoughts from a postnational and transnational understanding of language and culture, Risager (2007, p. 1) argues that 'modern languages studies […] have to break with the traditional national paradigm and start to define a transnational paradigm that places [English] language teaching in a transnational and global context.'
2. In Brazil, it is very common to have student-teachers enter university language courses with previous teaching experiences. Except for the public sector, it is very common to hire English teachers without a university degree, especially in language institutes. Later in their career, they decide to pursue a degree in order to apply for other opportunities in the field.
3. www.peopleinlevels.com—an interactive page for learners of English from around the world to write personal stories in that language. The content is organised by level.

References

Adichie, C. N. (2014). *We should all be feminists*. Vintage Books.
Alred, G., Byram, M., & Fleming, M. (Eds.). (2006). *Education for intercultural citizenship*. Multilingual Matters.
Anzaldúa, G. (1987). *Borderlands/La Frontera—The new mestiza*. Spinsters/Aunt Lute Book Company.

Baik, M. J. (1994). *Language, ideology, and power: English textbooks of two Koreas* (p. 415). Unpublished PhD Dissertation, Graduate College of the University of Illinois at Urbana-Champaign, Urbana, Illinois, United States of America.

Baker, W. (2018). English as a lingua franca and intercultural communication. In J. Jenkins, W. Baker, & M. Dewey (Eds.), *The Routledge handbook of English as a lingua franca* (pp. 25–36). Routledge.

Blommaert, J. (2010). *The sociolinguistics of globalization.* Cambridge University Press.

Bohn, H. (2003). The educational role and status of English in Brazil. *World Englishes, 22*(2), 149–172.

British Council. (2014). *Learning English in Brazil: Understanding the aims and expectations of the Brazilian emerging middle classes.* A report for the British Council, 1st Ed. São Paulo, Brazil: Data Popular Institute. Available at: britishcouncil.org.br/sites/default/files/learning_english_in_b razil.pdf. Accessed 22 Dec 2018.

Cogo, A., & Siqueira, S. (2017). "Emancipating myself, the students and the language": Brazilian teachers' attitudes towards ELF and the diversity of English. *Englishes in Practice, 4*(3), 50–78.

De Swaan, A. (2001). *Words of the world: The global language system.* Polity Press.

Estermann, J. (2010). *Interculturalidad: Vivir la diversidad.* Instituto Superior Ecuménico Andino de Teología.

Fay, R., Sifakis, N., & Lytra, V. (2016). Interculturalities of English as a lingua franca: International communication and multicultural awareness in the Greek context. In P. Holmes & F. Dervin (Eds.), *The cultural and intercultural dimensions of English as a lingua franca* (pp. 50–69). Multilingual Matters.

Gramsci, A. (1971). *Selections from the prison notebooks.* International Publishers.

Guilherme, M. (2002). *Critical citizens for an intercultural world—Foreign language education as cultural politics.* Multilingual Matters LTD.

Guilherme, M. (2019). Intercultural. *Dicionário Alice.* Available at: http://alice.ces.uc.pt/dictionary/?id=23838&pag=23918&id_lingua=1&entry=24306. Accessed 24 Mar 2019. ISBN 978–989–8847–08–9.

Holmes, P., & Dervin, F. (2016). Introduction—English as a lingua franca and interculturality: Beyond orthodoxies. In P. Holmes & F. Dervin (Eds.), *The cultural and intercultural dimensions of English as a lingua franca* (pp. 1–30). Multilingual Matters.

Kachru, B. B. (1985). Standards, codification and sociolinguistic realism: The English language in the outer circle. In R. Quirk & H. Widdowson (Eds.), *English in the world: Teaching and learning and literatures* (pp. 11–30). Cambridge University Press.

Kamhi-Stein, L. D., Maggioli, G. D., & de Oliveira, L. C. (Eds.). (2017). *English language teaching in South America: Policy, preparation, and practices.* Multilingual Matters.

Kimura, D., & Canagarajah, S. (2018). Translingual practice and ELF. In J. Jenkins, W. Baker, & M. Dewey (Eds.), *The Routledge handbook of English as a lingua franca* (pp. 295–308). Routledge.

Kubota, R. (2015). Inequalities of Englishes, English speakers, and languages: A critical perspective on pluralist approaches to English. In R. Tupas (Ed.), *Unequal Englishes: The politics of Englishes today* (pp. 21–41). Palgrave Macmillan.

Kumaravadivelu, B. (2006). Applied Linguistics in an age of globalization. In L. P. da Moita Lopes (Ed.), *Por uma linguística aplicada indisciplinar* (pp. 129–148). Parábola Editorial.

Kumaravadivelu, B. (2008). *Cultural globalization and language education.* Yale University Press.

Kumaravadivelu, B. (2012). Individual identity, cultural globalization and teaching English as an international language: The case for an epistemic break. In L. Alsagoff, W. Renandya, G. Hu, & S. L. Mckay (Eds.), *Teaching English as an international language: Principles and practices* (pp. 9–27). Routledge.

Liddicoat, A. J., & Scarino, A. (2013). *Intercultural language teaching and learning.* Wiley-Blackwell.

Mendes, E. (2012). Aprender a ser e a viver com o outro: materiais didáticos interculturais para o ensino de português LE/L2. In D. Scheyerl & S. Siqueira (Eds.), *Materiais didáticos para o ensino de línguas na contemporaneidade: contestações e proposições* (pp. 355–377). Edufba.

Nault, D. (2006). Going global: Rethinking culture teaching in ELT contexts. *Language, Culture and Curriculum, 19*(3), 314–328.

Parry, M. (2003). Transcultured selves under scrutiny: W(h)ither languages? *Language and Intercultural Communication, 3*(2), 101–107.

Phillipson, R. (1992). *Linguistic imperialism.* Oxford University Press.

Rajagopalan, K. (2003). The ambivalent role of English in Brazilian politics. *World Englishes, 22*(2), 91–101.

Rajagopalan, K. (2004). The concept of 'World English' and its implications for ELT. *ELT Journal, 58*(2), 111–117.

Risager, K. (2007). *Language and culture pedagogy: From a national to a transnational paradigm*. Multilingual Matters.

Risager, K. (2016). Lingua francas in a world of migrations. In P. Holmes & F. Dervin (Eds.), *The cultural and intercultural dimensions of English as a Lingua Franca* (pp. 33–49). Multilingual Matters.

Siqueira, S. (2018a). Inglês como Língua Franca Não é Zona Neutra, é Zona Transcultural de Poder: Por Uma Descolonização de Concepções, Práticas e Atitudes [ELF is not a neutral zone; it is a transcultural zone of power: For the decolonization of conceptions, practices and atitudes]. *Línguas & Letras, 19*(44), 93–113.

Siqueira, S. (2018b). English as a lingua franca and teacher education: Critical educators for an intercultural world. In T. Gimenez, M. S. El Kadri, & L. C. S. Calvo (Eds.), *English as a lingua franca in teacher education—A Brazilian perspective* (pp. 87–114). De Gruyter Mouton.

Spitzberg, B. H., & Changnon, G. (2009). Conceptualizing intercultural competence. In D. Deardoff (Ed.), *The Sage handbook of intercultural competence* (pp. 2–52). Sage.

Vertovec, S. (2007). Superdiveristy and its implications. *Ethnic and Racial Studies, 30*(6), 1024–1054.

Warschauer, M. (2000). The changing global economy and the future of English teaching. *TESOL Quarterly, 34*(3), 511–535.

Widdowson, H. (1994). The ownership of English. *TESOL Quarterly, 28*(2), 377–389.

Young, T., & Sercombe, P. (2010). Communication, discourses and interculturality. *Language and Intercultural Communication, 10*(3), 181–188.

4

Interculturality and Professional Identity: Exploring the Potential of Telecollaboration in Foreign Language Teacher Education

Joanna Pfingsthorn, Anna Czura, Christian Kramer, and Martin Štefl

Introduction

An important prerequisite for facilitating the development of students' interculturality lies in intercultural communicative competence and awareness that foreign language (FL) teachers themselves bring into the classroom. Interculturality, understood here as 'a dynamic process by

J. Pfingsthorn
University of Bremen, Bremen, Germany
e-mail: pfingsthorn@uni-bremen.de

A. Czura (✉)
University of Wrocław, Wrocław, Poland
e-mail: anna.czura@uwr.edu.pl

C. Kramer
University of Oldenburg, Oldenburg, Germany

M. Štefl
School of Business, University of Chemistry and Technology, Prague, Czech Republic

M. Victoria and C. Sangiamchit (eds.), *Interculturality and the English Language Classroom*, https://doi.org/10.1007/978-3-030-76757-0_4

which people draw on and use the resources and processes of cultures with which they are familiar but also those they may not typically be associated with in their interactions with others' (Young & Sercombe, 2010, p. 181) can be perceived as an element of teachers' professional identities, i.e. frameworks that provide them with ideas how to do their work and how to understand their place in society (cf. Sachs, 2005, p. 15). Such frameworks have been shown to shape the dispositions as well as classroom and professional development choices of teachers (Coldron & Smith, 1999; Hammerness et al., 2005). It has been widely accepted that the interplay of cultural, social and political contexts in which individuals are embedded as well as their interaction with other individuals act as crucial factors that shape the development of teachers' professional identity (Winograd, 2003).

One way in which FL teachers can develop their own interculturality as an aspect of their professional identity is through the engagement in telecollaboration. In language learning contexts, telecollaboration, also referred to as an Online Intercultural Exchange (OIE) or virtual exchange, has generally been understood as online communication between individuals with different cultural backgrounds, set in some institutionalized context and aiming at the development of intercultural communicative competence (Belz & Thorne, 2006; Guth & Helm, 2010). In this sense, one of the main goals of telecollaboration has been to help educate 'intercultural speakers', who can 'see and manage the relationships between themselves and their own cultural beliefs, behaviors and meanings [...] and those of their interlocutors' (Byram, 1997, p. 12).

Prior to starting a telecollaborative project that would involve student teachers from our three institutions, we wished to gain insights into student teachers' intercultural experiences, familiarity with telecollaborative projects and their perceptions of possible intercultural and professional gains that can be derived from participating in such a project. Additionally, in order to determine the role of interculturality in the participants' professional identity, they were asked to elaborate on the principles, skills, duties and goals that they considered important in the teaching profession. With this in mind, we designed and distributed a questionnaire that aimed to explore the potential benefits and challenges associated with creating a culturally diverse platform for student FL teachers through telecollaborative means, which, by allowing them to engage in intercultural communication and exchange their ideas on their future profession with fellow student teachers, potentially shapes their professional identities and enhances their interculturality. The recommendations based on the findings were intended to inform the planning and administration of our future telecollaborative project and may be of interest to other teacher educators taking their first steps in virtual exchanges.

Theoretical Background

Professional Teacher Identity and Teacher Education

According to Sachs (2005, p. 15),teachers' professional identity 'provides a framework for teachers to construct their own ideas of "how to be", "how to act" and "how to understand" their work and their place in society'. Teachers' professional identities 'shape their dispositions, where they place their effort, whether and how they seek out professional development opportunities, and what obligations they see as intrinsic to their role' (Hammerness et al., 2005, pp. 383–384). They also exert an impact on how classroom practice is shaped (Coldron & Smith, 1999). In addition, they provide a ground for understanding, explaining and justifying oneself in relation to others (Maclure, 1993). Consequently, it is to be expected that teachers' professional identities exert an impact on their ability and willingness to recognize various forms of learner diversity as a valuable resource, thereby following the principles of inclusive education. This poses the question of whether and how teachers' professional identities can be shaped to meet this goal.

The formation of professional identity is believed to be an intersectional process extending over the social, cultural and political contexts teachers find themselves in as well as their beliefs, attitudes, narratives and biographies (Rodgers & Scott, 2008; Sachs, 2005; Winograd, 2003). In this sense, professional development of teachers takes place both on the affective and cognitive levels, as it often requires the engagement with new and differing ideas about education as well as emotional adjustments when teachers' personal beliefs are challenged (Bell & Gilbert, 1994; Day & Sachs, 2004; Stoll et al., 2012). Clarke and Hollingsworth (1994, p. 950) suggest in addition that the personal domain (teachers' knowledge, attitudes and beliefs) continuously interacts with the experiences gathered within the domain of teaching practice, the domain of consequence (salient outcomes) as well as the external domain (sources of information, stimulus or support).

Yet, professional development programmes have often proven ineffective in their attempts to affect and effect teacher change. What has been suggested is a shift in focus away from the conception that change is something that is done to teachers, who act as relatively passive participants. Instead, professional development, adjustment or change is to be seen as a complex process in which teachers develop a sense of agency and become active learners, who shape their professional growth through reflective participation (Fullan & Stiegelbauer, 1991; Guskey, 1986; Hal & Loucks, 1977; Johnson, 1996). As Little (1995, p. 180) puts it, '[…] teacher education should be subject to the same process of negotiation as are required for the promotion of learner autonomy in the language classroom'.

Telecollaboration and Teacher Education

The international ELT (English language teaching) community seemed to have been relatively quick to embrace and develop various forms of virtual exchange (O'Dowd, 2015); however, notwithstanding its explosive growth and success of projects such as eTwininng, it is safe to say that 'telecollaboration has not yet been mainstreamed into higher education' (Helm, 2015, p. 197). A similar picture can be observed in the broadly defined pedagogy of online intercultural exchange, where 'the literature and tools related to teacher training and CALL have not paid great attention to the challenges of establishing and running telecollaborative exchange projects in the foreign language classroom' (O'Dowd, 2015, p. 64).

Reflecting on this situation, researchers in the field of CALL and telecollaboration generally recommend a more systematic incorporation of virtual exchanges into teacher training programmes (Guichon & Hauck, 2011; Helm, 2015; O'Dowd, 2015, 2017; O'Dowd & Waire, 2009). This need seems acute for two reasons. First, telecollaboration is viewed as an 'inclusive practice that can offer future teachers the opportunity to engage constructively with difference and contribute to the creation and maintenance of welcoming, inclusive spaces as they interact and collaborate online' (Virtual Exchange, p. 4), i.e. as a practice valuable to teacher trainees (of any stage and experience) at professional, personal and intercultural levels. Second, representing a step away from a rigid lesson plan and requiring considerable flexibility on the part of the teacher, telecollaboration is perceived as arguably one of 'the most difficult and complex CALL methods' which requires a 'complex array of skills, knowledge, and attitudes that teachers are expected to bring to online intercultural exchange projects' (O'Dowd, 2015, p. 65).

Speaking about the necessary pedagogical skills, O'Dowd (2015) identifies four main teacher competences necessary for telecollaboration: (a) organizational, (b) pedagogical, (c) digital competences and (d) attitudes and beliefs allowing them to negotiate the details of a telecollaborative exchange with the partner teacher. As O'Dowd and Waire (2009, p. 185) recommend, 'preparing educators for implementing successful telecollaborative projects needs to involve the development of an online collaborative competence for teachers as well as developing their awareness of the different options available in telecollaborative task design'.

The slowly but surely emerging training opportunities in telecollaboration for both pre- and in-service teachers exist in two parallel though often complementary lines: (a) traditional institutional training provided by pedagogical faculties, which includes either telecollaboration as such (e.g. Sadler & Dooly, 2016) or provides training in necessary pedagogical skills and competencies ranging from intercultural communicative competence and 'adequate training programmes for CALL and CMC-based language teaching informed by pedagogical considerations and suitable theoretical frameworks' (Guichon & Hauck, 2011, p. 189) to multimodal communicative competence, multiliteracy and learner autonomy training (Fuchs et al., 2012, p. 83); and (b) training facilitated and shared through professional communities of learning, empowering interested teachers by organizing conferences, sharing best practice, creating teacher tutorials, blueprints for online projects and teaching manuals, and facilitating telecollaboration by bringing together potential telecollaborative partners. Examples of such professional communities include Telecollaboration for Intercultural Language Acquisition (TILA), UNICollaboration or EVALUATE.

The Significance of Interculturality/Diversity in Teacher Education

The current educational policy of the European Commission with respect to competences that should be developed and fostered in the provision of teacher education puts a strong emphasis on the notion of diversity as well as tolerance and respect, following for instance the *diversity education* approach (cf. Blell, 2013, p. 230). The EU and its member states recognize the need to 'empower and equip teachers to take an active stand against all forms of discrimination, to meet the needs of pupils from diverse backgrounds, to impart common fundamental values and to prevent racism and intolerance' (PPMI, 2017, p. 13). The argumentation rests on the premise that social transformations taking place in Europe such as intra-continental mobility, international migration but also asylum seeking create culturally and diverse communities, in which addressing the needs of all learners becomes a necessity (PPMI, 2017).

Over the last few decades, the notion of cultural and linguistic diversity has also played an ever-increasing role in the academic and political discourse of the field of European foreign language education (e.g. Beacco et al., 2016; Blell, 2013; De Florio Hansen, 2011). The *Common European Framework of Reference for Languages* (CEFR), a pan-European guideline used to describe the achievements of foreign language learners in the subject matter, draws the attention to the fact that (Council of Europe, 2001, p. 2):

the rich heritage of diverse languages and cultures in Europe is a valuable common resource to be protected and developed, and that a major educational effort is needed to convert that diversity from a barrier to communication into a source of mutual enrichment and understanding.

The CEFR advocates the development of plurilingual and pluricultural competence, which it understands as the ability 'to use languages for the purposes of communication and to take part in intercultural action, where a person, viewed as a social agent, has proficiency, of varying degrees, in several languages and experience of several cultures' (Council of Europe, p. 168).

With this in mind, foreign language teachers need to assume a new role in the classroom: that of an 'intercultural mediator, able to act as an intermediary between their own and the L2 culture(s)' (Czura, 2016, p. 84); or that of a foreign language and intercultural competence teacher (cf. Sercu, 2006). (Future) teachers' own conceptualization of interculturality and their own intercultural communicative competence form important elements in the construction of their own professional identity, which in turn informs, shapes and influences their teaching practices in the multilingual and multicultural foreign language classrooms. What becomes evident here is that, while teachers' own professional identity as a whole shapes and influences their teaching practices in general, their intercultural competence understood as the 'ability to deal with differences that derive from everyday communication' (Magos & Simopoulos, 2009, p. 225) enables them to '(re)construct their identity as teachers of intercultural competence' (Ortactepe, 2015, p. 107). In consequence, (future) teacher's beliefs about these roles as well as interculturality and diversity 'need to be targeted, focused strategically, in order to facilitate professional development and foster effective classroom practice' (Sercu & St. John, 2007, p. 51). This needs to be reflected in the educational policy not only on the supranational level, as e.g. in the CEFR, but also on the national and institutional levels.

Concrete educational tools developed for teacher education purposes by the European Commission, such as e.g. the European Portfolio for Student Teachers of Languages (EPOSTL) developed at the European Centre for Modern Languages in 2007, encourage reflection on, among other competences, the extent to which language teachers feel competent to provide learners with materials and activities that foster their interculturality. Tools such as the EPOSTL thus address also 'how language teachers negotiate their identities as teachers of intercultural competence' (Ortactepe, 2015, p. 96).

On the state level, teacher education standards, at least in some member states, allude to different aspects of interculturality. In Germany, such standards are defined by the Standing Conference of the Ministers of Education and Cultural Affairs (KMK) and are recognized as guidelines by all the federal states. The standards describe requirements concerning competences, skills and attitudes of (future) teachers and educators. As such they also lay out the objectives for teacher education programmes (cf. KMK, 2014, p. 3). Among the eleven competence domains specified in the KMK standards for teacher education five allude to the importance of interculturality and diversity as well as institutional cooperation and mobility. As such, (future) teachers should know about the intercultural dimension in the design of educational and pedagogical processes (cf. KMK, 2014, p. 9), acknowledge diversity as an integral part of successful learning (cf. KMK, 2014, p. 10), be informed about theoretical concepts and aspects of diversity/heterogeneity (cf. KMK, 2014, p. 11), know that cooperation with other educational institutions comes with potentially differing perspectives on behalf of the involved cooperation partners (cf. KMK, 2014, p. 11), be able to reflect upon the challenges that diversity and heterogeneity pose for the teacher profession (cf. KMK, 2014, p. 13), and be accustomed to organizational requirements and conditions regarding intra- and inter-institutional cooperation structures (cf. KMK, 2014, p. 13). All could be realized via virtual exchange and telecollaboration. The KMK standards for teacher education emphasize that educators need to be able to mediate interculturality and diversity in their own (professional) identity as well as in the identities of their (future) students as a valuable resource and an asset for learning as well as teaching processes. Additionally, they point out the importance of the ability of (future) educators to carry out cooperative measures with other educational institutions bearing in mind that such cooperation requires an intercultural understanding of each other.

Research Methodology

Research Objectives

The study sets out to explore potential benefits and challenges that student teachers of foreign languages associate with intercultural telecollaborative exchanges within their occupational group. Our specific research interest focused on their perception of potential intercultural gains that such an opportunity could provide them with. In addition, we encouraged our participants to reflect on their professional identity as a future foreign language teacher. In particular, the participants were prompted to elaborate on the principles, skills, duties and goals that they considered important and to reflect on their ideas of 'how to be', 'how to act' and 'how to understand' their work as future teachers and their place in society. Based on the answers to both closed-ended and open-ended parts of the questionnaire, it was also expected to gain insight into the student teachers' understanding of the concept of interculturality and its role in foreign language teaching. In this paper we focus on the following research questions:

1. To what extent do student teachers from three European countries assume that their potential engagement in telecollaborative exchange with peers in their (future) profession can be associated with gains in their interculturality?
2. Is there any correlation between specific aspects of their professional identity (or their professional identity profiles) and their evaluation of potential gains within their own understanding of interculturality associated with telecollaboration?
3. To what extent do student teachers consider themselves as teachers of intercultural communicative competence?

Participant Profiles and Context

The study was conducted among 44 Polish and 65 German student teachers pursuing their under- and post-graduate degrees in

English/American studies as well as 25 Czech in-service teachers pursuing their post-graduate teacher degrees in English. In the Polish context, the undergraduate and post-graduate students of the English Philology programme can choose an optional FL teaching course to obtain full nationally acknowledged qualifications to teach English in primary and secondary education, respectively. The teaching course consists of psychology and pedagogy training, TEFL (teaching English as a foreign language) classes, supervised teaching and teaching internships in schools at the respective levels of education. The teacher training programme in the Czech institution is a 4-semester, distance study training for both in-practice teachers and graduates from non-pedagogical faculties. The programme was created in response to specific legislative changes introduced by the Czech Ministry of Education in 2004 and 2005 which make it mandatory for all language teachers to obtain a Qualifications Certificate to teach English at elementary and/or high schools. Participants of this course are either English teachers (often with many years of teaching practice) who already teach but lack any formal qualification or certified teachers of other subjects who wish to extend their certification to be able to teach English. In the German context, the undergraduate study programme for English includes obligatory introductory as well as elective advanced courses/seminars on TEFL. On the graduate level, students of English can choose between several programmes which are tailored towards different school forms (e.g. Master of Education for Primary School, Lower and Upper Secondary School, or Special Educational Needs). The different graduate teacher training programmes all include pedagogy and education science training, courses on TEFL as well as supervised teaching and research internships at schools of up to 18 weeks of length.

One particularly striking aspect of the participant profiles was the time they had spent abroad prior to the study. While many German participants (46%) reported having spent more than 6 months abroad in an English-speaking country, only (12%) of the Polish participants provided the same answer. About a third of the Czech in-service teachers (33%) reported having spent more than 6 months abroad in an English-speaking country. The high level of German students' mobility may stem from the fact that the students who want to become English teachers are required to spend a compulsory stay abroad (three months) in an English-speaking country before they finish their studies.

Before data collection started, we presented the idea of telecollaboration to the participant group as an Internet-based exchange, which engages students from different geographic locations to work on joined projects or tasks under the supervision of educators. In the case of our project, this meant that various forms of communication (e.g. chat, teleconferencing tools, forums, wikis, Facebook or other social networks) would be used in order to establish a way for (student) teachers coming from different geographical locations to exchange their ideas, tips or opinions about their (future) profession.

Instruments

The data were collected by means of a written questionnaire in English that consisted of closed-ended and open-ended questions. Following a set of items that explored participants' educational, cultural and linguistic backgrounds, the instrument included questions that were aimed to measure the level of participants' familiarity with the concept of telecollaboration as well as their intrinsic motivation to engage in intercultural telecollaborative projects that deal with their (future) profession. Subsequently, the participants were faced with a series of statements that described various advantages and challenges that telecollaboration could be associated with in the sphere of intercultural gains. Selected items were loosely based on Byram's model of intercultural communicative competence (Byram, 1997) as this model is widely cited in FL pedagogical literature and frequently used in the FL classroom (Matsuo, 2012). At the same time, it should be mentioned that Byram's model has been subject to vocal criticism for a number of reasons, in particular for its identification of culture with the so-called national culture (Matsuo, 2012), its perpetuation of the Cartesian/Enlightenment metaphor of the rational thinking subject, its lack of attention to the 'hybrid and shifting nature of the self and the socially constructed nature of language' (Ferri, 2014, p. 18) and dialogic perspective (Hoff, 2014; Matsuo, 2015), as well as for its inability to productively work with 'elements of contention and disagreement' (Hoff, 2014, p. 515). These objections to Byram's model, however, do not directly affect the findings of the survey as they do not seem to directly problematize professional teacher identity or telecollaborative task design except in cases addressed below. Our participants were asked to express the degree to which they agree or disagree with said items (Likert scale: 1 = strongly disagree, 5 = strongly agree).

The participants were then asked to describe their professional identity as (future) teachers. First, the informants were requested to evaluate themselves on a set of semantic differential scales following survey suggestions by Clément et al., (1994). Each of these scales represented a dimension with pairs of opposites and seven points in between, e.g.

Imaginative   __/ __/ __/ __/ __/ __/ __/ Unimaginative

The remaining dimensions included the following pairs: *consistent— inconsistent, enthusiastic—unenthusiastic, thorough—unsystematic, fair— unfair, aware of the local classroom context and its implications for teaching—unaware of the local classroom context and its implications for teaching, autonomous/self-endorsed in my classroom choices—dependent on external factors in my classroom choices, reflective—unreflective, familiar with subject teaching methodology—unfamiliar with subject teaching methodology, causal agent in the classroom—not having much influence in the classroom, inquisitive—non-inquisitive, interesting—boring, suited for the profession—unsuited for the profession.*

The participants were asked to rate how they see themselves as (future) teachers in view of the two poles. Finally, these data were supplemented with responses to the open-ended question, which asked the participants to further describe their professional identity as a (future) teacher. Here the participants described some of the principles, skills, duties and/or goals that they considered important. They were also requested to summarize their ideas of 'how to be', 'how to act' and 'how to understand' their work as teachers and their place in the society.

The collected quantitative data were subjected to statistical analysis of central measure tendencies, analyses of variance as well as correlations, whereas the open-ended responses were subjected to inductive content analysis.

Results

When asked whether they had heard of the concept of telecollaboration, a vast majority of the sample reported unfamiliarity with the idea (80% of the German sample, 72% of the Czech sample and 97.8% of the Polish sample were not familiar with the concept).

In order to assess whether student teachers from the three European countries assume that their potential engagement in telecollaborative exchange with peers in their (future) profession can be associated with gains in their interculturality, we asked the participants to express the extent to which they agree with a number of statements listed in Figs. 4.1, 4.2 and 4.3.

Figure 4.1 illustrates the level of agreement with the very basic and general assumption that telecollaboration (of the kind presented in the project) could lead to a development in the participants' intercultural

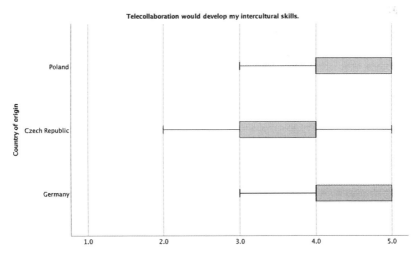

Fig. 4.1 Self-reported perception of the potential impact of telecollaboration on the development of intercultural skills

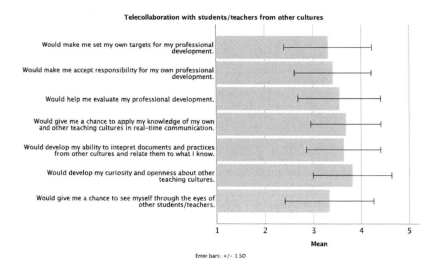

Fig. 4.2 Self-reported appraisal of the potential of telecollaboration

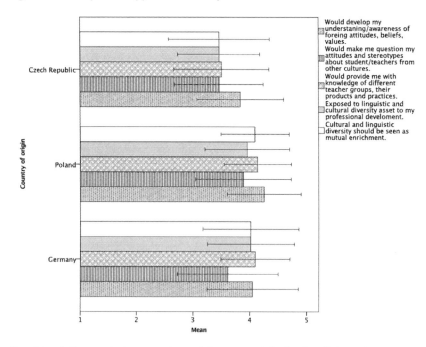

Fig. 4.3 Self-reported perception of the potential of telecollaboration

skills. Here we observe that the Polish and German participants seem to be quite positive that intercultural virtual exchange could lead to growth within their interculturality [M PL (mean in the Polish group) $= 4.21$, with standard deviation (SD) $= 0.67$; M DE (mean in the German group) $= 4.27$, SD $= 0.62$], while the Czech participants express more reservations [mean in the Czech group (M CZ) $= 3.51$, SD $= 0.62$].

Although this general trend may seem promising at first sight, a detailed analysis of a set of more concrete statements reveals growing levels of scepticism rooted within all participants regardless of their country of origin. As seen in Fig. 4.2, our participants only somewhat agree with the notion that telecollaboration would develop their curiosity and openness towards other cultures ($M = 3.83$, SD $= 0.83$). They also express less optimistic views ($M = 3.34$, SD $= 0.9$), when asked whether telecollaboration of (future) teachers would have the potential to encourage perspective switching and looking at oneself from the perspective of other teachers and students. Similarly, the participants are less optimistic with respect to the notion that their engagement in telecollaboration would help them interpret documents and practices from other cultures and relate them to what they already know ($M = 3.64$, SD $= 0.77$).

A comparably sceptical tendency could be observed with respect to the idea that virtual exchange of the proposed nature could be seen as a source of inspiration to set targets for the professional development of participants ($M = 3.31$, SD $= 0.91$) and as a motivating factor that would encourage taking responsibility for their own professional development ($M = 3.39$, SD $= 0.79$). The participants expressed similarly sceptical views concerning the prospect of developing their curiosity about and openness for other teaching cultures ($M = 3.83$, SD $= 0.83$) through telecollaboration and generally only somewhat agreed that virtual exchange would allow them to critically evaluate perspectives, practices and products in and of other teaching cultures ($M = 3.68$, SD $= 0.69$).

The data represented in Fig. 4.3 reveal some country-specific views with respect to some concrete aspects of the participants' perception of their own interculturality as well as the benefits of cultural and linguistic diversity that telecollaboration could offer. The Polish and the German student teachers generally somewhat agreed that cultural and linguistic diversity should be seen as a source of mutual enrichment (M PL = 3.9, SD = 0.82; M DE = 4.0, SD = 0.87), while the Czech sample expressed more scepticism (M CZ = 3.4, SD = 0.86). The Czech participants were also not as convinced that telecollaboration would provide them with knowledge of different teacher groups including their practices and products (M CZ = 3.4, SD = 0.82), and that it would make them question their stereotypes about students/teachers from other countries (M CZ = 3.46, SD = 0.78). In addition, the data revealed that both the Polish and the German sample generally somewhat agreed that exposure to linguistic and cultural diversity would be an asset to their professional development (M PL = 3.9, SD = 0.79; M DE = 4.0, SD = 0.77), while the Czech sample tended to be less convinced of that idea (M CZ = 3.4, SD = 0.76).

In order to assess whether there is any correlation between specific aspects of professional identity (or their professional identity profiles) and the evaluation of potential gains within participants' own concept of interculturality associated with telecollaboration, we computed the Pearson correlation coefficients for a set of professional identity markers as well as the evaluation of the statement '*Telecollaboration would develop my intercultural skills*'.

Table 4.1 lists all statistically significant instances of correlation between the level of agreement with the above statement and the various dimensions of professional identity for the three participant groups. All observed correlations were positive and ranging from low to moderate. The data revealed that Czech participants who considered themselves to be consistent, reflective, imaginative, interesting, inquisitive and/or aware of their local classroom context and its implications for teaching were more likely to agree that there is a potential link between engaging in telecollaboration with peers and the development of intercultural skills. For the Polish sample, perceiving oneself as an imaginative and interesting teacher seemed to be correlated with a more positive appraisal of the link between engaging in telecollaboration and growth within one's own interculturality. Furthermore, Polish participants who described themselves as enthusiastic were also more likely to agree with the idea of a link between telecollaboration and intercultural development. A similar

Table 4.1 Pearson's correlation coefficients for markers of professional identity and the agreement with the statement 'Telecollaboration would develop my intercultural skills', statistically significant with **p<0.001 and *p<0.005

	Germany	Poland	Czech Republic
Consistent	–		0.539**
Enthusiastic	–	0.349*	–
Thorough	–	0.438*	–
Fair	0.308*	0.323*	–
Aware of context	–	–	0.584**
Autonomous	–	–	–
Reflective	–	–	0.461*
Familiar w. methods	–	–	–
Imaginative	0.258*	0.411*	0.478*
Interesting	–	0.343*	0.426*
Suited for profession	0.3*	–	–
Causal agent	–	–	–
Inquisitive	–	–	0.399*

tendency was observed for Polish participants who perceive themselves as thorough and fair.

The German sample, in contrast, revealed few weak links between specific markers of professional identity and the appraisal of the potential positive impact of telecollaboration on intercultural growth. Here only the participants who considered themselves fair, imaginative and suited for the profession showed a higher likelihood of evaluating the link between telecollaboration and intercultural development in a positive way.

Through content analysis of the responses to the open-ended questions on participants' perceptions of their professional identity, we explored whether and to what extent the student teachers considered themselves as intercultural mediators responsible for not only communicative but also intercultural development of FL learners. In total, 47 German (72%), 40 (91%) Polish and 4 (16%) Czech student teachers provided responses to this question. The responses revealed that irrespective of the country of origin, the participants most often referred to creating interesting and safe environment in order to motivate and engage learners as the most important element of their teaching. The second most frequently recalled feature was fairness and consistency

(15 DE, 9 PL and 1 CZ). Teachers' engagement and enthusiasm as well as their willingness to play the role of a causal agent, that is someone responsible for learners' development and motivation to engage in the learning process, also appeared of importance to a large group of participants.

As regards the content of learning, the participants mainly focused on developing language skills. Three persons pointed to communicative competences as an important objective of teaching and individual respondents emphasized the need to develop general competences (PL83), critical thinking (CZ124), lifelong learning (CZ114) and creativity (CZ120). Interculturality and plurilingualism were mentioned only by participant DE26, who noted 'I want students to understand the importance of being able to speak and communicate in different languages. To have an understanding for difference amongst cultures and people. To develop social competence'. The student teachers also seem to undermine their own intercultural communicative competence and its role in teaching—only one person considered 'Being aware of cultural backgrounds of students' (PL67) as an important element of professional identity. A few other participants underscored the significance of individualised learning (e.g. being fair, treat and see students as individuals, accept that there are many different people with different interests, strengths and motivations' (DE24), 'accept their individual identities, without basing my judgments on stereotypes or prejudice' (DE67); however, no clear reference to interculturality was made. In the statement, '"Inklusion" → some see it as a problem to have a heterogeneous classroom. I see it as a challenge that I definitely want to master!', participant DE42 referred to the notion of inclusive education; however, the terms 'inclusion' or 'heterogeneity' were not clearly specified and may, therefore, refer to, for instance, teaching students of different cultural and/or linguistic backgrounds, FL skills or learning difficulties. One of the participants observed that 'Since our society is going through a massive change of values, I think, being a teacher is also going to imply some significant image change' (DE22), which indicates the awareness of the changing nature of modern education; still, the character of these changes was not disclosed.

Discussion and Practical Implications

Telecollaboration and intercutural communicative competence

The results indicate that student teachers' understanding of interculturality is incomplete, which has a direct impact on its perceived importance in the FL classroom. Whereas the vast majority of participants consider telecollaboration as a potential tool for developing their own intercultural skills, the detailed questions concerning the value of such online exchanges in developing attitudinal elements (e.g. openness and curiosity) and skills (the ability to relate experiences and to adopt a critical stance towards one's own culture) (cf.Byram, 1997; Deardorff, 2011) proved less optimistic and, thus, suggest inconsistencies in student teachers' conceptualizations of intercultural communicative competence. This finding was confirmed by the analysis of the open-ended question which revealed that student teachers tended to emphasize their own ability to develop language skills and create a positive atmosphere in the classroom, and generally failed to perceive themselves as teachers of intercultural communicative competence (ICC).

The results of the present study, which was originally aimed to inform our instructional choices in the process of designing a telecollaborative project, turned out to shed light also on the role of teacher education at large in the investigated institutions and beyond, particularly in the light of the fact that a volume of studies (Bektaş-Çetinkaya, 2014; Czura, 2016; Larzén-Östermark, 2009; Sercu, 2005) have also reported on FL pre-service and in-service teachers' limited and inconsistent understanding of ICC.

Intercultural communicative competence and intercultural awareness are the 'buzz words' of modern foreign language teaching and constitute an important element of language policies. However, there seems to be a marked discrepancy between theory and practice. The participants of the study have most probably encountered these positively connotated terms in the course of their teacher education; however, the depth and the quality of the instruction in this area leave much to be desired. In the international investigation by Aleksandrowicz-Pędich et al. (2003), language teachers admitted that they had not received any explicit training on how to develop ICC in their students as a part of their teacher education programme. Instead, they had made inferences as regards the nature of ICC in an indirect way, through such university courses as sociolinguistics, literary studies and FL methodology. Taking these into account, it is clear that despite sustained efforts to promote ICC on European and national levels, teacher training programmes have not fully embraced the intercultural turn.

Student Teachers' International Experience

Another finding of the present study that should be reflected on is the respondents' relatively low level of long-term international experience. As Byram (1991) asserts, one of the factors that affects the quality of intercultural instruction is teachers' own international experience. If we assume that foreign language student teachers are in dire need to gain first-hand intercultural experience in order to grow professionally, it is clear that the majority of them seem to miss that opportunity on account of not being provided with the possibility to participate in an (obligatory or optional) stay abroad. Consequently, the provision of alternative practices that facilitate intercultural dialogue is absolutely necessary.

There is, therefore, an urgent need to redefine the objectives of FL teacher education courses in terms of ICC. Since the principles of developing ICC have been extensively presented both in theory and practice elsewhere (Byram, 1997; Garret-Rucks, 2016; Liddicoat & Scarino, 2013; McConachy, 2017), including a more detailed critique of Byram's model (Ferri, 2014; Hoff, 2014; Matsuo, 2012, 2015), in the context of the present study, we would like to focus on discussing telecollaboration as a tool promoting interculturality in teacher education. Telecollaboration is often seen as a preparatory step to a face-to-face mobility project or as an alternative opportunity for students who, for different reasons, do not want to or are unable to go abroad.

A telecollaborative project has the potential of bringing a two-fold benefit—on the one hand, by being exposed to an experiential and intercultural learning environment, student teachers have an opportunity to reflect on and develop their own intercultural skills; on the other, an online project provides participants from different cultural and linguistic backgrounds a platform for discussion related to teaching techniques and tools that aim at developing intercultural competence in the FL classroom.

Naturally, it cannot be taken for granted that mobility experiences alone contribute to the development of intercultural competence. Studies report that participants of both face-to-face (e.g. Jackson, 2010; Ward & Rana-Deuba, 1999) and virtual exchanges (Clavel Arroitia & Pennock-Speck, 2016) may experience a number of intercultural communication problems, that may, in extreme cases, lead to even more ethnocentric attitudes. Jackson (2010) notes that the personal, linguistic and intercultural gains of a mobility project depend largely on the participants' previous intercultural experiences, sociocultural knowledge, initial level of intercultural awareness, openness and tolerance. Our results partially corroborate these findings. They suggest that Polish and Czech (student) teachers whose appraisal of their own professional identity is based on such positive traits as e.g. being consistent, reflective, imaginative, interesting, enthusiastic, inquisitive and/or aware of their local classroom context are somewhat more likely to agree that there is a potential link between engaging in telecollaboration with peers and the development of intercultural skills. For German student teachers, this link between positive evaluations of their own professional identity as a teacher with the perceived benefits of telecollaboration is less apparent.

Maximizing the Benefits of Telecollaboration

To maximize learning benefits of a telecollaborative project at both intercultural and professional level, ongoing support and guidance involving content, tasks, experiences and cultural experiences at different stages of a virtual exchange are recommended (Egli et al., 2015; Sadler & Dooly, 2016). Engagement in collaborative discussions and exchanges of thoughts on selected facets of ICC with student teachers and/or practitioners from other countries may encourage (future) teachers to reflect in a greater depth on their own experiences.

This can be achieved through a set of carefully designed telecollaborative activities, which 'generally involve different linguistic and cultural communities and thereby have a strong possibility of producing negotiation of meaning and providing opportunities for the exploration of different cultural perspectives' (O'Dowd & Lewis, 2009, pp. 174–175). Each category of telecollaborative tasks defined by O'Dowd and Lewis (2009) serve different communicative purposes and can be used to touch upon different aspects of ICC. In *information exchange tasks* telecollaborative partners exchange information about themselves, their immediate surroundings and local culture. Simple as it seems, this type of a task requires participants to analyse, take a critical stance and select appropriate aspects of their own culture before presenting them to telecollaborative partners. As O'Dowd and Lewis (2009) indicate, conducting such tasks in a form of an ethnographic interview additionally requires the participants to be able to discover and interpret new cultural information in a sensitive and respectful manner. The objective of *comparison and analysis tasks* lies in looking for similarities and differences between the cultures through engagement in dialogic exchanges (O'Dowd & Lewis, 2009). Consequently, through engagement in such activities, the participants have an opportunity to question their attitudes to and stereotypes about the other culture(s) as well as to develop a greater awareness of their own and partners' cultural background. A word of warning should be added here: as this task type involves comparison of cultures, its success depends on a careful task design and teacher's guidance that would prevent the formulation and formation of essentialist views of culture and categorization, as such approach is often encouraged by instrumental and 'Model Type' conceptualizations of culture including, among others, Byram's model of intercultural communication which has been often criticized specifically for perpetuating a rather reductive identification of nations with cultures and thinking of and envisioning cultures as 'containers', i.e. as hermetically sealed units (Matsuo, 2012, p. 350).

Finally, in *collaborative tasks* telecollaborative partners work together towards the completion of a concrete linguistic or cultural outcome (O'Dowd & Lewis, 2009). Such activities involve a great deal of cooperation and negotiation of meaning, whose success is to a large extend conditional on the participants' attitudes of openness, tolerance and mutual respect. As can be seen, the task types presented above can be and have been (for a review see O'Dowd & Lewis, 2009) successfully exploited to develop intercultural knowledge, skills and attitudes both in the FL classroom and in teacher education programmes.

In line with the 'experiential modelling approach' (Guichon & Hauck, 2011, p. 195), student teachers are more likely to use a particular teaching tool or technique in their teaching if they have a chance to experience them themselves in the course of their teacher education programme. It applies to both pre- and in-service teachers (both novice and experienced) and rests on the assumption that 'once educators have carried out a telecollaboration exchange, they will likely continue' (Helm, 2015, p. 203). It must be noted, however, that student teachers' extensive cross-cultural contact or a high level of ICC may not automatically translate into the ability to develop this construct in future learners. A study aimed to investigate the impact of FL student teachers' international experience and their beliefs about developing ICC revealed that the participants, by and large, associated ICC with the ability to communicate cross-culturally; however, regardless of the time spent abroad, they were at a loss with what intercultural learning should look like in practice (Czura, 2018). It indicates that neither study abroad nor telecollaborative exchanges should be treated as ultimate solutions to the inadequacies in teacher education programmes. There is therefore a need to include intercultural modules in FL teacher education that would offer comprehensive instruction on both theoretical and practical aspects of developing ICC. That being the case, in order to support future teachers' professional development, in a course involving a telecollaborative exchange, student teachers should ideally be given an opportunity to reflect on their own intercultural experiences and develop professional skills that will help them design and implement telecollaborative modules on conceptual, organizational and technological levels (cf. Egli et al., 2015; Vinagre, 2016).

Conclusions

Nowadays teachers are required to assume the role of an intercultural mediator in order to prepare language learners for intercultural communication. Intercultural communicative competence can therefore be expected to constitute an important element of teacher identity. Telecollaboration has the potential to serve as a valuable tool for developing ICC in teacher education programmes, provided student teachers are guided and supported in the process in terms of professional, digital and intercultural competences. As communities of practice such as student teachers may not necessarily be aware of the full potential that telecollaborative exchanges may have for the process of professional identity formation, it is especially advisable to engage such groups in explicit discussions of the goals as well as benefits associated with such virtual learning environments. Telecollaborative exchanges may undoubtedly bring an added value to FL teacher education programmes; however, they should be seen as a valuable addition and not a replacement for explicit training in intercultural teaching skills.

Recommended Texts

1. PluriMobil: Plurilingual and intercultural learning through mobility

PluriMobil is a freely accessible teaching tool that offers activities and materials to support the plurilingual and intercultural learning of students for the phases before, during and after a mobility activity. It can be adapted to multiple virtual and face-to-face mobility projects across all educational levels, including teacher education. The PluriMobil resources devoted to developing intercultural competence encourage future teachers to reflect on how their mobility experiences affect their understanding of the importance and the role of interculturality in the foreign language classroom.

The materials for student teacher training programmes include a handbook, that which provides information on mobility activities in teacher education, a quick start guide for first time users and 14 lesson plans with practical, hands-on exercises and photocopiable resources. PluriMobil website: https://plurimobil.ecml.at/.

2. O'Dowd, R., and T. Lewis (2016), *Online intercultural exchange: policy, pedagogy, practice.* New York: Routledge. 308 pp.

This volume offers insights into a broad range of topics related to Online Intercultural Exchange (OIE), such as a research-based conceptualization of telecollaboration (Chapter 1, O'Dowd & Lewis), the development of Intercultural Communicative Competence (ICC) in University-based telecollaboration (Chapter 7, Müller-Hartmann & Kurek), and a number of descriptive accounts of different projects related to OIE.

3. Hagley, E. (2016), Making virtual exchange/telecollaboration mainstream—large scale exchanges. In Jager, S.; Kurek, M., and B. O'Rourke (eds.), *New directions in telecollaborative research and practice: selected papers from the second conference on telecollaboration in higher education.* Research-publishing.net. 225–230. https://doi.org/10.14705/rpnet.2016.telecollab2016.511 (22/01/2019).

This article gives an overview of a large-scale Virtual Exchange (VE) including more than 1500 students and 53 teachers from six different countries. Next to insights into advantages and disadvantages of the VE, as well as student engagement and participation, it offers access to a Single Language Virtual Exchange (SLVE) platform to educators interested in VE.

4. Guth, S. and F. Helm (2010). Telecollaboration 2.0: Language, literacies and intercultural learning in the 21st century. New York: Peter Lang. 475 pp.

This volume discusses telecollaboration in the wake of the Web 2.0 digital shift focusing—among many other things—on its potential for the development of intercultural communicative competence by exploring student and instructor roles, relevant assessment formats and task design.

> 5. EVALUATE—Evaluating and Upscaling Telecollaborative Teacher Education

This European Union project aims to explore the impact of telecollaboration on pre-service student teachers in terms of intercultural, foreign language and digital-pedagogical competences. The project and the final report offer practical recommendations on telecollaborative exchanges in teacher education.
Project website: http://www.evaluateproject.eu/.

> 6. ASSESSnet project—assessment in virtual exchange

The ASSESSnet project aims to support foreign language practitioners in the process of assessing student learning in virtual exchange/telecollaboration, particularly in terms of selecting appropriate assessment content, criteria (including intercultural components) and tools. The website additionally showcases a collection of promising assessment practices in telecollaboration at tertiary level. Website: https://www.assessnet.site.

Engagement Priorities

1. As the data suggest, there are some discrepancies between the three different participant groups. For instance, whereas the Polish and the German participants express some agreement with respect to their perception of cultural and linguistic diversity as a resource of mutual enrichment and an asset for their own professional development, the data from the Czech sample indicate more scepticism towards these statements. (Compare the results section for detailed information).

   Debate possible causes for these discrepancies. How can this information be used to improve pre- and in-service teacher education courses and education policy in your context?

2. As the data further suggest, the Polish and Czech participants show a broader range of significant correlations between agreement levels regarding the statement 'Telecollaboration would develop my intercultural skills' and particular professional identity markers reported by the participants as important for their (future) profession compared to the German sample.

   Debate possible causes for the correlations between agreement levels and particular professional identity markers (such as fair, imaginative, aware of local classroom context). What are their implications for teaching and teacher education? Sketch out a potential research design in order to investigate your assumptions and hypotheses (e.g. open-ended questionnaire or interview design).

3. Below you find some exemplary excerpts from participants' descriptions of their future profession/their professional identity. Discuss how these statements could be used as a starting point for a teacher education module, training or programme that emphasizes the importance of intercultural competence and interculturality in foreign language teaching and learning.

Statement I: "[…]I want students to understand the importance of being able to speak and communicate in different languages. To have an understanding for difference amongst cultures and people. To develop social competence."

Statement II: "I think my work as a teacher can be very influential for my future students. My choices and way of communication can influence their future. I think it is very important to work closely together with other organisations and with the families to support students. School is only one part of their lives which, however, has a lot of influence on their lives.

Statement III: "Treat the students fair, accept their individual identities, without basing my judgements on stereotypes or prejudice".

Statement IV: "[S]ince our society is going through a massive change of values, I think being a teacher is also going to imply some significant image change. For me being a teacher would mean to be useful in the process of learning, useful to my students. I cannot help them to learn everything but I can help when they learn something."

Further Research

Further research could include:

1. An interview study to get an in-depth picture of how student teachers envision and construct their own professional identity: Such a study could be turned into a formative assessment procedure to be used in a telecollaborative project. It could also provide more insight into subjective views regarding particular topics and concepts such as interculturality, telecollaboration, digitalization or intercultural competence as well as to analyse to what extent and in which ways participants draw on these concepts when constructing their own professional identity.
2. An expansion of the data pool in terms of the involved countries as well as in terms of involved institutional 'types' in (foreign language) education (e.g. pre-service and in-service teachers in primary education, secondary education, tertiary education, vocational schools, university education).
3. A follow-up study focusing on participants' understanding and conceptualization of interculturality and intercultural competence followed by qualitative analysis in order to ascertain possible (mis)matches between participants' subjective theories and research-informed conceptualizations.
4. A longitudinal study that would explore the impact of participating in a telecollaborative exchange on student teachers' conceptualization of intercultural competence and the perceived usefulness of such exchanges in professional development.

References

Aleksandrowicz-Pędich, L., Draghicescu, J., Issaiass, D., & Sabec, N. (2003). The views of teachers of English and French on intercultural communicative competence in language teaching. In I. Lázár (Ed.), *Incorporating intercultural communicative competence in language teacher education* (pp. 7–37). Strasbourg: Council of Europe.

Beacco, J-C., M. Byram, M. Cavalli, D. Coste, M. Egli Cuenat, F. Goullier, & Panthier, J. (2016). *Guide for the development and implementation of curricula for plurilingual and intercultural education* (2nd ed.). Council of Europe.

Bektaş-Çetinkaya, Y. (2014). Extension of teacher knowledge: Developing the intercultural competence of pre-service foreign language teachers in Turkey. *Novitas-ROYAL (research on Youth and Language), 8*(2), 153–168.

Bell, B., & Gilbert, J. (1994). Teacher development as professional, personal, and social development. *Teaching and Teacher Education, 10,* 483–497.

Belz, J. A., & Thorne, S. L. (2006). *Internet-mediated intercultural foreign language education.* Heinle & Heinle.

Blell, G. (2013). Diversity Education im Fremdsprachenunterricht. In K. Hauenschild, S. Robak, & I. Sievers (Eds.), *Diversity Education. Zugänge – Perspektiven – Beispiele* (pp. 228–240). Brandes & Apel.

Byram, M. (1991). Teaching culture and language: Towards an integrated model. In D. Buttjes & M. Byram (Eds.), *Mediating languages and cultures: Towards an intercultural theory of foreign language education* (pp. 17–30). Multilingual Matters.

Byram, M. (1997). *Teaching and assessing intercultural communicative competence.* Multilingual Matters Ltd.

Clarke, D. J., & Hollingsworth, H. (1994). Reconceptualising teacher change. In G. Bell, B. Wright, N. Leeson, & J. Geake (Eds.), *Challenges in mathematics education: Con- straints on construction. Vol. 1. Proceedings of the 17th annual conference of the of the Mathematics Education Research Group of Australasia.* Southern Cross University.

Clavel Arroitia, B., & Pennock-Speck, B. (2016). Analysis of teacher roles in telecollaboration in the context of a European Funded project (TILA Project). In A. L. Lafuente & M. D. Dolores Porto Requejo (Eds.), *English and American studies in Spain: New developments and trends* (pp. 189–196). Universidad de Alcalá.

Clément, R., Dörnyei, Z., & Noels, K. A. (1994). Motivation, self-confidence and group cohesion in the foreign language classroom. *Language Learning, 44,* 417–448.

Coldron, J., & Smith, R. (1999). Active location in teachers' construction of their professional identities. *Journal of Curriculum Studies, 31*(6), 711–726.

Council of Europe. (2001). *Common European framework of reference for languages: learning, teaching, assessment.* Cambridge University Press.

Czura, A. (2016). Major field of study and student teachers' views on inter-cultural communicative competence. *Language and Intercultural Communication, 16*(1), 83–98. https://doi.org/10.1080/14708477.2015.1113753.

Czura, A. (2018). Student teachers' international experience and their beliefs about developing intercultural communicative competence. In M. Pawlak & A. Mystkowska-Wiertelak (Eds.), *Challenges of second and foreign language education in a globalized world* (pp. 327–344). Springer.

Day, C., & Sachs, J. (2004). *International handbook on the continuing professional development of teachers*. Open University Press.

Deardorff, D. K. (2011). Assessing intercultural competence. *New Directions for Institutional Research, 149*, 65–79.

De Florio Hansen, I. (2011). *Towards multilingualism and the inclusion of cultural diversity*. Kassel University Press.

Egli Cuenat, M., Brogan, K., Cole, J., Czura, A., Muller, C., Szczepańska, A., … Wolfer, B. (2015). *Plurilingual and intercultural learning through mobility: Practical resources for teachers and teacher trainers*. Council of Europe.

Ferri, G. (2014). Ethical communication and intercultural responsibility: A philosophical perspective. *Language and Intercultural Communication., 14*(1), 7–23. https://doi.org/10.1080/14708477.2013.866121

Fuchs, C., Hauck, M., & Müller-Hartmann, A. (2012). Promoting learner autonomy through multiliteracy skills development in cross-institutional exchanges. *Language Learning & Technology* [Online Journal],*16*(3), 82–102. Available at http://oro.open.ac.uk/35595/8/fuchsetal.pdf. Accessed 13 Nov 2018.

Fullan, M., & Stiegelbauer, S. (1991). *The new meaning of education*. Teachers College Press.

Garret-Rucks, P. (2016). *Intercultural competence in instructed language learning:Bridging theory and practice*. Information Age.

Guichon, N., & Hauck, M. (2011). Teacher education research in CALL and CMC: More in demand than ever. *ReCALL* [Online Journal], *23*(3), 187–199. Available at https://hal.archives-ouvertes.fr/hal-00806415. Accessed 8 Nov 2018.

Guskey, T. R. (1986). Staff development and the process of teacher change. *Educational Researcher, 15*, 5–12.

Guth, S., & Helm, F. (2010). *Telecollaboration 2.0, language, literacies and intercultural learning in the 21 st century*. Peter Lang.

Hal, G. E., & Loucks, S. F. (1977). *A longitudinal investigation of individual implementation of educational innovations*. The University of Texas.

Hammerness, K., Darling-Hammond, L., Bransford, J., Berliner, D., Cochran-Smith, M., McDonald, M., & Zeichner, K. (2005). How teachers learn and develop. In L. Darling-Hammond & J. Bransford (Eds.), *Preparing teachers for a changing world. What teachers should learn and be able to do* (pp. 358–389). Jossey-Bass.

Helm. F. (2015). The practices and challenges of telecollaboration in higher education in Europe. *Language Learning & Technology* [Online Journal], *19*(2): 197–217. Available at http://llt.msu.edu/issues/june2015/helm.pdf. Accessed 8 Nov 2018.

Hoff. H. E. (2014) A critical discussion of Byram's model of intercultural communicative competence in the light of Bildung theories. *Intercultural Education* [Online Journal], *25*(6), 508–517. https://doi.org/10.1080/146 75986.2014.992112.

Jackson, J. (2010). *Intercultural journeys: From study to residence abroad.* Palgrave Macmillan.

Johnson, K. (1996). *Language teaching and skill learning.* Blackwell.

KMK Standing Conference of the Ministers of Education and Cultural Affairs of the Länder in the Federal Republic of Germany. (2014). *Standards für die Lehrerbildung: Bildungswissenschaften.* Berlin: Sekretariat der Ständigen Konferenz der Kultusminister der Länder in der Bundesrepublik Deutschland.

Larzén-Östermark, E. (2009). Language teacher education in Finland and the cultural dimension of foreign language teaching—A student teacher perspective. *European Journal of Teacher Education, 32*(4), 401–421.

Liddicoat, A. J. & Scarino, A. (2013). *Intercultural language teaching and learning.* Wiley-Blackwell.

Little, D. (1995). Learning as a dialogue: The dependence of learner autonomy on teacher autonomy. *System, 23*(2), 175–182.

Maclure, M. (1993). Arguing for your self: Identity as an organising principle in teachers' jobs and lives. *British Educational Research Journal, 19*, 311–322.

Magos, K., & Simopoulos, G. (2009). 'Do you know Naomi?' Researching the intercultural competence of teachers who teach Greek as a second language in immigrant classes. *Intercultural Education, 20*(3), 255–265.

Matsuo, C. (2012). A critique of Michael Byram's Intercultural Communicative Competence model from the perspective of model type and conceptualization of culture. *Fukuoka University Review of Literature & Humanities, 44*, 347–380.

Matsuo, C. (2015). A dialogic critique of Michael Byram's Intercultural Communicative Competence model: Proposal for a dialogic pedagogy.

conference paper. [Online]. Available at https://www.researchgate.net/pub
lication/309634615_A_Dialogic_Critique_of_Michael_Byram's_Intercultu
ral_Communicative_Competence_Model_Proposal_for_a_Dialogic_Peda
gogy.

McConachy, T. (2017). *Developing intercultural perspectives on language use.*
Multilingual Matters.

O'Dowd, R. (2015). Supporting in-service language educators in learning to
telecollaborate. *Language Learning & Technology* [Online Journal], *19*(1),
64–83. Available at http://llt.msu.edu/issues/february2015/odowd.pdf.
Accessed 13 Nov 2018.

O'Dowd, R. (2017). Exploring the impact of telecollaboration in initial teacher
education: The EVALUATE project. *The EUROCALL Review* [Online
Journal], *25*(2), 38–41. Available at https://polipapers.upv.es/index.php/eur
ocall/article/view/7636/9679. Accessed 13 Nov 2018.

O'Dowd, R., & Waire, P. (2009). Critical issues in telecollaborative task design.
Computer Assisted Language Learning [Online Journal], *22*(2), 173–188.
Available at https://doi.org/10.1080/09588220902778369. Accessed 12 Jan
2015.

Ortactepe, D. (2015). EFL teacher's identity (re)construction as teachers of
intercultural competence: A language socialization approach. *Journal of
Language, Identity & Education, 14*(2), 96–122.

PPMI Public Policy and Management Institute/European Commission.
(2017). *Preparing teachers for diversity: the role of initial teacher education*
(Final Report to DG Education, Youth, Sport and Culture of the European
Commission) Available at: https://publications.europa.eu/en/publication-
detail/-/publication/b347bf7d-1db1-11e7-aeb3-01aa75ed71a1. Accessed 29
Jan 2019.

Rodgers, C. R., & Scott, K. H. (2008). The development of the personal
self and professional identity in learning to teach, In M. Cochran-Smith,
S. Feiman-Nemser, D. J. McIntyre and K. E. Demers (Eds.). *Handbook of
research on teacher education.* Abingdon: Routledge. Routledge Handbooks
Online.

Sachs, J. (2005). Teacher education and the development of professional identity: Learning to be a teacher. In P. M. Denicolo, & M. Kompf (Eds.),
*Connecting policy and practice: Challenges for teaching and learning in schools
and universities* (pp. 5–21). Routledge: Taylor and Francis Group. https://
doi.org/10.4324/9780203012529.

Sadler, R., & Dooly, M. (2016). Twelve years of telecollaboration: What we
have learnt. *ELT Journal, 70*(4), 401–413.

Sercu, L. (Ed.). (2005). *Foreign language teachers and intercultural competence: An international investigation.* Multilingual Matters.

Sercu, L. (2006). The foreign language and intercultural competence teacher: The acquisition of a new professional identity. *Intercultural Education, 17*(1), 55–72.

Sercu, L., & St. John, O. (2007), Teacher beliefs and their impact on teaching practice: A literature review. In: M. Jiménez Raya & L. Sercu (Eds.), *Challenges in teacher development: Learner autonomy and intercultural competence* (pp. 41–64). Peter Lang. Pages.

Stoll, L., Harris, A., & Handscomb, G. (2012). *Great professional development which leads to great Pedagogy: Nine claims from research.* National College for School Leadership.

Vinagre, M. (2016). Training teachers for virtual collaboration: A case study. *British Journal of Educational Technology, 47*(4), 787–802. https://doi.org/10.1111/bjet.12363

Virtual Exchange and 21st Century Teacher Education. [Online]. Available at: https://www.evaluateproject.eu/evlt-data/uploads/2018/09/EVALUATE_Findings_Report.pdf Accessed 20 Dec 2018.

Ward, C., & Rana-Deuba, A. (1999). Acculturation and adaptation revisited. *Journal of Cross-Cultural Psychology, 30*(4), 422–442 https://doi.org/10.1177/0022022199030004003.

Winograd, K. (2003). The functions of teacher emotion: The good, the bad, and the ugly. *Teachers College Record, 105,* 1641–1673.

Young, T., & Sercombe, P. (2010). Communication, discourses and interculturality. *Language and Intercultural Communication, 10*(3), 181–188. https://doi.org/10.1080/14708470903348523

Part II

Integrating Interculturality in ELT Textbooks

5

Teaching Global Issues for Intercultural Citizenship in a Tunisian EFL Textbook: "Skills for Life"

Nadia Abid

List of Acronyms

ICC Intercultural Communicative Competence
EFL English as a Foreign Language
ELT English Language Teaching

Introduction

In their attempt to adapt foreign language teaching to the requirements of intercultural communication, intercultural educationalists and
researchers working within the framework of the Council of Europe have
adopted, since the 1990s, an intercultural approach to foreign language
teaching. The outcome of this approach is the acquisition of intercultural

N. Abid (✉)
University of Sfax, Sfax, Tunisia

M. Victoria and C. Sangiamchit (eds.), *Interculturality and the English Language
Classroom*, https://doi.org/10.1007/978-3-030-76757-0_5

communicative competence (ICC) (Byram, 1997, pp. 32–38) which enables learners to communicate effectively interculturally.

However, Byram (1997, 2008, 2012) and Porto et al. (2017, p. 2) argue that foreign language education should be concerned with not only the linguistic but also the educational dimension for a better preparation of learners for intercultural encounters. This involves learning universal values of justice and human rights as well as the skills necessary to live responsibly in a globalized world. Byram (2008, p. 160) suggests the concept of intercultural citizenship to take into account both the instrumental and educational objectives of foreign language teaching (Porto et al., 2017, p. 2). Byram (2008, p. 216) and Wagner and Byram (2017, p. 1) argue that learning to be an intercultural citizen in a foreign language class requires the acquisition of ICC. This entails the learners' exposure to culture and global issues (Cates, 1990, p. 41) as well as their engagement in activities promoting global/intercultural skills (Byram, 2008; Cates, 1990), which can be done through textbooks and other teaching materials.

Textbooks' contents and activities, for instance, can play a significant role in raising learners' awareness of these issues and developing their global skills. Despite the important role of textbooks in exposing students to global issues, few studies (Cates, 1990; De La Caba Collado & Atxurra, 2006; Hosack, 2011) have been conducted on their representation and the ways they are taught in foreign language textbooks. The Tunisian context is no exception. Although global issues are included as topics in English language textbooks, EFL teachers, to the best of my knowledge, have been using them more as contexts for language teaching than as a springboard for the development of global and citizenship skills. In addition, concepts such as intercultural citizenship, intercultural communication and intercultural competence have not yet been introduced to the Tunisian educational system and to the English language curriculum as no reform has been advocated since 2006. Statements in the Education and School Instruction Law (2002–2007) stress the importance of the global dimension and openness to the world's cultures in young people's education. However, this importance is not reflected in school subjects, including English, where priority is given to language proficiency over the intercultural dimension.

This chapter argues for the importance of textbooks in teaching global issues and developing intercultural citizenship competences in the Tunisian context and other contexts worldwide. This is done through the evaluation of a Tunisian ELT textbook's potential to develop intercultural citizenship competences through its representation and teaching of global issues in its content and activities. The textbook "Skills for Life" was analysed based on my belief in the crucial role that EFL textbooks can play in exposing students to global issues, especially in foreign language contexts where such exposure is limited. In fact, well-designed globally oriented textbooks can connect learners to the world, develop intercultural skills, and foster feelings of belonging to a wider community with whom they share different concerns (Byram, 2008; Cates, 1990, 2002). The results of the evaluation will give Tunisian teachers and other EFL teachers insights on how to teach global issues and use the textbook's content and activities. The results will also help EFL teachers worldwide develop skills as well as criteria for the evaluation of the textbooks and other teaching materials they use in classes to teach global issues, and find better ways for materials selection and design.

The chapter comprises two major sections. The first section situates teaching global issues within its theoretical framework. It defines the concepts of interculturality and intercultural citizenship education and highlights their relationship to foreign language teaching in general and to foreign language textbooks in particular. The section also sheds light on the importance of those concepts in the Tunisian education system. The second section reports on the study, discusses its findings, and suggests ways to improve English language teaching and materials so that they fit in the new developments in foreign language education.

Interculturality and Intercultural Citizenship

Due to political, economic, and technological globalization, contacts between people of different cultural backgrounds have become easier and more frequent than ever. Interculturality has consequently become a feature characterizing people's communication and relations. Indeed, people of different cultural and linguistic backgrounds interact, meet differences, and negotiate cultures and images of themselves and of others (Dervin & Liddicoat, 2013; Liddicoat, 2015; Young & Sercombe, 2010).

At the heart of interculturality is culture. Dervin (2016) argues that the definition of interculturality depends on the way culture itself is defined. Solid interculturality is based on the view of culture as static and deterministic of interaction and human behaviour, and of the individual as the representative of the group, thus, undermining individual differences (Dervin, 2016). A more recent approach is liquid interculturality which views culture as diverse, unstable, and variable. Individuals are perceived as members of diverse social and cultural groups and as having multiple identities (Dietz, 2018). This variation is, according to Dervin and Liddicoat (2013, p. 7), "a constituent part" of interculturality which, therefore, has come to be defined as "an interaction between diversities where different perspectives are exchanged and negotiated" (ibid., p. 7).

The notion of interculturality as diversity and variability has influenced the state-centred conception of citizenship (Hosack, 2011, p. 127) and the concept of national identity which started to be deconstructed with the increasing multiracial and multicultural character of modern societies (Byram, 2012, p. 91). People belong to different groups inside or outside their countries for different reasons, and may identify with those groups or see themselves as citizens of the world rather than of a particular nation (Osler & Starkey, 2015, p. 33). This shift in the perception of one's identity leads to questioning the nature of the national identity which has become more globally oriented (De La Caba Collado & Atxurra, 2006, p. 206). Osbourne (2000, p. 72) asserts that: "citizenship is not one single locus of identity. Citizens can be members of different overlapping communities- local, regional, national and global".

This change in the nature of culture, identity and citizenship has led to questioning the role of education in creating a new form of citizenship beyond the national boundaries (Alfred et al., 2006; Byram, 2008). Communicative language teaching tradition has adopted an essentialist view of culture where the national culture of the target language country was exclusively portrayed in textbooks (Wagner & Byram, 2017). However, as Wagner and Byram (2017) argue, foreign language teaching in the contemporary world should adopt a liquid interpretation of culture and interculturality.

Byram (1997, 2008, 2012) and Porto et al. (2017) also observe that foreign language teaching, given its potential to connect people and cultures, should go beyond preparing students for intercultural interaction and focus more on its educational aspect which encompasses learning universal values of justice and human rights as well as skills. In this respect, Byram and Wagner (2018) argue that foreign language teaching should promote the development of intercultural communicative competence (ICC) which enables language learners to think, feel, and behave as intercultural citizens.

Byram's (2008, p. 160) concept of intercultural citizenship takes into account both the instrumental and educational objectives of foreign language teaching (Byram 2008; Porto et al., 2017; Wagner and Byram, 2017). Being an intercultural citizen means acquiring and possessing the skills, attitudes, and knowledge necessary to act as a citizen of one's community and the world. Foreign language teaching, like other school subjects such as history and civic education, has the potential to teach the fundamental values and skills upon which citizenship is founded. Byram (2008, p. 216) and Wagner and Byram (2017, p. 1) argue that learning to be interculturally competent and learning to be a citizen are similar processes and have similar outcomes.

Global or intercultural citizenship education adopts an intercultural and humanistic approach that aims to achieve cognitive, affective, and behavioural objectives (Byram, 2008; Cates, 2000, p. 214). Byram (2008, p. 216) provides a comprehensive account of the intercultural/global orientation of his concept of intercultural citizenship. Similarly, Cates (1990, 2000) argued for the importance of global issues in developing global citizenship but gave a more detailed account of the content and methods of globally oriented foreign language education. There is an agreement that global topics enable learners to understand issues shared by people across the globe, develop feelings of empathy, and acquire skills of critical thinking, problem-solving, decision-making, managing conflicts, etc.

Intercultural Citizenship in Foreign Language Education

Language learning and citizenship are closely related. It is with language that individuals learn to be citizens of their own country or of other countries enjoying the rights given to all its members (Davies, 2006, p. 8). Language is one of the instruments used to teach citizenship thanks to its potential to create membership and reinforce the sense of belonging to a nation. Today, English plays a significant role in connecting people and increasing their sense of belonging to the world, thus leading to the emergence of a new form of citizenship that Byram calls intercultural citizenship (Byram, 2008). English is "a window to the world" (Cates, 2000, p. 241) that offers students and teachers a wide variety of topics (Cates, 1990, 2000, 2002; Jacobs & Cates, 1999; Yakovchuk, 2004) enriching students' knowledge of cultures and understanding of matters shared by people across the globe such as social justice and the environment (Rauschet & Byram, 2018).

Intercultural citizenship is the contribution of foreign language teaching to education and the development of individuals and societies as a whole (Porto et al. 2017, p. 2). An intercultural citizenship-oriented foreign language education is responsible for the promotion of shared identity and belonging to the world community, the appreciation of diversity, the respect for difference, and the commitment to taking action in the interest of their own communities and the world as a whole (Guiherme, 2007, p. 82). Similar assumptions are suggested in Cates' argument for global education as an approach to foreign language teaching. He (2000, p. 241) identifies the goals of global education as: (1) Knowledge, about the world countries and cultures, and about global problems, their causes, and solutions; (2) Skills of critical thinking, co-operative problem-solving, conflict resolution, and seeing issues from different perspectives; (3) Attitudes of global awareness, cultural appreciation, respect for diversity, and empathy; and finally (4) Action, i.e. thinking locally and acting globally.

Byram (2008, p. 216) advanced similar objectives for intercultural citizenship education. He focused on the necessity of teaching global issues to prepare foreign language learners to act and live responsibly as global/intercultural citizens. Byram's model of intercultural citizenship (2008, p. 216), a modified version of his 1997's model, is based on the development of ICC and other competences inspired from citizenship education (Alfred et al., 2006, pp. 177–178). The model includes five objectives or orientations, namely the cognitive orientation, evaluative orientation, action orientation, comparative orientation, and linguistic orientation. They are described by Alfred et al. (2006, pp. 177–178) as follows:

- The cognitive orientation refers to the knowledge that learners should acquire in a foreign language class about other countries and his own, and about the present world, principles, and values of human rights and democratic citizenship.
- The evaluative orientation: refers to the attitudes of curiosity, openness, and tolerance of difference and those of respect for persons, acceptance of law, and recognition of pluralism. It also refers to critical cultural awareness, that is, learners' adherence to the values of freedom, equality, and solidarity as well as their valorization of mutuality and trust.
- The action orientation: refers to the acquisition of skills of discovery and interaction and political/instrumental competences. The skills of discovery and interaction include the learners' ability to elicit concepts and values, identify processes of interaction, and use knowledge and skills in real time. The instrumental competences include the ability to take others' opinions seriously, cooperate and tolerate divergence, and find compromise and group responsibility.
- The comparative orientation: like ICC, it refers to the acquisition of skills of interpreting and relating which mean the learner's ability to identify areas of misunderstanding and mediate between conflicting interpretations.
- The linguistic interpretation: it includes the development of linguistic competence, sociolinguistic competence, and discourse competence.

Byram's modified model of ICC (2008) was criticized on its neo-essentialist view of culture (Hoff, 2014; Matsuo, 2012). According to Hoff (2014) and Matsuo (2012), the model's equation of culture with the national culture confines culture within the boundaries of the nation-state, thus undermining intra-cultural differences and the social, economic, and political contexts influencing intercultural communication. In the teaching practice, the conception of culture as rigid and homogenous is translated into the delivery of ready-made form of cultural facts that does not trigger learners' critical thinking and creativity (Matsuo, 2012).

The evaluative or attitudinal dimension is also questioned in terms of its development of ICC. In this respect, Hoff (2014) believes that promoting tolerance and acceptance of difference should not mean engaging in a one-sided and imbalanced relationship where the learner aims to adapt to the other, missing meanwhile the opportunity to take a critical stance towards the other's culture. However, despite the pertinent critique to two dimensions of ICC, Hoff (2014) and Matsuo (2012) agree that critical cultural awareness, or the evaluative orientation, can be considered as a tool and an objective that, once used and reached, can develop in language learners independent critical thinking and rational argumentation. It has a political, and human rights dimension including freedom, equality, and solidarity (Alfred et al., 2006; Byram, 2008).

Byram's model is used as a framework for the interpretation of the results of the textbook evaluation for two main reasons. First, the study is concerned with global issues rather than intercultural understanding. Therefore, the evaluative dimension can serve as a suitable tool for the development of intercultural citizenship skills. Second, its concern with universal values of solidarity, equality, freedom, and human rights, and critical and reflective skills needed by an intercultural citizen overlap and reinforce citizenship competences stipulated by the UNESCO (2014).

Because global issues and intercultural citizenship are taught and developed in foreign language classes, an English language class with an intercultural dimension is potentially an appropriate and favourable context for teaching them. As English is taught as a compulsory subject in Tunisian students' curricula, it can also be a context to promote intercultural citizenship. The Tunisian EFL programmes, however, do not include statements about developing intercultural citizenship. Teaching materials, namely textbooks, include cultural references without actual teaching of culture through activities. The focus is placed more on language proficiency and the acquisition of language skills (Abid, 2012, 2018, 2019). Given the importance of textbooks in developing intercultural citizenship competences, the following section will deal with how textbooks' content and task can represent global issues for teaching intercultural citizenship.

Intercultural Citizenship Education in Textbooks

Foreign language textbooks, as pedagogic tools, help determine the type and the extent of knowledge that students can develop in the classroom (Mendez Garcia, 2005, p. 59) as well as the type of skills to be developed through activities. This can also be determined by teachers' use of textbooks, which is, in turn, influenced by their perceptions of intercultural teaching (Sercu, 2006). In the context of intercultural citizenship education, the Common European Framework of Reference has provided teachers with a common basis for the elaboration and design of language syllabuses and textbooks in the perspective of preparing students to be agents of change in their communities and the world as a whole.

According to intercultural educationalists, global issues should be part of the contents and activities. For instance, Cates (2000, p. 241) asserts that a global education approach in foreign language teaching (FLT) should integrate a global perspective into classroom instruction through lessons built around global issues, and classroom activities linking students to the wider world and concepts such as social responsibility and world citizenship. Global issues may include topics such as: discrimination, equal opportunities, racism, human rights, globalization and world economy, the impact of the media, consumer education, health care, environmental concerns, conflict and peace, poverty, use and misuse of natural resources, peoples of the world, social injustice, homelessness, perceptions and stereotypes, refugees, war, participation and democratic responsibility, identity, diversity, etc. (Yakovchuk, 2004, p. 33). Equally important to the study of global issues is the acquisition of global values which offer opportunities for mutual understanding, effective cooperation between different nations, and living in a peaceful world. Those values include values of justice, freedom, peace, dignity, equality, rights, democracy, social responsibility, tolerance, independence, environmentalism, multiculturalism, anti-consumerism.

Byram (2008) argues that teaching global issues is part of the development of ICC which is in turn a prerequisite for being and becoming an intercultural citizen. Raising learners' intercultural awareness in textbooks is achieved through the realistic representation of the target culture, international cultures and the learners' own (Byram & Esarte-Sarries, 1991; Sercu, 2000; Risager, 1991) and global issues (Risager, 1991, 2007; Sercu, 2000) as well as activities teaching citizenship skills. These activities can take different forms such as case studies, critical analysis, problem-solving, comparison between cultures, cooperative work (Jacobs, 2003, p. 119), inquiring about cultures, etc. Different activities can be used in the foreign language class to promote citizenship skills by creating opportunities to stimulate learners' interactions and initiative (De La Caba Collado & Atxurra, 2006, p. 207). Such activities can develop students' active and autonomous learning inside and outside school through telecollaboration projects (Porto, 2018), cooperative learning, and extracurricular activities (Keser et al., 2011), and service learning (Rauschet & Byram, 2018).

Research on the impact of those activities has shown that they could raise learners' intercultural awareness, develop attitudes of respect of difference (Rauschet & Byram, 2018; Porto, 2018), and enhance criticality, social responsibility, and a sense of community (Porto, 2018). Many studies have evaluated EFL textbooks' promotion of ICC through the analysis of their representation and teaching of culture (Arslan, 2016; Baskin, 2018; Byram & Esartes Sarries, 1991; Sercu, 2000; Shin et al., 2011; Tüm & Ugūz, 2014), however, the global dimension of textbooks has scarcely been given attention. Topics such as climate change, human rights, peace and war, and pollution (Hosack, 2011, p. 129) are barely represented and superficially tackled (Cates, 1990, p. 43). In the Tunisian context, Melliti (2012) analysed the global course book "Headway Intermediate" in terms of its globality according to the criteria of connectedness, appropriacy, and inclusivity. He found that the textbook is partially global and recommended that it should be adapted to the needs of the local users, i.e. Tunisian learners of English. They should be glocalized, that is to say, they have to meet the needs of the local users, keeping meanwhile their connection to the world (Melliti, 2012, p. 12).

Research on global issues in textbooks is limited. Collado and Atxurra (2006, pp. 220–223), for instance, examined the extent to which primary school textbooks in Spain incorporate the ideals of democratic education and citizenship. The results of the analysis of five topics— responsibility, participation, conflict resolution, diversity, and human rights showed that these topics were unevenly dealt with, and some were barely represented. In the Tunisian context, Abid's (2019) study on global issues in four Tunisian secondary school EFL textbooks revealed that the textbooks had low potential to develop intercultural citizenship skills. Because of their underrepresentation of globally and interculturally oriented content and activities, textbooks failed to provide learners with opportunities to acquire and develop citizenship skills and values.

To the best of the researcher's knowledge, Abid's (2019) evaluation of global issues in Tunisian EFL textbooks might be the only one carried out in this respect. Therefore, given the lack of research on that particular issue in the Tunisian context and lack of focus on it in the Tunisian EFL programmes, the study reported in this chapter aims to be a modest contribution to the identification and understanding of the weaknesses of Tunisian EFL textbooks in terms of their potential to promote intercultural citizenship education among Tunisian learners. The development of intercultural citizenship in Tunisian young people is considered necessary especially after the 2011 revolution where the country witnessed political liberalization (UNESCO, 2014). To support their role in the democratic transition, Tunisian young people need to be equipped with skills and values that enable them to live and act as citizens of their country and the world (UNESCO, 2014).

The following section reports on the evaluation of a Tunisian EFL textbook's content and activities in terms of their teaching of global issues and skills. The evaluation aims to determine the extent to which globally oriented content and activities can contribute to the development of intercultural citizenship in Tunisian English language learners.

Intercultural Citizenship in a Tunisian EFL Textbook: "Skills for Life"

In the Tunisian educational system, the relationship between education and intercultural citizenship is reflected in the educational act's (2007) emphasis on the interaction between national and the universal values of freedom, democracy, social justice, and human rights. However, interculturality does not figure among the objectives of the English language curriculum. It makes no reference to the global/intercultural dimension of English language teaching (ELT) despite its use of the British and American cultures as context for language teaching and its representation of topics with global orientation (Official programme, 1998).

Given this gap in the system and my strong belief in the educational mission of EFL textbooks to educate EFL learners to become citizens of the world, I evaluated a textbook's cultural content and activities to determine the extent to which it promotes intercultural citizenship. The textbook analysed, "Skills for life", was locally designed by Tunisian EFL teachers and teacher trainers. It is used by all Tunisian EFL teachers and all fourth form Tunisian secondary school students. The textbook is made up of an introductory unit, four main topics, and an add-ons section focusing on vocabulary and grammar review. As stated in the textbook's introduction, the texts are meant to be contexts for teaching language as structure and as a means of communication. No reference is made to the cultural dimension of the textbook's content or activities in the introduction. Although intercultural learning and citizenship education are not mentioned as objectives to be achieved by the textbook, cultural information, and global issues are included in the four main topics. For this reason, I found it relevant to examine the textbook's representation of global issues and their potential to teach intercultural/global citizenship that is the skills, attitudes, and knowledge that enable the learners to become global citizens.

Textbook Content

Using content analysis, the textbook is evaluated in terms of its representation of culture, global issues, and activities promoting global/intercultural skills (Sercu, 2000, p. 253). Using the text as a unit of analysis, the analysis of the textbook is based on calculating the frequency distribution of global issues in comparison with other types of cultures, and the distribution of global issues over their types. The evaluation seeks to determine whether global issues are equally represented in the textbook in comparison with other topics using Mark's (1993) and Swenson and Cline's (1993) classification (cited in Yakovchuk 2004, p. 32). The authors classified global issues into the following four groups:

- Environmental issues: pollution, deforestation, endangered animals, global warming, recycling, natural disasters, etc.
- Peace education issues: wars, nuclear arms race, refugees, etc.
- Human rights issues: racism, gender issues, children's rights, etc.
- Intercultural communication issues: cultural issues, global citizenship vs. national identity, multiculturalism, etc.
- Socio-economic issues: poverty, wealth, consumer society, advertising, immigration, etc.
- Health concerns: drugs, AIDS, etc.
- Linguistic imperialism.

The results of the evaluation of the content in Table 5.1 show that there is a clear imbalance in the representation of culture and global issues. The target cultures, namely the American and the British, are more represented than the other types (50, 60%), whereas the learners' culture, that is the Tunisian culture, is absent. In fact, the textbook comprises four

Table 5.1 The distribution of cultures according to their types in "Skills for Life"

	Source culture	Target culture	Other cultures	Culture free	Global issues	Total
Frequency	0	42	11	15	17	83
Percentage	0%	50.60%	13.25%	18.07%	20.48%	100%

main topics which are art shows and holidaying, educational matters, life issues, and creative and inventive minds. All the texts, whether written or audio, discussed those topics in American, British, and culture free contexts. No text has dealt with these issues in Tunisia.

With reference to Byram's (2008, p. 216) framework for intercultural citizenship education, the cognitive orientation or the knowledge component includes the learners' knowledge of their own and other cultures as well as knowledge of the world (civility, social inequality, law, order, etc.) and principles of human rights. The content of "Skills for Life" does not seem to develop knowledge of culture and other issues shared by other people in the world due to their imbalanced representation of the different categories. The absence of the learners' culture and the dominance of the target culture may not promote interculturality, in the sense of the potential for the acquisition of intercultural knowledge, attitudes, and intercultural/global skills such as the comparison of cultures and critical thinking.

The inadequacy and lack of variety of the contact situations portrayed provide learners with limited opportunities for the development of the knowledge, attitudes, and skills of an intercultural citizen. In addition, the lack of frequency and variety of contacts may negatively influence the learners' perception of possible contacts they can have with people other than the native speakers of English. This is a reductionist view of intercultural knowledge and contact that does not fit in an increasingly intercultural world nor does it take into account the learners' reality where intercultural communication on social media is a common daily practice.

Generally speaking, the textbook's representation of contacts as well as the focus on the target culture provides an essentialist stance that treats culture as static and homogeneous, emphasizes difference, and undermines the variation inside cultures themselves (Dervin, 2016; Holliday, 2010). This essentialist view may decrease willingness to interact with the other (Holliday, 2010) and enhance the formation of stereotypes.

In comparison with the other categories, target, native, and other cultures, global issues seem to be more represented, although that representation cannot be said to be significant. In terms of variety, a limited range of global issues was represented in the textbook (see Table 5.2).

Table 5.2 The distribution of global issues according to their types in "Skills for Life"

Type	Frequency	Percentage (%)
Environmental issues	2	11.76
Peace education issues	0	0
Human rights issues	2	11.76
Intercultural communication	0	0
Socio-economic issues	11	64.70
Health concerns	1	05.88
Linguistic imperialism	1	05.88
Total	17	100

In fact, most topics belong to the socio-economic category dealing with issues such as consumerism, technology, international immigration, etc. Few issues as health concerns (smoking and other health problems) are hardly represented and those related to intercultural communication and peace education are absent.

Given the limited number of global issues in the textbook analysed (e.g. intercultural communication and human rights), these issues cannot be attended to by learners and can consequently impede their acquisition of intercultural/global skills and universal values required to get engaged in actions across geographical and cultural boundaries (Byram, 2008; Cates, 1990, 2000; Guiherme, 2002).

Textbook Activities

Content analysis is used to analyse the activities in terms of their distribution over the different types: language aspects (grammar, vocabulary, and pronunciation), language skills (reading, listening, speaking, and writing), and global skills. The activities teaching global skills are evaluated on the basis of Cates' (1990, p. 45) and Cabesudo et al.'s (2008, pp. 30–31) classification which includes:

- communication through simulations and role plays,
- critical and creative thinking,
- cooperative problem-solving,
- non-violent conflict resolution,

● informed decision-making,
● seeing issues from multiple perspectives,
● projects (interviews, surveys, and oral presentations).

This classification which was published by the council of Europe in the "Global Education Guidelines" applies to the European context and any other context, including the Tunisian one, because global issues are shared by people all over the world.

Results (see Table 5.3) showed a clear imbalance in the distribution of activities according to the skills they aim to develop. The reading skills are more emphasized than the rest of the skills, and the language aspects are not given importance except for vocabulary. In comparison with the activities teaching language skills, those developing global skills are very limited in number and constitute only 3.55% of the total number of the textbook's activities.

The distribution of activities promoting global skills over their types (Table 5.4) demonstrates their lack of variety. For instance, settling conflicts, communicating across cultures, and adopting multiple perspectives do not figure as potential global skills to develop. The most represented global skills are critical and creative thinking which is developed in speaking, reading, and writing activities. Examples of these include writing a letter to the World Bank to discuss its view of brain drain in developing countries, and expressing agreement or disagreement and justifying with convincing arguments.

Table 5.3 The distribution of the textbook's activities according to their types

	Frequency	Percentage (%)
Pronunciation	42	6.22
Vocabulary	113	16.74
Grammar	48	07.11
Listening	54	08.00
Writing	35	05.18
Speaking	67	09.92
Reading	292	43.25
Global skills	24	03.55
Total	675	100

Table 5.4 The distribution of global skills over their types in "Skills for Life"

	Frequency	Rate (%)
Critical and creative thinking	19	79,16
Communication through simulations and role plays	0%	0
Cooperative problem-solving	4	16.16
Non-violent conflict resolution	0%	0
Informed decision-making	1	0.41
Seeing issues from multiple perspectives	0%	0
Total	24	

The evaluation of the textbook in terms of its teaching of global skills highlights the inadequacy of activities dealing with global issues in terms of frequency and variety. However, the textbook's activities, according to Cates (1990), should invite learners to reflect on global issues, relate them to their local problems, find solutions, and take decisions that are beneficial for their own and other communities.

The Tunisian educational system emphasizes the role of education in forming citizens who are proud of their national identity and loyal to their country, while being open to the world's cultures and universal values. It also points out the notion of dialogue between the Tunisian culture and international ones and its role in the enrichment of the national culture by adding a universal dimension. Those objectives were made clear by the educational law of 2002–2007 and should normally be taken into consideration in teaching different subjects at school including English. Although the objectives of the system are clear about being a world's citizen, the English language textbook's content and activities do not seem to help learners attain those objectives due to the essentialist view of culture it embodies and the inability to observe the intercultural nature of communication.

The gap is clear between the requirements of the educational system and the actual implementation of its requirements in the English language syllabus reflected in the textbook's content and methods. It is necessary, then, to bridge the gap between educational objectives and the actual implementation and make textbooks more intercultural and global in their contents and methods of teaching. If English language teaching in Tunisia intends to prepare learners to live in today's world and cope with the everyday changes and challenges, it is necessary to teach them global values and skills. They do not only need to communicate effectively interculturally using English, but also to build and maintain relationships with other people outside their national boundaries. Living in an intercultural world requires them to mediate between different cultures to be able to manage cultural misunderstanding and conflicts.

Teaching English as a foreign language should focus on developing intercultural citizenship competences as much as they focus on achieving instrumental objectives. Teachers of foreign languages in Tunisia and abroad should be invited to use teaching techniques that are appropriate to the development of intercultural citizenship such as project work, collaborative learning, problem-solving activities, the use of ICT, virtual intercultural exchanges, extracurricular activities, etc.

Conclusion

Intercultural citizenship education is a recent development of teaching for ICC which aims to prepare learners to be active citizens of the world. Being a citizen implies learning knowledge, attitudes, and skills to be able to communicate successfully and maintain relationships with culturally different people and have interest in understanding and solving global issues. Foreign language education can play an important role in that by promoting the intercultural/global dimension of teaching and textbooks' contents and activities. For these reasons, this study undertook the evaluation of a Tunisian EFL textbook's potential for the development of ICE through the analysis of global issues in texts and activities.

The analysis and evaluation suggest that the textbook's cultural content presented an essentialist and solid view of culture by depicting the British and American cultures, while undermining the Tunisian culture. Cultures were depicted as separate and independent entities that did not interact or connect. The underrepresentation of other cultures and the learners' own on the one hand, and the absence of intercultural interaction and communication in the textbooks' activities, may reduce the textbook's potential to promote ICE. The limited number and the lack of variety of global issues and activities teaching intercultural/global skills do not provide the learners sufficient opportunities to acquire the skills. The activities promoting global skills were few, which in turn may limit learners' engagement in performing tasks and learning skills they may need in living and communicating with other people from different cultural backgrounds. In order to bridge the gap between the weaknesses of textbooks and teaching English in general in terms of the promotion of ICE, the researcher suggests recommendations for Tunisian teachers and others around the world. These are stated in detail in the following section.

Recommendations

Through the evaluation of the textbook's potential to promote the acquisition of intercultural citizenship through global issues, this chapter has raised important issues in relation to interculturality. The findings showed the limitations of the textbook to develop ICC, the author proposes some recommendations to language policymakers in her country, material developers, and English language teachers nationally and internationally.

The author suggests that language policymakers take measures to adopt and implement an intercultural approach in English language teaching with focus on global aspects. Following that the already existing textbooks should be improved or completely changed by adopting a more liquid approach to interculturality that facilitates the acquisition of flexible attitudes, intercultural skills, and knowledge of culture, intercultural communication, and universal values and issues. The textbooks' content should represent cultural diversity and give a multiperspectival representation of culture. In terms of activities, the promotion of global skills should be given more importance.

As far as material developers are concerned, cross-curricular cooperation is recommended. They can draw on contents and methods used by subjects teaching citizenship such as history, geography, and civic education. To increase the effectiveness and appropriateness of activities in teaching global skills, material developers should draw on different checklists either of the content or for the activities or for the skills to be developed. Some of the toolkits are mentioned in this chapter and used for the evaluation of the textbooks. Others are suggested by UNESCO (2014) and the catalogue produced by a group of researchers and published by the Centre for Universal Education at Brookings (2017). Because global issues and global/intercultural citizenship are and should be of concern to many educational systems, those toolkits which are designed by an international organization are useful to material developers all over the world.

Although teachers should comply with the requirements of the objectives, methods, and materials decoded by the curriculum designers and textbook developers, they can take initiatives to make their teaching more interculturally and globally oriented. They are advised not to restrict their teaching practice to the contents and activities in the textbooks they use. They can select their texts from other sources and design suitable activities they think achieve the envisaged goal that is the promotion of intercultural citizenship.

The activities should be more varied using developed technologies. Information and Communication Technology (ICT) is powerful in bringing students from different countries together either for language learning or for the development of ICC and intercultural citizenship. Telecollaboration such as e-twinning and Erasmus+virtual exchanges provide authentic contexts for exchange, interaction with people from different cultural backgrounds, and intercultural learning. They also offer opportunities to link the local issues to global ones developing meanwhile citizenship skills such as conflict management, problem-solving, taking informed decisions about an issue, taking actions.

E-twinning is a practical telecollaboration that brings together two groups of students from two different countries to work on a project with a determined outcome. For instance, students in both groups can deal with a topic such as school violence. Each group read documents and conduct interviews with schoolmates about the topic, and then they report their findings to the other group. Students in both groups will get new knowledge about the topic from another perspective, identify differences and similarities between the two perspectives, and end up finding solutions. The outcome can be concretized in the form of a brochure sensitizing students in both schools about the dangers of school violence and its negative impact on students' lives, relations, and academic achievements.

The benefits of this project work include raising learners' intercultural awareness, acquiring knowledge of other perspectives, and developing feelings of empathy, cooperation, solidarity, sharing, and respect. By doing something for other students in another country, learners develop a strong sense of belonging to a wider community than his/her own. Project work can also develop, while cooperating, skills of negotiation, discussion, reconciliation of different points of view, and settling conflicts when they happen.

Added to that, activities should develop agency and autonomy, and go beyond the classroom setting to involve students in community service, fieldwork research, and voluntary work. Jacobs and Cates (1999, p. 46) suggest that teachers can encourage students to write letters to governments and national and international organizations to ask them to take actions to protect the environment and help children in poor countries. They can as well participate in fundraising and voluntary actions. Extracurricular activities such as intercultural service learning (Rauschet & Byram, 2018) might be very beneficial for the promotion of students' language proficiency, critical thinking, intercultural competence, and autonomous learning. Doing online project with citizenship focus can integrate the promotion of linguistic proficiency and other skills such as research skills, informed decision-making, critical thinking, problem-solving, etc.

Given the lack of research on global issues in textbooks in foreign language education, teachers in Tunisia and in countries where intercultural approach and ICE is not adopted yet, should take into account how to use the textbook and adapt it so that it can respond to their learners' needs. Training teachers on the selection and the design of materials and the teaching methods to develop ICC might be an urgent requirement. Global issues and skills should be emphasized to raise learners' awareness of the fact that their local problems are shared by other people in the world and that solving those problems can also be shared.

Recommended Texts

1/ Alfred, G; Byram, M. and Fleming, M. (2006). Education for Intercultural Citizenship: concepts and comparisons.

This book can be helpful to foreign language teachers thanks to its comprehensive explanation of intercultural citizenship education, its relationship with interculturality and education, and its implementation in the classroom as well as in curriculum and syllabus design.

2/ Byram, M. (2008). From foreign language education to education for intercultural citizenship: Essays and Reflections. Clevedon: Multilingual matters Ltd.

This book is important for foreign language teachers and researchers as well because it provides a framework for intercultural citizenship education, a detailed description of its objectives and principles, and the characteristics of possible curricula for intercultural citizenship as well as methods of assessing intercultural competence and intercultural citizenship.

3/ Dervin, F. (2016). Interculturality in Education: A Theoretical and methodological Toolbox. London: Palgrave Pivot.

The book is a guide to teachers, students, and education policymakers to better understand and adopt a new view of the issue of interculturality in education.

4/ Global Citizenship Education. Preparing Learners for the Challenges of the Twenty-First Century (2014). Paris: UNESCO.

This book is UNESCO's report on global citizenship education in practice. It is of importance to teachers as it enhances understanding of global citizenship education and its relevance to understand and resolve global issues. The report provides teachers with guidance on the already existing as well as new good approaches to teaching global issues and global citizenship.

Engagement Priorities

1. If you teach global issues in your English language classes, which techniques and strategies do you think are appropriate for teaching global issues and skills?
2. What challenges may you face in implementing activities with a global citizenship orientation?
3. If you find the textbook inadequate for developing global skills and you intend to use materials other than the textbook, which criteria would you use for the selection or design of appropriate materials?
4. If an English class teaches intercultural citizenship, do you think that it should draw on other subjects teaching citizenship such as history and geography?
5. The study shows that developing intercultural citizenship skills requires learners' exposure to a balanced representation of different cultures including the learners' own. Which cultures are represented in the textbooks you use in your context? Do you think the cultural content of the English textbooks you use is appropriate and adequate for the development of intercultural citizenship skills?

References

Abid, N. (2012). *Intercultural language learning in Tunisian EFL textbooks: 6th, 7th, 8th, and 9th form basic education pupils as a case study*. Unpublished doctoral dissertation. University of Lorraine and University of Sfax.

Abid, N. (2018). Developing national and intercultural identities in Tunisian EFL classes. A study of English textbooks, teachers' and learners' attitudes. In M. Guirat (Ed.), *Politics and Poetics of Belonging* (pp. 169–196). Newcastle upon Tyne: Cambridge Scholars Publishing.

Abid, N. (2019). Global issues in EFL textbooks for Tunisian secondary school students. In Ch. Smaoui, S. Abid, A. Bennani, & M. Romdhani (Eds.), *Humanising ELT. Proceedings of TATE's 6*[th] *International Conference* (pp. 44–64). Imprimerie Reliure d'Art.

Alfred, G., Byram, M., & Fleming, B. (2006). *Education for intercultural citizenship: Concepts and comparisons*. Multilingual Matters Ltd.

Arslan, S. (2016). An analysis of two Turkish EFL books in terms of cultural aspects. *Procedia—Social and Behavioural Sciences, 232*, 217–225.

Baskin, S. (2018). Which cultural aspects do the textbooks of teaching Turkish to foreigners transfer? *Advances in Language and Literary Studies, 9*(2), 131–137.

Byram, M. (1997). *Teaching and assessing intercultural communicative competence*. Clevedon: Multilingual Matters.

Byram, M. (2008). *From foreign language education to education for intercultural citizenship*. Multilingual Matters.

Byram, M. (2012). Conceptualizing intercultural communicative competence and intercultural citizenship. In J. Jackson (Ed.), *The Routledge handbook of language and intercultural communication* (pp. 85–97). Routledge.

Byram, M., & Esarte-Sarries, V. (Eds.). (1991). *Investigating cultural studies in foreign language teaching*. Clevedon: Multilingual Matters.

Byram, M., & Wagner, M. (2018). Making a difference: Language teaching for intercultural and international dialogue. *Foreign Language Annals, 51*(1), 140–151.

Cabesudo, A., Chritidis, Ch., Demetriadou-Salte, T., Halbartschlager, F., & Mihai, G. P. (2008). *Global education guidelines: Handbook for educators to understand and implement global education*. The North-South Centre of the Council of Europe.

Cates, K. A. (1990). Teaching for a better world: Global issues and language education. *The Language Teacher*, 41–52.

Cates, K. A. (2000). Entry for 'global education.' In M. Byram (Ed.), *The Routledge encyclopaedia of language teaching and learning* (pp. 241–243). Routledge.

Cates, K. A. (2002). Teaching for a better world: Global issues and language education. *Human Rights Education in Asian Schools*, 41–50.

Davies, L. (2006). Global citizenship: Abstraction or framework for action. *Educational Review, 58*(1), 5–25.

De La Caba Collado, M., & Atxurra, R. L. (2006). Democratic citizenship in textbooks in Spanish primary curriculum. *Journal of Curriculum Studies, 38*(2), 205–228.

Dervin, F., & Liddicoat, A. (2013). *Linguistics for intercultural education*. Amsterdam: John Benjamins Publishing Company.

Dervin, F. (2016). *Interculturality in education: A theoretical and methodological toolbox*. London: Palgrave Macmillan.

Dietz, G. (2018). Interculturality. In H. Callan (Ed.), *The international encyclopaedia of Anthropology* (pp. 1–19). Wiley.

Education and School Instruction Law (2002–2007). Ministry of Education

Ferri, G. (2014). Ethical communication and intercultural responsibility: A philosophical perspective. *Language and Intercultural Communication, 14*(1), 7–23.

Guiherme, M. (2002). *Critical citizens for an intercultural world: Foreign language education as cultural politics*. Multilingual Matters Ltd.

Guiherme, M. (2007). English as a global language and education for cosmopolitan citizenship. *Language and Intercultural Communication, 7*(1), 72–90.

Hoff, H. E. (2014). A critical discussion of Byram's model of intercultural communicative competence in the light of bildung theories. *Intercultural Education, 25*(6), 508–517.

Holliday, A. (2010). Complexity in cultural identity. *Language and Intercultural Communication, 10*(2), 165–177.

Hosack, I. (2011). Foreign language teaching for global citizenship. 政策科学, *18*(3): 125–140.

Ichilov, O. (1998). *Citizenship and citizenship education in a changing world*. The Woburn Press.

Jacobs, G. M. (2003). Cooperative learning to promote human rights. *Human Rights Education in Asian Schools, 6*, 119–129.

Jacobs, J. M., & Cates, K. (1999). Global education in second language teaching. *KATA, 1*(1), 44–56.

Keser, F., Akar, H., & Yildirim, A. (2011). The role of extracurricular activities in active citizenship education. *Journal of Curriculum Studies, 43*(6), 809–837.

Liddicoat, A. J. (2015). Interculturality. In K. Tracy, C. Ilie, & T. Sandel (Eds.), *The international encyclopaedia of language and social interaction* (pp. 1–5). Wiley.

Mark, K. (1993). Some thoughts about 'global content.' *The Language Teacher, 17*(5), 37–40.

Matsuo, C. (2012). A critique of Michael Byram's model of intercultural communicative competence from the perspective of model type and conceptualization of culture. *Fukuoka University Review of Literature & Humanities, 44*, 347–380.

Measuring global citizenship education: A collection of Practices and Tools. (2017). Centre for Universal Education at Brookings.

Melliti, M. (2012). *Globality in global textbooks: Principles and applicability: The case of Headway Intermediate (Soars & Soars, 2003)*. Verlag: Lap Lambert Academic Publishing.

Mendéz García, M. D. (2005). International and intercultural issues in English teaching textbooks: The case of Spain. *Intercultural Education, 16*(1), 57–68.

Osbourne, K. (2000). Public schooling and citizenship education in Canada. *Canadian Ethnic Studies Journal, 32*(1), 8–37.

Osler, A., & Starkey, H. (2015). Education for cosmopolitan citizenship: A framework for language learning. *Argentinean Journal of Applied Linguistics, 3*(2): 30–39.

Porto, M. (2018). 'Yo antes ya reciclaba y esto me cambio por complete la consencia': Intercultural citizenship education in the English classroom. *Education 3–13, 46*(3): 317–334.

Porto, M., Houghton, S. A., & Byram, M. (2017). Intercultural citizenship in the (foreign) language classroom. *Language Teaching Research, 22*(5), 484–498.

Rauschet, P., & Byram, M. (2018). Service learning and intercultural citizenship in foreign language education. *Cambridge Journal of Education, 48*(3), 353–369.

Risager, K. (1991). Cultural references in European textbooks: An evaluation of recent tendencies. In D. Buttjes & M. Byram (Eds.), *Mediating languages and cultures* (pp. 181–192). Clevedon: Multilingual Matters.

Risager, K. (2007). *Language and culture pedagogy from national to transnational paradigm*. Clevedon: Multilingual Matters.

Sercu, L. (2000). *Acquiring intercultural competence from textbooks. The case of Flemish adolescent pupuls learning German*. Belgium: Leuven University Press.

Sercu, L. (2006). The foreign language and intercultural competence teacher: The acquisition of a new professional identity. *Intercultural Education, 17*(1), 55–72.

Shin, J., Eslami, Z. R., & Chen, W. (2011). Presentation of local and international culture in current international English-language teaching textbooks. *Language, Culture and Curriculum, 24*(3), 253–268.

Swenson, T., & Cline, B. (1993). Global issues in content-based curriculum. *The Language Teacher, 17*(5), 27–40.

Tüm, G., & Ugūz, S. (2014). An investigation on the cultural elements in a Turkish textbook for foreigners. *Procedia- Social and Behavioural Sciences, 158*, 356–363.

UNESCO. (2014). *Global citizenship education: Preparing learners for the challenges of the twenty-first century*. Paris.

Wagner, M., & Byram, M. (2017). Intercultural citizenship. In Y. Y. Kim & K. L. McKay (Eds.), *The international encyclopaedia of intercultural communication* (pp. 1–6). Wiley-Blackwell.

Yakovchuk, N. (2004). Global issues and values in foreign language education: Selection and awareness-raising. *ELTED, 8*, 28–47.

Young, T., & Sercombe, P. (2010). Introduction: Communication, discourses and interculturality. *Language and Intercultural Communication, 10*(3), 181–188.

6

Intercultural Competence in the Curriculum and in Textbooks—Which Lessons Can Be Learnt from EFL Textbooks in Norwegian Schools?

Helen Margaret Murray

Introduction

Interculturality in the language classroom refers to the processes in which pupils learn both about other cultures and about how they relate to their own cultures. These involve a two-way interaction between known and unknown cultures, where pupils 'draw on and use the resources and processes of cultures with which they are familiar but also those they might not typically be associated within their interactions with others' (Young & Sercombe, 2010, p. 181). To those working with young people in the English language classroom, these ideas are very relatable to class experience. We teach our pupils to approach interactions with an understanding based not only on their own cultural experiences but also with a new understanding of cultures based on what they have learnt in our

H. M. Murray (✉)
Department of Teacher Education, Norwegian University of Science and Technology (NTNU), Trondheim, Norway
e-mail: helen.m.murray@ntnu.no

© The Author(s), under exclusive license to Springer Nature
Switzerland AG 2021
M. Victoria and C. Sangiamchit (eds.), *Interculturality and the English Language Classroom*, https://doi.org/10.1007/978-3-030-76757-0_6

classrooms. Language teaching is not only about learning the form of the language itself, but also the cultural understandings that are inherent in the language and its usage.

This idea of interculturality can be seen in the Norwegian curriculum from 1990s onwards, influenced by the Council of Europe's Common European Framework of Reference for Languages (Council of Europe, 2001). Curriculum goals require pupils to connect their own linguistic and cultural backgrounds with the target languages and cultures. For example, a fourth grader (10 years old) will be required, according to the curriculum, to 'converse about some aspects of different ways of living, traditions and customs in English-speaking countries and in Norway' (The Norwegian Directorate for Education and Training, 2013). To achieve this curriculum goal, the learners can use their own cultural backgrounds and experiences as a point of reference when attaining new knowledge about English-speaking worlds.

While the term 'interculturality' is not used in the EFL curriculum in Norway, 'intercultural understanding' is directly mentioned (The Norwegian Directorate for Education and Training, 2019). This 'intercultural understanding' in the classroom involves pupils developing competence in communication with people of different cultural and linguistic backgrounds. When two people from different cultures are speaking together, their cultural backgrounds affect what they say, how they say it and how they interpret the responses that they get from the other person. Cultural backgrounds in this context, can refer to a combination of the following aspects:

> personal cultural realities can be made up of a variety of things such as religion, ancestry, skin colour, language, discourse, class, education, profession, skills, community, family, activities, region, friends, food, dress, political attitudes, many of which can cross national boundaries. (Holliday, 2010, p. 263)

'Intercultural competence' is the knowledge and skills needed to use cultural awareness actively in communication with others (Byram et al., 2002). It is important to avoid a prescriptive approach in the acquirement of this knowledge and these skills. Cultural identities are complex and in flux, and individuals will have multiple identities depending on their situation at the time. Intercultural competence will therefore consist of 'contradictions, instabilities and discontinuities' (Dervin & Gross, 2016, p. 6).

While a textbook cannot, in itself, teach intercultural competence, as this is a personal skill developed by the learner, it can contribute to the development of intercultural competence in pupils by creating an awareness of own and other cultures in the texts and tasks in the learning materials on offer. This awareness is an essential stepping-stone in developing intercultural competence. However, it is to be noted that working with textbooks is seldom enough to develop intercultural competence in pupils, and the teacher must supplement with discussion and with authentic materials in the classroom.

This chapter will focus on to what extent the development of intercultural competence is encouraged in textbooks used in EFL teaching in Norway, relating to the demands of the curriculum. These examples can be used by teachers worldwide to assess the teaching materials used in their own classrooms for suitability in developing these skills.

Background

The Norwegian Education System

Compulsory education in Norway is from ages 6 to 16 and free for all pupils. Compulsory schooling is divided up into grades 1–7, which are primary education, and grades 8–10, which are lower secondary education. A vast majority of pupils stay on at school after age 16 and have the right to take three years upper secondary education before the age of 19. This upper secondary education is divided into theoretical courses, which prepare pupils for further study, and vocational courses, which prepare pupils for apprenticeships or other vocational careers.

Compulsory education is based on a common curriculum that is taught in all Norwegian schools. Pupils in Sámi schools[1] and pupils with sign language as their first language have their own adjusted curriculum. The curriculum consists of two parts. The first part is a general section explaining the aims of education as a whole while the second part is subject specific, and consists of the purpose of the subject, main areas, skills to be learnt, goals for different age groups and how assessment in the subject should happen. Principles of equality in education are fundamental in the common curriculum, which in practice means that pupils of all abilities and backgrounds will meet the same curriculum and achievement goals at school. All pupils will participate in the sharing of common knowledge, cultural experiences and values. The current curriculum was created in 2006 and revised in 2013 (The Norwegian Directorate for Education and Training, 2013). A new curriculum has been launched and will be gradually implemented from August 2020.

English is taught as a foreign language in Norwegian schools from grade 1 onwards. It is a compulsory subject from grades 1–10, and all pupils will follow the same curriculum. The final course in compulsory English is taken at upper secondary school, either over one or two years, depending on the course of study followed. The teacher can tailor the content of this course towards their pupils' studies to a certain degree, although large parts are identical for all pupils no matter their studies.

Intercultural Competence and Textbook Representations of Cultures

According to Byram et al. (2002), the development of intercultural competence can be divided into several different aspects that pupils should explore in the classroom. While Byram's theories have been challenged and modified since first publication, the different aspects of intercultural competence are still present in the Norwegian EFL curriculum. The first aspect is the development of attitudes, that is a curiosity and openness about the world rather than a belief that one's own values and cultural background are superior or 'correct'. Secondly, is having knowledge of how social groups and identities function and interact, including the development of own and other's identity. Thirdly, is the development of specific communicative skills. Pupils must learn how to look at cultures from diverse perspectives and understand how people from different social groups might interpret the same situation in multiple ways. Furthermore, learners also need skills in being able to acquire new knowledge and add or amend existing knowledge. Finally, pupils need to develop a critical awareness of their own cultures, and how their own beliefs and values affect how they view other people's (Byram et al., 2002, pp. 11–13). While a single text or task is unlikely to cover all these aspects, they should be evident in some form in the compete plan of class activities aimed at promoting the development of intercultural competence.

However, it is also important to avoid an 'essentialist' view when working with cultural topics in the classroom, that is the idea that 'a person from a given culture is essentially different from someone with another cultural background' (Hoff, 2018, p. 73). Cultures should rather be seen as 'non-essentialist', meaning that they are dynamic and complex and cut across national boundaries. Individuals are unique, moving in and out of different roles depending on context. Therefore, it is important to be aware that cultural background is not the same as a national identity. Individuals can have membership in multiple cultures and can emphasise and utilise these differently, depending on setting. So, for example, the same person can be a Norwegian, a European, a football player, a pupil, a family member. It is notable here that not all these cultural identities relate to nationality or ethnic backgrounds. Different aspects of these identities will be brought into play or discarded depending on the interaction (Zhu, 2015, pp. 72–73). A teacher needs to be aware of these different identities within the classroom. Especially with modern global communications, pupils can have strong identities that are transnational, for example, due to taking part in online gaming. To some, these identities and cultures may take precedence over ties to state or nationality.

While it is important to focus on similarities between peoples and cultures, at the same time there should be a recognition that differences do exist, as to ignore these can be to create and perpetuate power imbalances. Especially when working with topics involving peoples who historically have experienced oppression by another cultural group, for example, indigenous peoples, an awareness of difference can bring inequalities to light. An understanding of the fluid, dynamic and transnational aspect of cultures can help people accept that others are neither worse nor better than themselves, which can in turn lead to a revision of unequal power relations (Dervin & Gross, 2016, p. 6).

Developing intercultural competence in the language classroom should aim at creating learners who can engage with multiple identities. Pupils enter the classroom with different viewpoints and cultural backgrounds, as well as academic levels, meaning there is no common starting point for the development of intercultural competence. Pupils develop skills at different rates, making intercultural competence a lifelong learning goal, part of a never-ending cycle where previous knowledge is gradually replaced with new (Moeller & Nugent, 2014, pp. 5–6), rather than the aim of a particular semester or school year.

In the classroom, focus on the development of intercultural competence will affect the teaching methods and the kinds of materials used. Teachers must be aware of the dangers of creating and reinforcing stereotypes, that is seeing a single person or social group as representative of a culture. Studies of textbooks reveal that one-sided or stereotypical representations are not uncommon, and a critical engagement with the textbook as 'cultural artifact and bearer of messages' (Gray, 2000, p. 280) is necessary.

Textbooks contain artificially created secondary environments in which cultures are represented in various ways—through the creation and/or inclusion of multiethnic characters, through the choices made in what to include and exclude as examples of the target cultures, the ways in which gender and sexual orientation are presented, etc. These constitute 'very particular constructions of reality in which English is given a range of specific associations' (Gray, 2010, p. 12). Teachers should be careful that materials used in class do not imply that identified cultural features are common to citizens of a country or cultural background, reducing individuals to single stereotypes (Young & Sercombe, 2010, p. 182). Instead, teachers should aim to give pupils access to as wide a range of perspectives as possible. Pupils should engage with 'diversities' rather than a single 'diversity' (Dervin, 2016, p. 28), as the latter encourages pupils to see minorities as a homogenous group, rather than encouraging meaningful interaction with the multiplicity of perspectives that exist.

Pupils will be living their adult lives in an ever-changing world. Social identities are not static, and pupils will develop their own and meet others of different and changing identity throughout their lives. Activities in the classroom should be tailored to developing pupils' intercultural competence through exposure texts and tasks that raise intercultural awareness, exposing pupils to as wide a range of voices and experiences as possible, and letting them experience a variety of social identities as well as exploring their own. Learning activities that promote dialogue are essential, as it is in the meeting with others that intercultural competence can develop.

Intercultural Competence in the Norwegian EFL Curriculum

The influence of theories on intercultural competence is visible in the Norwegian national curriculum (2006/2013). In the introduction to the English subject curriculum, one of the aims of the subject is: 'Development of communicative language skills and cultural insight can promote greater interaction, understanding and respect between persons with different cultural backgrounds' (The Norwegian Directorate for Education and Training, 2013). This introductory paragraph to the whole curriculum reflects ideas that are covered in specific curriculum goals for the different grades.

The Norwegian Department of Education has released a new curriculum which will be gradually implemented in the coming years, starting in August 2020. The position of intercultural competence is strengthened in curriculum. The opening paragraph explaining the purpose of learning English states that,

> The subject shall give pupils a basis for communication with others locally and globally, independent of cultural and linguistic background. English will contribute to developing pupils' intercultural understanding of different ways of living, thinking and patterns of communication (The Norwegian Directorate for Education and Training, 2019).

The English curriculum is divided into four main areas (these will be revised in the new curriculum), 'Language Learning', 'Oral Communication', 'Written Communication', and 'Culture, Society and Literature'. This final area is where the influence from theories on intercultural competence is most noticeable, for example, in the focus on developing knowledge to understand and respect other people's cultures, as shown in the quotation from the curriculum below:

> … working with and discussing expository texts, literary texts and cultural forms of expression from different media. This is essential to develop knowledge about, understanding of and respect for the lives and cultures of other people (The Norwegian Directorate for Education and Training, 2013).

Here it is also notable that pupils are expected to meet a wide range of materials in their English education and gain insight into a range of genre and cultural expressions. This breadth of material is reminiscent of the third of Byram's aspects of intercultural competence, referring to how pupils should gain awareness of a wide range of perspectives and understand how people from different social groups might interpret the same situation in multiple ways (Byram et al., 2002, pp. 11–13). However, the teacher should be aware of how they represent 'lives and cultures of other peoples', so that they include diversities of opinions and perspectives within the social groups, to avoid portrayal of a single, homogenous group and stereotyping of individuals (Dervin, 2016, p. 28).

There are five basic skills that pupils are to acquire, according to the English curriculum (oral, written, reading, numeracy, digital skills). The influence of theories on intercultural competence can be seen in the references to the communication types and situations pupils should master under the section 'Oral Skills':

> …be able to listen, speak and interact using the English language. It means evaluating and adapting ways of expression to the purpose of the conversation, the recipient and the situation (The Norwegian Directorate for Education and Training, 2013).

While 'listen, speak and interact' involve meaningful dialogue between individuals, it is in the point involving 'evaluating and adapting ways of expression' that the influence of intercultural competence can be clearly seen. This includes consideration of personal perspectives, the many different aspects that constitute a person's cultural background, and how these can lead to multiple interpretations and responses to the same situation. It will also involve an understanding of the dynamic and fluid nature of cultural identity, meaning the same individual can change role and cultural affiliation depending on the situation (Hoff, 2018; Zhu, 2015).

The points made above refer to the general curriculum for the English subject in Norwegian schools. As well as containing this general section, the curriculum is also divided up into goals to be reached by the end of grades 2, 4, 7, 10 and the end of the final year of compulsory English teaching. These curriculum goals do not specify exactly what should be taught but give general themes that must be covered by all Norwegian schools. It is not within the scope of this chapter to show all the influence from intercultural competence throughout the curriculum, however, an extract from the English curriculum (Appendix 1) can show how skills related to the development of intercultural competence are found and developed in the section on 'Culture, Society and Literature' (The Norwegian Directorate for Education and Training, 2013).

It is interesting to note the depth of engagement required by the curriculum goals increases as pupils move up the grades. Pupils start off by 'conversing' about topics, later they 'discuss and elaborate' and 'describe and reflect'. Along with this development of skills, is an increase in the complexity of engagement with the topics. From starting off with 'everyday life' for children in the lowest grades, the curriculum goals move on to general ways of life, culture and society and social conditions. It is notable that while the focus of English teaching is the world outside of Norway, three of the five grade levels given include pupils discussing ways of living, traditions and customs in Norway. This inclusion reflects several aspects of intercultural competence, including the final of Byram's aspects as mentioned previously, which requires pupils to develop both a curiosity about other cultures, and critical awareness of own cultures and how these affect their viewpoints (Byram et al., 2002, pp. 11–13).

Intercultural Competence in Norwegian EFL Textbooks

Methodology

To consider how the development of intercultural competence is encouraged in textbooks, extracts from two textbooks used in English teaching in Norway are considered here. These books are used in grades 8 and 10 (lower secondary age). Textbooks for these levels have been chosen as the pupils will be intermediate language learners at this point and should be capable of expressing themselves with some complexity and engaging with challenging ideas in the English language. According to the curriculum, the pupils at this level should learn to 'discuss and elaborate' on the way people live and relate to one another in English-speaking countries, and 'describe and reflect' on the situation of indigenous peoples (The Norwegian Directorate for Education and Training, 2013).

Techniques in discourse analysis are used in analysing the examples from the textbooks. Discourse analysis is the study of language in social context, specifically how it is used to "do things", such as construct realities and create and maintain social relationships. While some approaches focus on the details of the language (grammar, syntax, etc.), other approaches, such as the one used in this article, concentrate on how ideas and themes are constructed and maintained in speech and in writing (Gee, 2011, p. ix). This article will also touch briefly upon Critical Discourse Analysis, which looks more specifically at the ways in which language 'both shapes and is shaped by society' (Machin & Mayr, 2012, p. 4). CDA looks at the interrelationship between power, ideology and language, and how power balances and imbalances are created and sustained through language. Texts that appear neutral on the surface, can contain ideas, assumptions and representations of cultures that maintain stereotypes and outdated attitudes.

While a full analysis of discourse is beyond the scope of this chapter, points concerning the focus of texts and tasks will be mentioned in connection with raising intercultural awareness and aiding the development of pupils' intercultural competence. It is also interesting to consider why the authors have designed and built a text in one particular way.

Insight into the cultural assumptions and attitudes of the author can be given by considering what could have been said, and what was the aim and meaning of what is actually said (Gee, 2011, p. 55). Certain aspects of the power relations revealed within the texts will also be discussed, and how these relate to the development of intercultural competence.

Analysis of Extracts from EFL Textbooks

Stages 8
The first book considered is *Stages 8*, a textbook used in grade 8 (13 years old) (Areklett et al., 2013). In the introductory pages of the first chapter of the book, which aim to introduce pupils to the themes they will cover in the school year, there are photos showing six people from different ethnic backgrounds. All the pictures are of people smiling or laughing and all are shown from the same camera-angle (centre/front). The questions alongside ask:

a. What do you think this person might be like?
b. Why do you think so?
c. What can we learn about people from what they look like?
d. What can we not learn? (Areklett et al., 2013, p. 16).

Regarding the development of intercultural competence, what is positive about these questions is that firstly, pupils are asked to consider their own attitudes by stating their immediate reaction. Rather than stopping there, the second question requires pupils to reflect in more depth over why they responded the way they did to the first question. This encourages a critical awareness of pupils' own opinions and attitudes, by reflecting over where they originated. Questions c and d develop this critical reflection further, asking pupils to consider what appearance can and cannot say about a person. If these questions are used as a starting point for dialogue between pupils, this consideration of own attitudes and how they are formed may also encourage an understanding of differing attitudes and how and why they exist.

Opportunities for interesting discussion, such as the one above, are not given elsewhere in the same textbook. Chapter three, 'Rule Britannia', is about the United Kingdom (Areklett et al., 2013, pp. 76–131). In this chapter, there is great potential to talk about how people live and relate to one another in the UK. The chapter starts off by presenting the four countries of the UK. These representations are largely factual in content, but the text does note that:

> Each of the countries in the United Kingdom is unique. Scotland, Wales and Northern Ireland all have their own versions of Celtic languages in addition to distinct accents when they speak English. They have their own histories, cultures, food and tradition (Areklett et al., 2013, p. 76).

This extract from the final paragraph of the introduction suggests that there will be information about different societies and their unique aspects in the following pages. However, this potential is largely unfulfilled. In the section on Scotland (half a page long), the following topics are mentioned: bagpipes, kilts, the Highlands, clan names, the biggest cities, and the Loch Ness Monster (Areklett et al., 2013, p. 79). These topics, while touching on the traditional cultures of Scotland, do not give an impression of the people who live there and their diversity. In fact, these topics could be considered stereotypical of Scotland and of Scottish people. Other countries are dealt with similarly. For example, Wales is described in terms of: Cardiff, Roald Dahl, sheep, castles, music festivals, choirs, the Welsh language (learning it in school, alphabet, longest place name in the world) (Areklett et al., 2013, p. 81). Here there is an opportunity to discuss the importance of the Welsh language for national identity, but it is not explored further.

The tasks for this text are similarly fact-focused. The first task, entitled 'Understanding', consist of 11 questions, three of which start with 'Which', six of which start with 'What' and two of which start with 'Where'. All these questions involve finding factual information in the text. It is notable that there are no 'Why' or 'How' questions that demand a greater level of independent thought and understanding.

The final two tasks are 'Writing Workshop' and 'Explore More'. The 'Writing Workshop' involves finding out information about a number of historical or geographical sites in the UK, and answering the questions: 'What is it? Where is it? How old is it? Why is it important?' (Areklett et al., 2013, pp. 82–83) The 'Explore More' section involves planning a short holiday to a city in the UK. Neither of these tasks encourage pupils to move beyond the gathering of information. Both of these sections could have contained tasks that would raise intercultural awareness. The 'Writing Workshop' could, for example, have encouraged reflection on the pupil's own country and comparison with the UK, or could have involved personal response to what they have read about the UK. It could also have invited discussion of the stereotypes presented in the text, and the problems with thinking in stereotypes, both those about people from the UK and from the pupil's own cultural background.

The example given above is repeated in slightly different versions throughout this chapter in *Stages 8*. The people, customs and identities of the UK are never explored in more depth, nor do the tasks require any particular degree of reflection over own cultures and attitudes. Of the 57 pages that make up the chapter on the UK, thirty-three of them focus on British history and six on the weather.

If we consider the curriculum again, there are two points (of six under 'Culture, Society and Literature' altogether) referring to the UK:

● Explain features of history and geography in Great Britain and the USA
● Discuss and elaborate on the way people live and how they socialise in Great Britain, USA and other English-speaking countries and Norway (The Norwegian Directorate for Education and Training, 2013).

Regarding the text and tasks discussed above, the first of these curriculum goals is covered well, but it seems to be at the cost of covering the second point, as very little is focused on the way people live and their social interactions, and even less on comparison with the situation in Norway. This chapter on the UK from *Stages 8*, has the potential to encourage intercultural awareness, but its tasks and texts would need to be reworked to focus on pupils' development of intercultural competence. In general, there are not enough texts about people and societies. What there is, is largely presenting stereotypical views of the four nations that make up the UK, rather than the diversity of the modern British society. There needs to be movement from questions and tasks that focus on factual information, towards tasks that focus on 'why' and 'how'. These questions will encourage pupils to consider in greater depth the attitudes that they are meeting in the texts and also explore their own reactions. Further exploratory tasks could focus on studying cultures and societies within the UK in more depth, or in comparison with own experiences and societies.

Stages 10

Another textbook in the same series, *Stages 10*, aimed at pupils in grade 10 (16 years old) (Areklett et al., 2015), has a much greater focus on intercultural awareness and developing skills. Chapter four, 'Indigenous Peoples', focuses on learning about indigenous cultures and societies in the English-speaking world. This relates mainly to the curriculum goal:

- Describe and reflect on the situation of indigenous peoples in English-speaking countries (The Norwegian Directorate for Education and Training, 2013).

It is notable here that when working with this curriculum goal, indigenous peoples in the modern world, rather than historically, should be the main focus. Pupils must 'describe and reflect' on the materials covered in class, requiring depth in study and real engagement in the topic.

One chapter in *Stages 10* (48 pages in length) looks at indigenous peoples in North America, Australia and New Zealand. This chapter commences with a general introduction to different indigenous peoples, followed by an extract from the United Nations Declaration on the Rights of Indigenous Peoples. This inclusion of the UN Declaration is important, as it is an extract from an authentic text, and one that is highly relevant for indigenous peoples in modern day societies. The focus of this introductory text is on the indigenous cultures, societies and their histories, rather than on the European account, giving pupils access to a wide range of opinions and perspectives.

The tasks relating to this text also encourage greater pupil engagement than in the examples from *Stages 8*. A section in the tasks entitled

'Viewpoints' considers issues raised in the text. Pupils are asked to discuss questions such as.

- Why do you think the authorities of many countries tried to suppress or even eliminate the indigenous cultures?
- Do you know of any suppression of discrimination against the Sámi people of Norway? If so, what do you know?
- What would we lose if any of the endangered indigenous cultures and languages disappeared?
- How can an indigenous culture be a valuable enrichment to a society? (Areklett et al., 2015, p. 154).

These four questions, taken as examples from seven questions in total, exemplify how developing intercultural competence can be encouraged in textbooks. Firstly, there is the exploration of current attitudes and knowledge in the first 'Why' question. Pupils are encouraged to think about what they already know. The second question shows a clear link to own cultural backgrounds, where pupils relate their new knowledge to their own cultures and knowledge of the treatment of indigenous peoples in Norway. The final two questions encourage a further development of thoughts and attitudes, as pupils reflect over indigenous people's contribution to society. The use of 'we' and of 'valuable enrichment' here avoids an 'othering' (viewing a group of people as essentially different to oneself) and devaluing of indigenous peoples and cultures.

Further tasks relating to this first text are a mixture of factual and discursive exercises. In the 'Writing Workshop', pupils are asked to either 'Write a factual article about the Sámi people' or 'Write a five-paragraph essay where you argue for the importance of the UN Declaration on the Rights of Indigenous Peoples' (Areklett et al., 2015, p. 156). While the second task encourages a discussion of different perspectives, the first task could be developed further. What sort of facts are pupils to find out? How can pupils avoid reproducing stereotypes? A better task would be to find out about specific areas of Sámi cultures and create an overview in class together, so that there is balance in the portrayal, or to compare aspects of Sámi cultures with own or with other indigenous cultures. Finding similarities rather than differences between cultures can promote better understanding and avoid the reproduction of power relations where historically there has been an imbalance between the Sámi and the Norwegian state.

A few texts included in the chapter are by indigenous writers, such as an extract from Sherman Alexie's *The Absolutely True Story of a Part-Time Indian* (Alexie, 2007) about Alexie's own experience growing up on the Spokane Indian Reservation in Washington State, and Archie Roach's song about the Stolen Generations in Australia, *Took the Children Away* (Roach, 1990). The inclusion of material by indigenous authors is important as it enables pupils to engage with indigenous peoples in a more authentic way than in texts produced by the textbook writers (assuming they are not indigenous themselves). This can also be a first step towards an 'indigenization' of teaching materials (Olsen, 2017, p. 72), that is, a curriculum and textbook reform where equal weight is given to indigenous as to non-indigenous voices.

Before the extract from the novel *The Absolutely True Diary of a Part-Time Indian* (Alexie, 2007), there is a 'Starting Off' activity, showing an illustration from the book (drawn by Ellen Forney) about the contrast between being white and being Native American (Areklett et al., 2015, p. 162). This illustration (the person is divided in two with the left half dressed as 'White' and the right half dressed as 'Indian') exemplifies both the difference between the two cultures, and how they interact with each other. Examining illustrations like this one can open a classroom discussion of both cultural differences and similarities.

The tasks after the literary extract once again encourage reflection. In a set of tasks entitled 'Viewpoints', pupils must first discuss the issues raised in the text, focusing on the 'why' of the events which happened, for example,

- Why do you think Mr. P goes to visit Junior at home?
- Why do you think the teachers at school let the kids pick on Junior? (Areklett et al., 2015, p. 167).

These questions do not focus on only the factual side of the text, but also ask the pupils to explore the attitudes that the characters in the story show. An understanding of the different identities in the story and how they relate to each other, promotes intercultural awareness. The final questions in this task move on to more general discussion:

* What gives people hope in their lives?
* What makes people give up and feel defeated? (Areklett et al., 2015, p. 167).

These questions show a shift away from an understanding of the others' social identities and attitudes to a greater awareness of own attitudes. New knowledge gained from working with the story is brought back to encourage critical awareness of own beliefs and values.

The texts and tasks from *Stages 10* fulfil the demands of the curriculum to a greater extent than those found in *Stages 8*. They cover the requirements of the curriculum goal in discussing modern day issues for indigenous peoples. The tasks require pupils to 'discuss and reflect', and to engage in the topics in greater depth. The development of intercultural competence is encouraged through these tasks, and in self-reflection over own cultures and attitudes. While there is still room for improvement in this chapter from *Stages 10*, it can be seen as a good example of how curriculum goals can be interpreted and how intercultural competence can be promoted in a textbook.

Discussion

What Can Be Learnt from the Norwegian Example?

This chapter has attempted to highlight the relation between curriculum requirements and textbook interpretations of curriculum goals when it comes to working with topics related to interculturality in the EFL classroom. While the focus has been on Norway, the points made here are relevant for teaching in all countries and settings where curricula and textbooks are used in EFL teaching.

It is important that school leaders make time available during the academic year for teachers to engage in discussion of curriculum requirements. Some curricula are very prescriptive and the exact points that the teacher needs to cover are clearly stated. However, some, like the Norwegian curriculum, are more open to interpretation. The terminology of the curriculum should also be discussed. What exact skills are the pupils required to develop? How can they be developed? There also needs to be an understanding of which educational theories have motivated the creators of the curriculum. Theories on the development of intercultural competence have had a clear influence on the Norwegian curriculum, and when it is considered in this light, the aims and goals of the curriculum can be discussed in more depth.

Most classes contain pupils with a range of abilities, requiring teachers to plan their class work to include pupils with all levels of linguistic competence. This demands the creation of tasks including in-depth reflection for both weaker and stronger pupils. While factual information about the target cultures can also be important to give pupils, the teacher needs to refer to the curriculum goals to check if that is all that is required of the pupils, or if they are expected to use the information in ways that include discussion, reflection or similar. In course planning, it is important that there is a clear development of skills throughout the school year, so that pupils can stretch themselves and gradually develop their skills.

Regarding textbooks, it is important that teachers maintain a critical awareness of the content of the books they use. Teachers should be aware that the texts given in textbooks often tend to be factual, rather than exposing pupils to a wide range of different opinions and attitudes. As can be seen in the examples from the two books given in this chapter, texts in textbooks can also tend towards stereotypical representations of countries and people, which hinder real cultural understanding. Teachers should approach textbooks with an awareness of their potential weaknesses and assess where the textbooks can be used well in class, and where additional materials and tasks are needed.

It is up to the teacher to take on the challenge of finding good teaching materials to work with these topics in the classroom. In developing intercultural competence, pupils need exposure to a wide variety of materials giving differing perspectives on the target culture. In the example from *Stages 10* in this chapter, indigenous voices are included in the textbook through extracts from literary works. The inclusion of literary texts in

English teaching can give the pupils excellent ways of connecting with cultural perspectives outside of their own experience. They can bring authentic voices from diverse cultures into the classroom, and can give pupils access to thoughts, ideas and belief-systems that can otherwise be difficult to access. Literary texts can play a vital role in the development of pupils' intercultural competence.

Engagement Priorities

This chapter aims to encourage teachers and student teachers in two ways. Firstly, to consider the curriculum used in the classes in which they teach, and secondly, to look at textbooks with a critical eye, and consider how well they contribute to covering the curriculum goals and what additional materials may be required. The following points are suggested as priorities for engaging with the topics discussed in this chapter:

Teachers should engage actively with the curriculum or course description by meeting regularly to discuss the content of curriculum. What skills should pupils develop and in what areas of knowledge? These skills may need to be broken down into smaller and achievable goals within the classroom. For pupils who are progressing through different grades within the education system, how does the curriculum build on what is already learnt, and how will it be built on in later years?

Teachers should consider what ideas lie behind the curriculum. Do theories on interculturality influence the curriculum, and what does that mean for teachers? It may mean that tasks need to be adjusted or supplemented to aid pupils develop intercultural competence. Teachers also should to be aware of the different aspects of intercultural competence and check that all aspects are covered in work done in class.

Looking at the textbooks used in the classroom, there needs to be an awareness of what kind of texts and tasks are there, and what they require of pupils. Are the texts and tasks fulfilling the curriculum goals, or are supplementary teaching materials required? Before choosing a textbook, the teacher should consider which attitudes are portrayed in the book towards other cultures. Are the attitudes realistic and related to modern life, or do they reinforce stereotypes? Do they encourage mutual respect, or reinforce unequal power relations between cultures? It may be necessary for the teacher to include other materials to bring authentic voices from the target cultures into the classroom. If so, what might these materials be and how can they be used?

Recommended Texts

This document gives an overview of what intercultural competence is, how teachers can teach it and how to overcome some common challenges:

Byram, M., Gribkova, B., & Starkey, H. (2002). *Developing the intercultural dimension in language teaching.* Strasbourg: Council of Europe.

This short article talks about how the curriculum can be reformed to integrate multicultural content:

Banks, J. A. (1989). Approaches to multicultural curriculum reform. *Trotter Review, 3*(3), 18–19.

Further discussion on representations of indigenous peoples in Norwegian textbooks (not EFL) is presented in this book chapter. It can give interesting insight into how to teach topics relating to indigenous peoples in general:

Olsen, T. (2017). Colonial conflicts: Absence, inclusion and indigenization in textbook presentations of indigenous peoples. In B. Andreassen, L. Lewis, & S. Thobro (Eds.), *Textbook violence* (pp. 71–86). London: Equinox.

It can be useful and interesting for teachers and students in teacher training programmes to learn to analyse their own textbooks. This book gives an easy-to-follow guide to analysing texts:

Gee, J. P. (2011). *How to do discourse analysis.* New York: Routledge.

For an introduction to Critical Discourse Analysis, this book can be useful:

Machin, D., & Mayr, A. (2012). *How to do critical discourse analysis.* London: Sage.

Note

1. The Sámi are the indigenous peoples who live in the area of northern Scandinavia called Sápmi, part of which is in Norway. Schools in Sámi administrative areas in Norway can choose to follow a Sámi version of the national curriculum, which includes increased Sámi content.

Appendix 1

Extract from English Curriculum used in Norwegian Schools (2013). Grade 2:

- converse about aspects of the day-to-day life of children in English-speaking countries.

Grade four:

- converse about some aspects of different ways of living, traditions and customs in English-speaking countries and in Norway.

Grade seven:

- converse about the way people live and socialise in different cultures in English-speaking countries and in Norway, including the Sami culture.

Grade ten:

- discuss and elaborate on the way people live and how they socialise in Great Britain, USA and other English-speaking countries and Norway
- describe and reflect on the situation of indigenous peoples in English-speaking countries.

Final year of compulsory teaching:

- discuss and elaborate on culture and social conditions in several English-speaking countries
- discuss and elaborate on texts by and about indigenous peoples in English-speaking countries.

Bibliography

Alexie, S. (2007). *The absolutely true diary of a part-time Indian*. Little, Brown and Company.

Areklett, K. K., Pettersen, S., Røkaas, F., & Tørnby, H. (2013). *Stages 8 textbook: Engelsk for ungdomstrinnet*. Aschehoug.

Areklett, K. K., Pettersen, S., Røkaas, F., & Tørnby, H. (2015). *Stages 10 textbook: Engelsk for ungdomstrinnet*. Aschehoug.

Byram, M., Gribkova, B., & Starkey, H. (2002). *Developing the intercultural dimension in language teaching*. Council of Europe.

Council of Europe. (2001). *Common european framework of reference for languages: Learning, teaching, assessment*. Council of Europe.

Dervin, F. (2016). *Interculturality in education*. Palgrave Macmillan.

Dervin, F., & Gross, Z. (2016). *Intercultural competence in education*. Palgrave Macmillan.

Gee, J. P. (2011). *How to do discourse analysis*. Routledge.

Gray, J. (2000). The ELT coursebook as cultural artefact: How teachers censor and adapt. *ELT Journal, 54*(3), 274–283.

Gray, J. (2010). *The construction of English: Culture, consumerism and promotion in the ELT global coursebook*. Palgrave Macmillan.

Hoff, H.E. (2018). Intercultural competence. In A.-B. Fenner & A. S. Skulstad (Eds.), *Teaching English in the 21st century* (pp. 67–89). Fagbokforlaget.

Holliday, A. (2010). Cultural descriptions as political cultural acts: An exploration. *Language and Intercultural Communication, 10*(3), 259–272.

Machin, D., & Mayr, A. (2012). *How to do critical discourse analysis*. Sage.

Moeller, A. K., & Nugent, K. (2014). Building intercultural competence in the language classroom. In *Faculty publications, department of teaching, learning and teacher education.* Department of Teaching, Learning and Teacher Education, Lincoln.

Olsen, T. (2017). Colonial conflicts: Absence, inclusion and indigenization in textbook presentations of indigenous peoples. In B. Andreassen, L. Lewis, & S. Thobro (Eds.), *Textbook violence* (pp. 71–86). Equinox.

Roach, A. (1990). *Took the children away.* Curtain Street Studios

The Norwegian Directorate for Education and Training. (2013). *English subject curriculum.* The Norwegian Directorate for Education and Training.

The Norwegian Directorate for Education and Training. (2019). *English subject curriculum.* The Norwegian Directorate for Education and Training.

Young, T., & Sercombe, P. (2010). Communication, discourses and interculturality. *Language and Intercultural Communication, 10*(3), 181–188.

Zhu, H. (2015). Negotiation as a way of engagement in Intercultural and Lingua Franca communication: Frames of Reference and Interculturality. *Journal of English as a Lingua Franca, 4*(1), 63–90.

7

Cultivating Critical Interculturality in Adult ESOL

Rob Sheppard

Abbreviations Used

CLT   Communicative Language Teaching
EAP   English for Academic Purposes
ELT   English Language Teaching
ESOL   English for Speakers of Other Languages
ELF   English as a Lingua Franca
EFL   English as a Foreign Language

R. Sheppard (✉)
Temple University Center for American Language and Culture (TCALC),
Philadelphia, USA

© The Author(s), under exclusive license to Springer Nature
Switzerland AG 2021
M. Victoria and C. Sangiamchit (eds.), *Interculturality and the English Language
Classroom*, https://doi.org/10.1007/978-3-030-76757-0_7

171

Introduction

There is a tendency for the field of English language teaching (ELT) to develop in silos: an important advancement in one context or domain can be slow to spread to others. This is certainly common in the subfield of ESOL for adult immigrants to the U.S., in which language and American culture are often bound up in a conventional sense that posits American culture as 'content' with an implicit (sometimes explicit) goal that immigrants adapt to or acquire 'American culture'. To many adult ESOL practitioners this may seem uncontroversial: after all, the thinking goes, students in these programs are typically permanent immigrants who need to understand certain aspects of life in America in order to navigate their new home.

There is a rich body of theory and research on the treatment of culture in adult ESOL. It is my contention, however, that *interculturality*—a term common in global English as a foreign language (EFL), but absent almost entirely from adult ESOL literature—has developed more rapidly and radically, folding in concepts and developments from other theoretical frameworks such as critical pedagogy and decoloniality. I argue that adult educators ought to incorporate the theory and vocabulary of interculturality into our practice so that we and our students can benefit from these developments. Certain insights from the literature of interculturality will force us to problematise the assumption that culture is a thing to be taught and learnt, and that acculturation is the desired outcome (House, 2007; Kramsch, 1995). Phillipson (1992) draws attention to 'how imperialistic even a pragmatic approach to teaching language can be if it assumes that universally shared basic human needs automatically correspond to universally shared ways of thinking and talking about those needs' (in Kramsch, 1995, p. 5). As I will show below, much work in adult ESOL assumes exactly that.

Interculturality is a notion that grew out of European English as a foreign language (EFL) classrooms and is still largely informed by that context (see, for example, Soler & Jordà, 2007). With the shift in EFL towards conceptualising English as a lingua franca (ELF), approaches to interculturality now often unbundle target language from Anglophone 'target cultures' (Akbari, 2008; Seidlhofer, 2001). Globally, this has been a welcome and necessary development. As the discourse evolves, we should consider what implications this has for other ELT contexts, including adult ESOL.

Here I argue that the goal of adult ESOL for immigrants is not assimilation or any of its ever-shifting euphemisms. It is not to produce a dubious and impossible cultural homogeneity. We may already know this declaratively, but much common practice in the adult ESOL classroom *does* implicitly promote acculturation towards a monolithic, monocultural norm. The goal of adult ESOL, I believe, is to equip newcomers with the skills and knowledge to thrive in their new home; it is to empower adult immigrants and their families to succeed on their own terms, as they themselves define success. As I have argued elsewhere (Sheppard, 2019) I believe the best way to prepare students to succeed in this way is to set a goal of informed self-advocacy, or 'justice-oriented citizenship', a term which Nash (2010) takes up from Mattson (2013).

The reason for teaching culture in the adult ESOL classroom, then, is to empower our learners to critically understand the culture—their own, as well as the cultures, plural and hybrid, that they will encounter in their new home—so that they may determine for themselves what they want their culture in America to look like, the ways in which and the extent to which they wish to adapt. This, I contend, requires a stance of critical interculturality, an approach to culture that entails challenging assumptions and monoliths, identifying unspoken implications, seeking manifold narratives and asserting one's own account.

My goal in writing this chapter is to introduce interculturality (a version that aligns closely with that articulated by Kramsch, 1999, 2009, 2013) into the context of adult ESOL and to spell out some of its implications for that context. The theoretical background will introduce a brief history of interculturality and intersecting concepts from decolonial theory and critical pedagogy, drawing them all together into a definition of critical interculturality. This, I will then link to Nash's (2010) work on civic engagement in adult education. The following section will turn a critical eye to the treatment of culture in several popular adult ESOL coursebooks in order to establish a baseline of how culture is often depicted in the adult ESOL classroom, and to consider whether these materials are likely to foster critical interculturality. The next section will lay out what a shift towards critical interculturality means in a theoretical sense, outlining several key aspects of the shift I propose. And a final section will spell out the practical implications of such a shift in adult ESOL programs, providing teachers and program administrators with activities and strategies for bringing a critical intercultural stance into our classrooms.

Theoretical Background

There is already a body of literature on the treatment of culture in the adult ESOL classroom (see, for just a few examples, Blatchford, 1973; Ilieva, 2000; Kegan et al., 2001; Rhodes, 2013; Valdes, 1986). The language of *interculturality*, however, is still largely absent from adult ESOL scholarship and classrooms. As one might expect, the two bodies of work—that on culture in adult ESOL and that on interculturality in English as a foreign language—share a great deal in common. But the discourse on interculturality has advanced further, having been more heavily influenced by important insights from critical pedagogy and decolonial thinking. I will provide a full working definition at the end of the literature review, but for the time being, let us understand *interculturality* to refer to the interaction between cultures.

This literature review will first introduce the origins of the concept of interculturality in the early European Union. I will then discuss the evolving use of the term, with special attention to the work of Claire Kramsch, whose notions of thirdness are fundamental to this chapter. The next two subsections introduce critical pedagogy and decoloniality, respectively, with a discussion of how those concepts relate to interculturality. The next subsection introduces the work of Nash on justice-oriented citizenship in adult ESOL. Finally, I will summarise the definition of critical interculturality that will be used throughout this chapter.

Interculturality in ELT

The dominant linguistic schools of thought from the 1950s through to the 1980s conceptualised language as 'primarily a social phenomenon, which is naturally and inextricably intertwined with culture' (House, 2007, p. 8). With the emergence of communicative language teaching (CLT), culture came to be seen as a necessary grounding for communication in the target language, an idea that was taken up by Canale and Swain in their seminal (1980) work on communicative competence. Some influential theorists associated with CLT stress the importance of teaching a 'target culture' alongside the language itself. Celce-Murcia (2007), for instance, wrote 'If the goal of language instruction is communicative competence, language instruction must be integrated with cultural and cross-cultural instruction', going on to list the history, geography, social structure, religion, holidays and customs of the 'target language community' (51).

Yet, as English has been reconceptualised as a global lingua franca, the bundling of English with a target culture has been called into question on various grounds. McKay (2003) argues that English has become an international language, and must be reconsidered in light of 'the diverse ways in which bilingual speakers make use of English to fulfil their specific purposes' (18). Seidlhofer (2001) explains that the practices of native speakers within their own communities are simply not a primary concern for those who use English as a lingua franca. Others go further, arguing that a critical examination of the treatment of target culture in English language materials reveals them to be imperialistic, hegemonic, or chauvinistic (for example, Canagarajah, 1999; Pennycook, 1998; Phillipson, 1992). An alternative to target culture, interculturality has emerged.

The term *intercultural* dates to the 1980s, when it was used to describe efforts to foster understanding across national borders in the lead-up to the formation of the European Union (Kramsch, 2013). In this context, one can think of interculturality as interaction across or between cultures. Dervin (2016) traces interculturality as an object of study (under other names) to the 1970s in Europe and the 1960s in the U.S. He rightly reminds us, however, that interactions across borders have existed for as long as borders themselves.

An important notion that emerges from the E.U. context is *savoir être*, 'knowing how to be'. The concept is treated at length in a number of papers commissioned by the Council of Europe. Byram et al. (2002), for example, define it as follows:

> willingness to relativise one's own values, beliefs and behaviours, not to assume that they are the only possible and naturally correct ones, and to be able to see how they might look from an outsider's perspective who has a different set of values, beliefs and behaviours. This can be called the ability to 'decentre'. (7)

Note that what is described here is an attitude. The literature associated with interculturality at the time in the Council of Europe papers break intercultural competence down into knowledge, skills, attitudes and values (Byram et al., 2002). Note also that these are notions that can be taught, acquired, performed and assessed. The emphasis is upon what one *has* or can *do*, rather than who one *is*.

In more recent literature, we can detect a shift away from interculturality as an attitude or skill. House (2007) speaks of *intercultural actants* who 'need to be conceived as independent of both their native culture (and language) and the new culture (and language) which they are trying to link, mediate, reconcile' (14–15). Baker (2009) describes *cultures themselves* as emergent, hybrid and dynamic. Kramsch (2009) speaks of the hybrid identities of immigrants, of intercultural speakers. In this later literature, interculturality is associated with the *identity* of individuals and communities, rather than simply a set of skills to be acquired. It is this conception of interculturality that has strong implications for adult ESOL.

The work of Kramsch warrants further discussion. She is perhaps the most prolific and influential theorist on interculturality, and it is her definitions that will most inform the rest of this chapter.

Kramsch (1993) also introduces to the context of language teaching the notion of *thirdness*, which has precedents in semiotics, philosophy and critical cultural studies, and whose history she traces explicitly in Kramsch (2009), citing the work of Peirce (1955), Bakhtin (1981), and Holquist (1990). Thirdness represents an attempt to question, move beyond and mediate binarisms such as L1 and L2, their cultural counterparts C1 and C2, native and non-native, Self and Other (1995, p. 238). She emphasises that striving for thirdness is not about abolishing these dichotomies, nor is it an idealistic attempt to gloss over difference or establish impossible universals. Rather, thirdness is a focus on what lies between the two poles of the dichotomy. It is a choice to explore the emergent, unstable 'in-between', fraught as it is with multiple meanings and ways of knowing, with tensions that can be a source of pain and also of creativity and insight (Kramsch, 1995, 2009). Importantly, the 'third place' is a metaphorical space in which critical dialogue about differences can occur. Indeed, the vital dialogue about our differences *becomes* the space that we share (Kramsch, 1995).

For Kramsch, identity is not fixed and intrinsic but always constructed in relation to context, and reconstructed in new encounters. Recognising thirdness allows one to step back from the ongoing reconstruction of identity to see ourselves at a distance, thereby strengthening our sense of identity and permanence (2009, pp. 234–235). Thus, thirdness can be an asset for those living in a new culture, developing a pluricultural sense of identity. Similarly, Zhu (2014) contends that one's cultural identity and frame of reference are continually negotiated; that is, one can situationally foreground or suppress their various cultural membership categories. Zhu is focused on ELF settings, but this work can surely be extended to the experience of adult immigrants, who also develop pluricultural identities.

Critical Pedagogy and Critical Interculturality

An assumption underrunning this chapter is that the aim of adult ESOL is not our students' assimilation into or their learning of a target culture, but their empowerment. Because immigrants are a systemically disempowered and marginalised population, their empowerment necessarily involves a transformation of existing power dynamics, and it is this focus on power dynamics that distinguishes *critical* interculturality from simple interculturality. The notion that education ought to be transformative and emancipatory can be traced to Freire's (1972) critical pedagogy. As Pennycook (1990) put it, critical pedagogy 'seeks to understand and critique the historical and sociopolitical context of schooling and to develop pedagogical practices that aim not only to change the nature of schooling, but also the wider society' (in Crookes & Lehner, 1998, p. 319).

Some teachers balk at such an overtly political understanding of their craft, seeing themselves and their work as apolitical. But, as Akbari observes, educational systems are a microcosm of society, and as such, they reproduce and reinforce the biases and inequities of that society, in terms of race, class and gender (2008, pp. 276–277). Through the lens of critical pedagogy, then, teaching is inescapably political.

In terms of classroom practice, critical pedagogy means putting local needs at the centre of our practice (Akbari, 2008; Banegas & Villacañas de Castro, 2016), helping students to locate their experience in a broader context, and identifying systemic oppression (Rivera, 1999). Crookes and Lehner (1998) apply critical pedagogy directly to English language teaching, arguing that it 'takes as joint goals the simultaneous development of English communicative abilities and the ability to apply them to developing a critical awareness of the world and the ability to act on it to improve matters' (320). In the final section of this chapter, I will outline several practical strategies for fostering this critical awareness in adult ESOL classrooms.

Dervin (2016) observes that the notion of interculturality is unstable, both personal and political. 'Like many other important notions in education', he observes, 'interculturality tends to be polysemic, fictional and empty at the same time, conveniently meaning either too much or too little.' Dervin (2017) brings together notions of criticality and interculturality into critical interculturality, 'a never-ending process of ideological struggle against solid identities, unfair power differentials, discrimination and hurtful (and often disguised) discourses of (banal) nationalism, ethnocentrism, racism and various forms of -ism' (1). In the instability and negotiation that define interculturality, Dervin seems to see an opportunity to resist injustice and hegemony, an idea that is further developed in the decolonial project.

The Decolonial Turn

The *decolonial turn* is a line of argumentation that has developed independent of interculturality and critical pedagogy, but with parallel aims. Efforts to 'decolonise curriculum'—decentring the white, European perspectives that tend to dominate the syllabus—have made great headway, even outside of academia, having made numerous headlines in *The Guardian*, *The Los Angeles Times* and *The Economist*. Although decoloniality is not focused on the immigrant experience, recent scholarship in decolonial thinking synthesises critical pedagogy and interculturality in a way that has implications for those who serve the immigrant community.

Coloniality refers to the lingering effects of colonialism and entails an enduring imbalance of power (Beltrán, 2016, p. 174). Although colonial powers may have relinquished their colonial hold upon former colonies, massive power differentials persist in other forms: cultural and linguistic hegemony, trade agreements, political interventions (Restrepo & Rojas, 2010). It is probably worth noting that these lingering effects ultimately ripple into our adult ESOL programs: economic conditions in former colonies force migration to economies with more opportunities, which are former colonial powers like the U.K., the U.S., and continental Europe. The very existence of ESOL is fundamentally and inextricably linked with coloniality.

The decolonial project, then, is an effort to dismantle colonial hegemony, and in doing so to 'recognize and disseminate the manifold forms of knowledge, ways of life, and hopes for the world [granting them] the same validity as those that come from the European and North American experience' (Beltrán, 2016, p. 174). Nuñez-Pardo (2018) applies this perspective to ESL materials, pointing to the biases, distortions, simplifications and omissions in the representation of culture in English coursebooks.

Beltrán (2016) makes a powerful argument for critical interculturality as a decolonizing tool. He contends that developing a critical consciousness—which entails cultivating an awareness of the self in social context; constructing one's own self-concept, free from externally imposed archetypes; recognising subjectivities, multiple narratives and multiple ways of constructing knowledge—is a key strategy in reshaping power dynamics. I will take up many of these ideas in the final section of this chapter.

Justice-Oriented Citizenship

Finally, I would like to bring in the work of Nash (2010), who focuses on the role of civics education in adult education. Nash advocates an approach to civics that fosters critical thought aimed at systemic change, developing students into what Westheimer and Kahne call *justice-oriented citizens*. The justice-oriented citizen is one who seeks to critically understand systemic injustice and to pursue solutions that address not just symptoms but root causes (in Nash, 2010).

Though Nash is focused on civics, her argument can be extended to culture. Indeed, she mentions 'preserving important aspects of one's culture and identity' as a key feature of civics (2010, p. 2). She observes that the notion of *civics* has been interpreted in a number of ways, but that most programs focus on participation 'in the system as it is, accepting it as an effective, functional process' (2). I believe that teachers generally approach culture in the same problematic manner: we address opportune, pressing and practical cultural tidbits that can be applied in the short term—the holiday of the season, shaking hands at a job interview, current events, what Nuñez-Pardo (2018) calls 'superficial culture'—perhaps at the expense of opportunities to build towards broad, lasting change and to critically explore deep culture.

Defining Critical Interculturality for Adult ESOL

What, then, does critical interculturality mean for the context of U.S. adult ESOL? We will take interculturality to be a stance of openness—to perspectives, frames of reference and ways of knowing that may be different from one's own—which will serve immigrants as they communicate across cultural lines and iterate their identities in their new home.

This openness will be balanced with a criticality—an attitude of scepticism towards power imbalances, an inquiry that connects the immediate with the systemic, an understanding that an unjust status quo need not be accepted—that will prepare for self-advocacy in their day-to-day life, and for leadership and transformation in their community, should they choose to pursue it.

Culture in Adult ESOL Materials

What I propose is a shift in the treatment of culture in the adult ESOL classroom. In order to determine what exactly that shift entails, we first need to establish a baseline: What does the treatment of culture currently look like? It is beyond the scope of this chapter to conduct a formal survey of classroom practice in adult ESOL programs, so I take as a proxy an informal analysis of a number of the most popular adult ESOL coursebooks available.

The series I reviewed were some of the most widely used in U.S. adult education: *Future: English for Results* (Lynn et al., 2019), *English in Action* (Foley & Neblett, 2019), *Stand Out* (Jenkins & Johnson, 2019), and *Ventures* (Bitterlin et al., 2018). I did not review teachers' guides or supplementary materials.

My objective in analysing these texts was to determine the extent to which, taken at face value, they are likely to foster critical interculturality. I approached this task with a set of guiding questions, which I drew from the literature cited in the Theoretical Background. I have loosely grouped these into four broad areas:

Representation of U.S. culture	• Does the text treat U.S. culture as a 'target culture'? (Akbari, 2008; Seidlhofer, 2001) • Does the text treat U.S. culture as monolithic? (Kramsch, 1995; Nuñez-Pardo, 2018) • Does the text treat U.S. culture in a way that promotes cultural imperialism, hegemony, or chauvinism? (Canagarajah, 1999; Pennycook, 1998; Philipson, 1992)
Representation of the immigrant experience	• Does the text promote critical consideration of plural values, behaviours, ways of knowing? (Beltrán, 2016; Kramsch, 1995) • Does the text depict the realities of the immigrant experience and life in America as our students likely experience it? (Akbari, 2008) • Is the model for success based upon successful intercultural speakers? (House, 2007)
Promotion of dialogue	• Does the text invite or promote criticality and intercultural dialogue? (Kramsch, 2009)
Treatment of power dynamics	• Does the text invite criticism and transformation of the status quo, of current power dynamics? (Beltrán, 2016; Freire, 1972) • Does the text address ways in which students can become involved in their communities as agents of systemic change? (Nash, 2010)

Once I had determined these guiding questions, I turned to the coursebook series. For the questions related to representation of US culture and representation of the immigrant experience, I reviewed the units in each series on the topics of food and the home (found in the lower levels of each series). For questions related to the promotion of dialogue, I looked at the type of activities each series included. And for the treatment of power dynamics I reviewed units on civic life, community engagement, and government (generally in the higher levels of each series).

In the interest of brevity, I will characterise these texts generally wherever possible, noting illustrative examples from specific series. Where necessary, I will call attention to differences and noteworthy exceptions to the general trend.

I want to emphasise again that this is not intended to be a rigorous, systematic evaluation of adult ESOL coursebooks. The treatment of culture in coursebooks is a worthy subject in its own right. As Nuñez-Pardo (2018) begins her powerful critical piece on the topic, 'English textbooks are not neutral' (232). They have the power to privilege the dominant culture and marginalise local cultures by reproducing and reinforcing values, stereotypes, and ideologies. Future work should include formal evaluations of ESOL coursebooks; a good model for this work can be found in Tomlinson and Masuhara (2013), which served as a very loose model for my approach.

Representations of U.S. Culture

Some of these texts overtly teach American culture in the form of tips or even entire lessons. Scattered throughout *English in Action* and *Ventures*, for instance, are callout boxes on a range of topics—Writing Note, Word Partnerships, Useful Language, etc.—one of which is Culture Notes (both series use the same header). Many of these Culture Notes are life skills or tips for navigating systems (for example, 'When you visit a doctor's office for the first time, you must fill out a patient information form for yourself or your child'), but some are more clearly culture in an anthropological and pragmatic sense: 'People ask the age of a child. People do not usually ask the age of an adult' (Foley & Neblett, 2019, pp. 39, 219). In a *Ventures 1* Culture Note, we get a brief hint at something other than the monocultural norm—"Some people have two first names: Mei-hwa."—but this proves to be a single anomaly (Bitterlin et al., 2018, p. 9).

Elsewhere, the treatment of culture in each series is incidental. These texts are generally built around synthetic syllabi, divided into thematic vocabulary units, and many of these involve depictions of culture. I examined units on food, clothing and housing at the basic levels of each series.

In vocabulary lists in food units, we find a strong tendency towards treating American culture as the target culture. Produce items are bananas, potatoes, apples, oranges, grapes, lettuce, tomatoes, etc. While we must be careful not to treat individual produce items as culture-specific, it is impossible not to notice that the contents of these vocabulary lists represent the offerings of major American supermarket chains, as opposed to, say, the Indian, Korean, or Hispanic supermarkets at which our students often shop.

Depictions of bread products are worth noting: all four series depict the American Wonderbread norm: mass-produced, sliced, white sandwich bread. The only other images of bread in any of these units are hot dogs and hamburger buns.

There is a surface-level effort to depict 'international food', but this comes almost entirely in the form of foods that have long been a part of the American food landscape: tacos, sushi, egg rolls and spaghetti.

In units on clothing, vocabulary lists show an even stronger tendency towards American norms: *blouse, jeans, dress, skirt, tie, suit, shirt, shorts, high heels*. In none of these series is there any mention of, say, *sari, hijab,* or *dashiki*: daily garments in much of the world and common among immigrant groups in the U.S. Photos and illustrations also reinforce U.S. clothing norms and the American retail experience.

Units on the home mostly seem to be scrubbed of any specific cultural references. Walls are bare of art aside from abstract doodles. When there is enough detail to indicate anything about the people who might live there, we get the trappings of upper-middle class suburban American life: high-end furniture, a swimming pool, a fenced-in backyard, two sinks in a master bathroom, spacious living rooms and dining rooms. This is the norm across all series. Other types of housing—apartments, trailers, smaller houses—are generally only introduced to teach the vocabulary items *apartment, trailer, condo* and so on. These units certainly seem to confirm the concerns of Gray (2002) and Akbari (2008) that what is depicted in coursebooks is at a remove from the realities of our students' lives.

At higher levels there appears to be more departure from the mono-cultural American norm, but only slightly. A unit on weddings in *English in Action 3* features a single reading on Indian ceremonies, but the rest of the unit focuses on what has come to be known as 'American' wedding traditions. An advanced lesson on music in *English in Action 4* focuses on the Boston Symphony Orchestra, Carnegie Hall and Leonard Bernstein. Again, a single reading on the music of New Orleans briefly discusses the role immigrants and enslaved people played in the development of that culture (Foley & Neblett, 2019, pp. 158, 193–208). One-off examples like these are generally the most we get in terms of heterogeneity.

Stepping back, the cumulative picture of American culture that emerges from incidental depictions is indeed the monolithic, monocul-tural one that Kramsch warns against: Americans dress like this, eat like this, live like this (*this*, in these cases, being generally upper-middle class, consumerist, Anglophone, heteronormative).

Representations of the Immigrant Experience

Having looked at the treatment of culture in terms of objects and arte-facts, let us turn to the representation of people, their experiences and perspectives. At first glance these series fare somewhat better on this front. As far as I can tell, these series mostly avoid outright chauvinism. There is some diversity in terms of countries of origin: A quick tally of names shows that those that are presumably meant to imply immigrant backgrounds (for example, Yefim, Huynh, Raj, Miguel, and Ana) occur more frequently in examples and readings than typically Anglophone names. Illustrations and photos depicting people are also rather diverse in terms of race and ethnicity. Readings and listening texts sometimes tell the stories of immigrant families.

We must ask, however, whether Akbari's claim proves true, that pres-sure from publishers to avoid any potentially controversial content has led to the erasure of certain aspects of students' experience or identity (Akbari, 2008; Gray, 2002). Akbari calls out poverty, aging and mental health topics, but we could add to that, say, racism, religion and politics. These certainly figure as aspects of our students' experience and identity, but do coursebooks address them as such? For the most part, the answer is a rather resounding *No*.

Units in *English in Action 3* and *Ventures 4* discuss community college. They refer to realities such as part-time attendance, trade certifications, the need for basic skills courses, financial aid, the difficulty of balancing work and study, and being the first in one's family to attend college (Bitterlin et al., 2018, p. 18; Foley & Neblett, 2019, p. 28). The mention of these challenges is certainly a gesture in the right direction, but the treatment is entirely superficial. Follow-up activities do not grapple substantively with challenging issues, and no mention whatsoever is made of the structural and societal problems that give rise to them.

Another *English in Action 4* unit entitled 'Changing Lifestyles' focuses almost exclusively on cheerful life milestones: getting married, having a child, becoming a citizen, saving a lot of money (Foley & Neblett, 2019, pp. 33–49). Not only does the text not address the financial hardships that may surround these events for many immigrants in our classes, but the suggested vocabulary includes *maternity* and *paternity leave*, revealing a stark disconnect between the representations in text and the typical working conditions for immigrants in adult ESOL classes in the United States, virtually none of whom receive such benefits.

Stand Out 4 mentions credit card debt and living paycheck to paycheck, and, again, some aspects of these chapters are laudable. Readers are left with the implication, however, that all of one's financial problems come down to decisions entirely within their control. Tips include turning off the air conditioner and thinking about whether you really need something before purchasing it (Jenkins & Johnson, 2019, pp. 39–49). There is no mention of minimum wage or predatory lending habits, no hint whatsoever that anything other than personal responsibility factors into consumer debt.

There seems to have been some express effort in the reading passages of the *Ventures* series to represent a range of authentic immigrant experiences, including typical hardships (a language divide between generations, underemployment, poverty). In level 4 of the series, roughly one third of the readings deal with immigrant and intercultural experiences (this is a relatively high proportion, among the volumes reviewed), but the other levels in the series fall far short of this.

Throughout these series, the diversity of cities and American culture is often mentioned, but there is no serious mention of racism or discrimination, either individual or systemic. Units about moving make no significant mention of or reference to gentrification or rising rents; indeed, in two different texts living in a small space is not presented as a difficult necessity, but in the context of the tiny homes craze.

Struggles, hardships and trauma are rarely mentioned. When they are, it is almost always as early obstacles on the road to eventual success, and these stories often invoke the problematic trope of the ideal, hardworking immigrant. There is no invitation to question the systems that force people to work nights, endure poverty and be model immigrants in order to achieve the American dream. Furthermore, these obstacles almost always result from freak accidents or lone bad actors. This framing, of course, sidesteps any critical discussion of the systems and biases that so often work against immigrant families.

Treatment of Criticality

To this point, we have looked at representations of culture in texts and imagery. Because critical interculturality involves critical dialogue and analysis, I also want to take a closer look at what students are asked to *do* in activities. Do the activities encourage critical dialogue, critical inquiry, a critical questioning of the status quo? Do they encourage students to dig beneath the surface of the facts they are presented with to understand root causes, implications, interconnections, systems of power? To examine assumptions or consider alternate narratives?

The four series vary greatly when it comes to this issue, so I will look at representative units from each to give a broad-stroke picture of where they stand.

A unit in *English in Action 3*, entitled Life in the United States, approaches its topic largely from a statistical approach, presenting facts about 'the average American'. (Foley & Neblett, 2019, pp. 18–32). Even when presenting facts like 33% of Americans have a bachelor's degree and 40% do not vote, not once in the chapter are students encouraged to ask why. Nor are they asked to consider the consequences of these facts, or whether these are realities that we should work to change. By and large the activities merely ask students to look at charts and form factual sentences about them, along the lines of '60% of Americans vote in national elections'.

Future and *Stand Out* have a much narrower focus on the everyday realities of the immigrant experience, taking what can be called a navigating systems approach. Although broad underlying and systemic issues are sometimes mentioned, it is largely as background (having moved from a war-torn country or having lost one's job). Activities are geared almost exclusively towards immediate needs: reading housing advertisements, identifying community resources, completing paperwork, accessing healthcare and so on. Though these are decidedly important skills, the series presents things uncritically *as they are* in the U.S., without inviting students to question whether things could or ought to be otherwise.

Ventures, more than any of the series, avoid anything that might be considered political. A unit in *Ventures 4* that is labelled 'Community Involvement' discusses volunteering at a library, a nursing home called Quiet Palms, a Meals-on-Wheels program, and a literacy program— nothing whatsoever that intimates that these programs might be stopgaps for systemic issues (pp. 58–69). Worse, issues such as smog and global warming are chalked up to personal responsibility. Representative quotations include, 'If people drove less and used less electricity, I am sure our air quality would improve', and 'Since people are building homes in forests, animals are losing their natural habitats' (pp. 115; 118). There is no mention of corporations or profit; solutions are not regulation or legislation, but taking shorter showers and driving smaller cars.

Taking Action

At this point, we have seen that these coursebook series do little to encourage a critical stance towards culture. That being the case, it is rather safe to assume that they do not encourage students to transform the world they see around them, the former being a prerequisite for the latter. Still, several of these series have units on civics and civic engagement, as the goal in examining these texts is to set a baseline for change.

In *Stand Out*, there are a handful of units on civic responsibility. Again, these focus on navigating systems—getting a driver's licence and becoming a citizen—and civics is treated as content to be learned through a practical, rather than critical, lens. There are exceptions. One unit asks students to identify community problems, and then connects these problems to the election process, showing students how local politics can make a difference. Another encourages students to get involved with local civic organisations. These are valuable lessons indeed, but they treat systemic problems, criticality and action as a discrete thematic topic, addressed in a single unit, rather than a line of inquiry or a curricular strand. Other series take even more superficial approaches, teaching civics strictly as the way things are, encouraging neither criticality nor activism.

A unit in *Ventures 4* on the topic of 'Saving Our Planet' is a particularly baffling example of a missed opportunity to encourage criticality and local action. Global issues like climate change and pollution *are* linked to individual actions like choosing to recycle or buying energy-efficient appliances, but not once in the unit is the question raised as to whether political action or systemic change might be part of the solution. One reading for this unit, entitled All Things Are Connected, tells a story about a despotic king who orders all the frogs killed, thereby creating a mosquito problem. This fable practically begs for a critical connection between politics and environmental impact, yet what we get are simple comprehension checks and a few anodyne questions about peaceful conflict resolution. Another reading in the unit suggests that the root of the problem of smog is that 'we' do not carpool enough and use too much electricity. Read through the lens of criticality, it is hard not to wonder whether this unit was deliberately expurgated of any reference to industry or politics.

Establishing a Baseline

Again, the point here is not an evaluation or indictment of these books or their authors; rather, the point is to establish a sort of jumping-off point for the change that I will propose in the following section. And a shift is most certainly needed if we aim to foster critical interculturality in our classrooms.

American culture is depicted as largely homogenous, a monolith informed by white, upper-middle class America, just as Akbari warned (2008). The depiction of the immigrant experience is superficial and bowdlerised.

I do not know that true criticality is ever achieved in these series. We are shown that things *are* a certain way in America, but not encouraged to question *why* they are that way, whether they *ought* to be that way, whether another person with another way of knowing would characterise things differently. When serious problems are addressed, it is briefly, distantly, sometimes cartoonishly. At best there are general observations here and there that change can be achieved through involvement in local politics. But true criticality requires more than a single short activity; it must be a throughline. Most of the time, students are asked to look only at the immediate effects upon their own lives, taught to solve their immediate problems. Seldom are they pointed to root causes, systemic biases, or how to go about effecting transformative change. Students learn to navigate systems, not to change or even challenge them.

Towards a Critical-Intercultural Stance in Adult ESOL

Why This Shift?

Ibrahim (1999) concluded that language learning 'is neither aimless nor neutral, nor is it free of the politics of identity' (365). Acculturation and language acquisition involve the construction of an identity, as well as the risk that elements of identity can be lost (Aman, 2014). Life in a new nation inevitably entails new labels and roles, some of which will likely involve Othering (Ibrahim, 1999; House, 2007) and some of which means students may find stereotypes or identities ascribed to them that do not align with their own self-identity (Zhu, 2014).

For permanent immigrants to the U.S., critical interculturality is not just a hat one puts on for a leisurely trip abroad. For newcomers in a new home, it is an invaluable navigation tool and a matter of survival. It can also help our students to recognise themselves as constructors of knowledge, to assert the validity of their experience and their narrative, and to be, if they so choose, agents of change in their new home.

That *if they so choose* is a necessary qualifier for me. Critical interculturality is not about indoctrination or forcing students into transformative social action; it is about ensuring that they are equipped with the skills and knowledge to choose for themselves. Criticality is a prerequisite for transformative action, and without it, we are deprived of the choice to take action. Even for those students who are not inclined towards activism, criticality is a lens on the world that will serve them well, equipping them to stand up for themselves and their families, to maintain their culture as they see fit. Like any other Americans, they have a right to make their voice heard at town halls and P.T.O. meetings.

What Does This Shift Look like?

What I propose is a shift away from representing American culture as monolithic and monocultural, a target to be learned and adopted. It is a shift away from a deficit model that views students as recipients of cultural knowledge, vessels to be filled. It is also a shift away from reductive dichotomies—us/them, target/native, before/after, same/different— and from uncritically presenting the status quo. It is a shift away from a strict focus on satisfying immediate needs. It is probably a shift away from corporately produced materials, teacher-centeredness and top-down curricular decision-making.

What I propose is a shift *towards* multiple depictions of various ways to be American. It is a shift towards hybridity and recognising students as the multicultural speakers that they are, as co-constructors of knowledge. Towards the 'third place', where difference is explored and the goal is discourse itself. A shift towards questioning the assumptions and implications of the status quo, recognising subjectivities and seeking alternative narratives and ways of knowing. It is a shift towards local materials, student-generated texts. Towards successful intercultural speakers as models. Towards a contextualised, interconnected, structural focus. Towards an approach that helps students to satisfy immediate needs while also considering systemic problems and their role in addressing them.

When we dig deep into parsing the nuances of hyphenated jargon—as we have perhaps done in this section—we run the risk of floating off into the purely academic, leaving it unclear what all the theory means in the classroom. I want to be certain not to do that. The shifts discussed above need far more research and theoretical exploration in the context of adult ESOL. The following section will outline some steps that adult educators can take in their programs immediately to better address the concerns I have raised above.

Cultivating Critical Interculturality in the Adult ESOL Classroom

The shifts described above have direct implications for what we do in the adult ESOL classroom. Each teacher should of course apply these concepts as they see fit, if they see fit. In this section I will share a number of classroom practices that embody the shift towards encouraging a critical intercultural stance among adult students. While I will continue to focus on and use the language of adult ESOL, readers will likely find that the strategies discussed below could quite easily be adapted to a number of other contexts, particularly those in which culture is treated as content.

Below are five concrete changes that present themselves to me, comparing the current thinking on interculturality with the current state of adult ESOL. These are modelling criticality, selecting better examples, co-constructing knowledge, decentering monoculturalism and cultivating a dialogic community. This is not intended to be a complete framework or comprehensive list.

These suggestions are framed with the classroom practitioner in mind, but sustained systemic change will also require that program administrators, curriculum developers, teacher educators and researchers make an intentional shift in perspective and in practice. Further work should be done on the implications of critical interculturality for these roles.

Modelling Criticality

The first thing we can do in our classes is to model critical interculturality. This means we ourselves must develop and exhibit a critical consciousness, trading the 'assumption of similarity' for the 'exploration of difference' (Ware & Kramsch, 2005, p. 203). This means becoming keen observers of culture, developing an awareness of our own subjectivities through active self-scrutiny. In order for this to be successful and sustained, this awareness-raising ought to be approached as a broad self-improvement process, akin to the purging of sexist and heteronormative tropes from our personal vocabulary. Performing think-alouds in class can give learners access to the reasoning of critical interculturality.

In addition to a broad self-improvement process, opportunities for the exploration of difference can also be incorporated into lesson planning. In my own planning process, this takes the form of another scan over the texts, materials, and activities I have selected with a critical eye to cultural assumptions, points of departure for intercultural dialogue. In class, I also try to self-monitor. I find myself stopping mid-sentence sometimes, saying, 'Wait, maybe that is a stereotype. Maybe I shouldn't assume that. What do you think about this idea? Are there other ways to think about this concept'?

Selecting Examples

As we have seen, examples in adult ESOL coursebooks can come up short in terms of representing the immigrant experience. And, being conditioned by these coursebooks, some teachers might find ourselves defaulting to a monolingual, monocultural norm.

But how much will a refugee from Nicaragua with indigenous heritage, now learning her third language and culture, relate to the example of monolingual, monocultural Kyle who has never left Iowa? Even if the student's goals for herself and her family involve the adoption of certain aspects of American culture, successful interculturality for her is never going to look like Kyle. Examples, in everything from reading passages to pronunciation models, should include successful intercultural immigrants.

We must take what we know of our students' experiences and develop more authentic examples. Better yet, we can arrange for students to tell their own stories and work with them to turn those authentic, local experiences into the examples that we work with in future classes. A text written by an advanced student can serve as an excellent reading for an intermediate student. Students can bring in photos from the stores that they shop at, of the clothes in their closets. All the better if we can bring in that advanced student, program alumni, or other successful immigrant individuals or families as guest speakers, serving as entirely authentic, proximal role models for students. Learning from other immigrants' accounts 'acknowledges the significance of learners' experiences as legitimate departure points in any meaningful learning enterprise' (Akbari, 2008, p. 282).

When we come to units like those discussed above on topics like housing, food and clothing, we can assign students to bring in photos of their own homes, the stores they shop at, the foods that are staples of their diets, the clothing they wear here or in their native country.

Fighting the Wonderbread norm does not necessarily mean erasing or ignoring dominant American norms altogether. Rather, it is about decentering that norm and introducing plurality and discourse.

Co-Constructing Knowledge

As language teachers, we are probably wary of any approach that posits our students as vessels to be filled with our knowledge of English. In the teaching of language per se, we likely recognise language acquisition to be a process of ongoing, collaborative meaning-making. But we must ask ourselves whether we approach the teaching of culture in the same way, as Beltrán advises:

> 'It is important to recognize [students'] experiences since they inform teachers about how students apprehend and talk about the world and because, based on the understanding of these experiences, teachers can truly establish a process of co-construction of knowledge that accounts for students' cultures, topics, projects and languages'. (183)

One important way to do this is to abandon the 'English-only' policies that are still common in adult ESOL programs. This suggestion is likely to be met with some resistance, but the embrace of L1 in the classroom is nothing new in global EFL and gaining traction in ESOL. As far back as 1993, Auerback lamented that 'many U.S. ESL educators continue to uphold the notion that English is the only acceptable medium of communication within the confines of the ESL classroom' (1).

Rivera (1999) described how L1 use affords ESOL students the chance to construct and reconstruct knowledge from the basis of their own lived reality.

Co-constructing knowledge can take familiar forms: independent research projects, community interviews, etc. I would encourage teachers to add a critical aspect to this, even in basic classes, connecting accounts to *how*s and *why*s and *so*s. Rather than teaching students from our own knowledge and a coursebook how Americans celebrate Christmas or who Thomas Jefferson was, we can send students in search of multiple accounts, teach them to recognise the dominant account and alternative narratives, teach them the critical language to characterise and hedge these. Many adult educators will recognise that such a shift meshes very nicely with current shifts towards incorporating rigour in standards-based adult ESOL.

Ibrahim (1999) describes projects (drawing upon Freierian dialecticism) in which 'students can become their teachers. In practical terms, this might mean planning activities in which students explain to the teacher and to the rest of the class what rap and hip-hop are and what they represent to the students' (367). We can of course substitute in other aspects of culture.

I also propose that teachers make student ethnographies a part of their regular repertoire of projects. House wrote, 'cultural gaps can, in theory, always be bridged via ethnographic knowledge' (11). The concept of student-conducted ethnographic research is not nearly as daunting as the name might sound: this can be as simple a poster presentation or interview project, but with some basic anthropological principles at work. This type of project can be facilitated if teachers or program administrators are able to point students to diverse resources and allies in the community: program alumni, local politicians, leaders within the immigrant community, other teachers, librarians, etc. Establishing such a network from scratch could be daunting, but many adult ESOL programs are associated with community-based organisations that already maintain networks such as these. It should be uncontroversial to say that connecting students with these networks, beginning with small research projects, can have various untold benefits down the line for our students.

Rivera (1999) described the fascinating and inspiring El Barrio Popular Education Program in which Latina students used video to conduct bilingual community research projects in a way that values and validates the knowledge that they bring to the program, encourages them to tell their stories, and engages frankly with the real challenges that they face. They become producers of knowledge and organisers of their community, documenting and transforming their reality. Rivera's words really speak to the transformative power of this type of work: 'From their individual stories, students can make sense of the forces that have shaped their lives and affect their social reality' (Rivera, 1999, pp. 489–490). A program like this might have been difficult to develop with the technology available in 1999, but with today's mobile technology, a remarkable program like this could be more easily replicated.

Decentering Systemic Monoculturalism

The decentering of monoculturalism should not just be a matter for coursebook examples. Since we know that power differentials are perpetuated systemically, we must also strive to decenter monoculturalism at the systemic level.

Those of us who are program administrators, in a position to make hiring decisions, must recognise the value of hiring teachers and administrators who are themselves immigrants and successful intercultural speakers. Not only is this a way to bring multicultural perspectives into the decision-making process, it surrounds students with powerful role models for stable, successful interculturality.

We should also (following the advice of Akbari) take steps to decentralise curricular decision-making. Ensure that students have a voice in selecting topics, conduct ongoing needs analysis, use student-generated texts, encourage students to bring in texts and situations from their daily lives, and contrive scenarios that allow students to drive the content of the course.

Create an Explicitly Dialogic Community

We must also strive to actively and intentionally foster relationships and deliberately build the community that is our classroom or even program. The importance of community is stressed by Kramsch (2009), Freire (1972), and Nash (2010). We do this already, of course, building trust and rapport, agreeing upon classroom rules or values at the start of the year, making a point of using supportive refrains in our classroom talk. What is likely a change for many teachers is the express emphasis on critical dialogue. We can incorporate the value of multiple narratives, identifying subjectivity and sharing our stories into classroom values statements. We can include among our teacherly refrains questions like *Who has a different understanding of this?* We can put emphasis on language used for hedging, politely expressing a different account, asking critical questions. We can ensure that the first weeks with a new class include activities that help us and other students to become familiar with one another's backgrounds (tactfully and with respect for students who may not care to share).

Conclusion

Though culture is often a key component of adult ESOL programs, the language of interculturality is still largely absent from this context. As a consequence, adult ESOL is lagging behind other subfields in our treatment of culture. Examining current adult ESOL materials, we have seen one piece of that picture, but more formal work should be done to determine what is actually happening in the classroom.

I have argued that a critical interculturality is necessary for our students to become agents of change in their communities, and beneficial even for students who have no such aspirations. Though far more theoretical work is needed to elaborate the implications of critical interculturality for the adult ESOL context, I have presented a series of pedagogical shifts that I believe teachers can enact immediately to better cultivate a critical intercultural stance in their classrooms.

I encourage readers to explore the references included here and the Recommended Texts list below. Moreover, it is important that we as adult educators contribute our voices to the body of literature on interculturality.

Adult immigrants to the U.S. bring with them a host of skills, knowledge and experience, frames of reference and ways of knowing, poetry, art, songs, theatre, oral history. Newcomers do not need to be taught how to be American; by coming here, they deepen and expand and enrich what it is to be American.

I think most of us working in ESOL already know this and teach accordingly. Still, having a language in which to express it, the language of critical interculturality, can galvanise our practice and show us a clearer way forward.

Recommended Texts

Soler, E. A., and Jordà, M. P. S. (2007). *Intercultural language use and language learning*. The Netherlands: Springer.

This volume brings together a range of voices and implications for interculturality, beginning with a basic introduction to the term and its history.

Dervin, F. (2017). *Critical Interculturality*. Newcastle upon Tyne: Cambridge Scholars Publishing.

This is a more current work, integrating criticality with interculturality. Being a transcription of spoken lectures, it is somewhat more accessible than other works on the topic.

Kramsch, C. (1993). *Context and culture in language teaching*. Oxford University Press.

An earlier, book-length treatment of Kramsch's ideas on culture in the context of language teaching. A strong primer before reading Kramsch's later work.

Engagement Priorities

Do you subscribe to a target culture or critical interculturality approach to teaching culture?
Do current practices and materials foster an interculturality that will serve students in their educational goals?
What changes in classroom practice could be made to better foster critical interculturality?
What systemic and administrative changes could be made to better foster critical interculturality?

References

Akbari, R. (2008). Transforming lives: Introducing critical pedagogy into ELT classrooms. *ELT Journal., 62,* 276–283.

Aman, R. (2014). Why Interculturalidad is not Interculturality: Colonial remains and paradoxes in translation between indigenous social movements and supranational bodies. *Cultural Studies,* 1–24.

Baker, W. (2009). The cultures of English as a lingua franca. *Tesol Quarterly, 43*(4), 567–592.

Bakhtin, M. (1981). The Dialogic Imagination. Ed. Michael Holquist. Trans. Caryl Emerson and Michael Holquist. Austin: University of Texas Press.

Banegas, D. L., & Villacañas de Castro, L. S. (2016). Criticality. *Elt Journal, 70*(4), 455–457.

Beltrán, C. G. (2016). Critical interculturality: A path for pre-service ELT teachers. *Íkala, Revista de Lenguaje y Cultura, 21*(2), 171–187.

Bitterlin, G., Johnson, D., Price, D., Ramírez, S., & Savage, K. L. (Series Ed.). (2018). *Ventures* (3rd ed.). Cambridge University Press.

Blatchford, C. H. (1973). Newspapers: Vehicles for teaching ESOL with a cultural focus. TESOL quarterly, 145–151.

Byram, M., Gribkova, B., & Starkey, H. (2002). *Developing the intercultural dimension in language teaching: A practical introduction for teachers.* Council of Europe.

Canagarajah, A. S. (1999). *Resisting linguistic imperialism in English teaching.* Oxford University Press.

Canale, M., & Swain, M. (1980). Theoretical bases of communicative approaches to second language teaching and testing. *Applied Linguistics, 1*(1), 1.

Celce-Murcia, M. (2007). Rethinking the role of communicative competence in language teaching. In E. A. Soler & M. P. S. Jordà (Eds.), *Intercultural language use and language learning* (pp. 41–57). Springer.

Crookes, G., & Lehner, A. (1998). Aspects of process in an ESL critical pedagogy teacher education course. *TESOL Quarterly, 32*(2), 319–328.

Dervin, F. (2016). *Interculturality in education: A theoretical and methodological toolbox.* Springer.

Dervin, F. (2017). *Critical interculturality.* Cambridge Scholars Publishing.

Foley, B. H., & Neblett, E. R. (2019). *English in action* (3rd ed.). National Geographic Learning.

Freire, P. (1972). *Pedagogy of the Oppressed.* Harmondsworth: Penguin.

Gray, J. (2002). The global coursebook in English language teaching. *Globalization and language teaching*, 151–167.

Holquist, M. (1990). *Dialogism: Bakhtin and his World*. London: Routledge.

House, J. (2007). What is an 'intercultural speaker'? In E. A. Soler & M. P. S. Jordà (Eds.), *Intercultural language use and language learning* (pp. 7–22). Springer.

Hua, Z. (2015). Negotiation as the way of engagement in intercultural and lingua franca communication: Frames of reference and interculturality. *Journal of english as a lingua franca, 4*(1), 63–90. Chicago.

Ibrahim, A. (1999). Becoming black: Rap and hip-hop, race, gender, identity, and the politics of ESL learning. *TESOL Quarterly, 33*, 349–369.

Ilieva, R. (2000). Exploring culture in texts designed for use in adult ESL classrooms. TESL Canada journal, 15–20.

Jenkins, R., & Johnson, S. (2019). *Stand out: Evidence-based learning for college and career readiness* (3rd ed.). National Geographic Learning.

Kegan, R., Broderick, M., Drago-Severson, E., Helsing, D., Popp, N., & Portnow, K. (2001). Toward a New Pluralism in ABE/ESOL Classrooms: Teaching to Multiple Cultures of Mind. Research Monograph. NCSALL Reports# 19. National Center for the Study of Adult Learning and Literacy (NCSALL).

Kramsch, C. (1993). *Context and culture in language teaching*. Oxford University Press.

Kramsch, C. (1995). The cultural component of language teaching. *Language, Culture and Curriculum, 8*(2), 83–92.

Kramsch, C. (1999). Thirdness: The intercultural stance. *Language, culture and identity*, 41–58.

Kramsch, C. (2009). Third culture and language education. In V. Cook & L. Wei (Eds.), *Contemporary applied linguistics* (pp. 233–254). Continuum.

Kramsch, C. (2013, January). Culture in foreign language teaching. *Iranian Journal of Language Teaching Research, 1*(1), 57–78.

Lynn, S., Magy, R., & Salas-Isnardi, F. (2019). *Future: English for work, life, and academic success* (2nd ed.). Pearson.

McKay, S. L. (2003). Toward an appropriate EIL pedagogy: Re-examining common ELT assumptions. *International Journal of Applied Linguistics, 13*(1), 1–22.

Nash, A. (2010). *Thinking beyond 'increased participation': Integrating civics and adult ESOL*. World Education. Retrieved from http://nelrc.org/publications/cpandesol.html.

Nuñez-Pardo, A. (2018). The English textbook: Tensions from an intercultural perspective. *GIST Education and Learning Research Journal, 17,* 230–259.

Peirce, C. S. (1955). Philosophical writings of Peirce (Vol. 217). Courier Corporation.

Pennycook, A. (1990). Critical pedagogy and second language education. *System, 18,* 303–314.

Pennycook, A. (1998). English and the discourses of colonialism. London, UK; New York, NY: Routledge.

Phillipson, R. (1992). *Linguistic imperialism.* Oxford, England: Oxford University Press.

Restrepo, E., & Rojas, A. (2010). Inflexión decolonial. Fuentes, conceptos y cuestionamientos. Popayán: Universidad del Cauca; Instituto de Estudios Sociales y Culturales Pensar; Maestría en Estudios Culturales, Universidad Javeriana.

Rhodes, C. M. (2013). A study of culturally responsive teaching practices of adult ESOL and EAP teachers. *Journal of Research and Practice for Adult Literacy, Secondary, and Basic Education, 2*(3), 170–183.

Rivera, K. (1999). Popular research and social transformation: A community-based approach to critical pedagogy. *TESOL Quarterly, 22,* 485–500.

Seidlhofer, B. (2001). Closing a conceptual gap: The case for a description of English as a lingua franca. *International Journal of Applied Linguistics, 11*(2), 133–158.

Sheppard, R. (2019). *Action required: The adult educator as advocate.* In H. Linville & J. Whiting (Eds.) Advocacy in English Language Teaching and Learning. TESOL Press.

Soler, E. A., & Jordà, M. P. S. (2007). *Intercultural language use and language learning.* Springer.

Tomlinson, B., & Masuhara, H. (2013). Adult coursebooks. *ELT Journal, 67*(2), 233–249.

Valdes, J. M. (Ed.). (1986). *Culture bound: Bridging the cultural gap in language teaching.* Cambridge University Press.

Ware, P., & Kramsch, C. (2005). Toward an intercultural stance: Teaching German and English through telecollaboration. *The Modern Language Journal, 89*(2), 190–205.

Part III

The Role of English in the Learning and Teaching of Interculturality

8

The 'Intercultural' and English as a Lingua Franca in International Higher Education: Expectations, Realities and Implications for English Language Teaching

Pimsiri Taylor

Abbreviations

EAP   English for Academic Purposes
EFL   English as a Foreign Language
ELF   English as a Lingua Franca
ELT   English Language Teaching
EMI   English as a Medium of Instruction
EOP   English for Occupational Purposes
ESP   English for Specific Purposes
IC   Intercultural Competence
ICA   Intercultural Awareness
ICC   Intercultural Communicative Competence
IHE   International Higher Education

P. Taylor (✉)
Thammasat University, Bangkok, Thailand
e-mail: pimsiri.t@litu.tu.ac.th

© The Author(s), under exclusive license to Springer Nature
Switzerland AG 2021
M. Victoria and C. Sangiamchit (eds.), *Interculturality and the English Language
Classroom*, https://doi.org/10.1007/978-3-030-76757-0_8

Introduction

The past few decades saw a largely increasing trend of international higher education (or IHE) where higher education institutions adopt internationalisation strategies, part of which involve using English as a symbol of internationalisation (Duong & Chua, 2016). This has been especially noticeable amongst countries in which English is used as a second or foreign language. The South East Asian region which includes 10 ASEAN (The Association of Southeast Asian Nations) country members is likewise no exception. A recent study by the British Council (2018) has shown that there has been continuous growth in international engagement amongst higher education systems in ASEAN member states. Staff and student mobility is an explicit example of IHE, where the terms 'inter' and 'national' come into clear existence, but what about the terms 'inter' and 'cultural'? Are they directly concerned with the 'international' in the context of IHE? What are the fuzzy logics in understanding the 'intercultural' where English is used in IHE?

In order to understand the relationship between the English language and the 'intercultural' in IHE, it is necessary to review relevant concepts pertaining to the 'intercultural' such as 'intercultural communication', 'intercultural competence' and 'intercultural awareness'. Using international study programmes in universities in Thailand and Malaysia as contexts, I will explain how interculturality is constructed and enacted. As English is the common language used in these international settings, I will elaborate on the interplay between the English language and interculturality in these contexts. Is English being deployed not only as a 'lingua' franca but also as a 'cultural' franca (Sussex & Curtis, 2018)?

By drawing upon interview data collected from undergraduate students in IHE in Thailand and Malaysia I will discuss issues of English use found in such settings and how English can become a 'cultural franca', and a complex interaction site for nationality, language and identity. What are the expectations? What are the realities? As English language teachers, what can we do with our pedagogical practices? Whilst locally situated, what can we learn from these examples in order to embed interculturality in our teaching more widely?

The 'Intercultural'

Intercultural communication has become one key area which is important for a number of disciplines, and this is because it involves interactions of human beings. However, it is the term 'intercultural' which leads to arguments amongst academics and practitioners in various fields. First of all, it is 'culture' which can be interpreted in a number of ways. Geertz (1973, p. 89) proposed culture as 'a system of inherited conceptions expressed in symbolic forms by means of which men (sic) communicate, perpetuate, and develop their knowledge about and attitudes toward life'. D'Andrade (1990, p. 65), similarly, pointed out that cultures are:

> learned and shared systems of meaning and understanding, communicated primarily by means of natural language. These meanings and understandings are not just representations about what is in the world; they are also directive, evocative and reality constructing in character.

Being a learned and shared system implies that culture is a system of a social group, and this has led to an essentialist view of culture where people's behaviours are simply defined within the culture they live, compared with the 'other', often in the form of national culture (Holliday, 2011).

In intercultural studies, national culture still has its place in exploring intercultural communication (see Holliday, 2011 for 'a grammar of culture') but at the same time has been critiqued for its stereotypical framework in categorising individuals (e.g. as seen in the cultural dimension model, Hofstede, 1997). As we become more increasingly mobile, the static, homogenous view of national culture might no longer fit in today's globalised society. Rather, in understanding culture we can take Street's (1993) sociocultural view where culture is not a noun or a thing, but a '*verb*'. As a verb, culture is 'an active process of meaning making' (Street, 1993, p. 25). Because meaning-making is such a dynamic, hybrid process, defining 'culture' within the essentialist framework such as national culture can be problematic.

In addition to the term 'culture', the prefix 'inter' appearing in intercultural can also pose challenges. Since the term 'inter' literally means 'between', it implies the interactions of the 'two', be it nations or cultures. Given the 'transnational flows' (Risager, 2007) across national borders in today's globalised world, the term 'trans' may be more suitable due to its meanings of 'through' or 'across' (Baker, 2015). However, since the focus of this volume is on 'interculturality', the term 'intercultural' is used, instead of 'transcultural', in order to explore the possibilities as well as limitations of the 'intercultural', both between and across cultures. Moreover, using the term 'intercultural' can help us to explore how the concept of culture and its multifaceted aspects have developed over time. Since the initiation of the single culture notion, it is mostly this 'intercultural' paradigm which has grounded studies of human interactions and communication across cultures.

Amongst various 'intercultural' notions, two of the most common are intercultural competence (or IC) and intercultural communicative competence (or ICC). Both are found in literatures related to IHE (e.g. Deardorff, 2006; Gregersen-Hermans, 2016; Odağ et al., 2015; Otten, 2003; Zhou et al., 2008) as well as English language teaching (e.g. Byram, 1997; Byram et al., 2002; Young & Sachdev, 2011). In English language teaching, in particular, Byram's (1997) model is often discussed as a framework to develop L2 learner's ICC. Whereas IC is the 'ability to interact' in one's 'own language with the people from another country and culture', ICC emphasises 'the ability to interact with people from another country and culture in a foreign language' (Byram, 1997, p. 71). Despite the widespread application, Byram's (1997) IC and ICC concepts demonstrate the structuralist correlation between culture and nation/country (Baker, 2011, 2012, 2015; Holliday, 2011) and in categorising individuals by their country, the complexity and hybridity of culture are neglected. If our stance regarding intercultural and intercultural communication goes beyond the fixed paradigm of national language and national culture, how can we then understand the intercultural through the lens of language teachers?

To explore intercultural events, Holliday (2011, p. 4) called for an 'alternative grammar of culture', 'the loose, negotiated relationship between the particularities of national structures and cultural resources and the universality of small culture formation at a discoursal level'. Although national culture still exists in Holliday's (2011) framework, it is *only* a cultural resource which we partly draw upon in intercultural events. Essentially what we do or who we are is *not* always or necessarily defined by national culture. It could be derived from families, professional communities or other cultural groupings. The complexity, fluidity and multiplicity of cultures require L2 communicators to develop ICC which transcends national boundaries.

In addition, Kramsch (2011) also put forward the idea of teaching for 'symbolic competence' to complement intercultural competence in a foreign language classroom. Originally, Kramsch (1993) viewed that language learners' cultural identity was so increasingly complex and hybrid that it might no longer fit into the first language/second language (L1/ L2) or first culture/second culture (C1/ C2) paradigm. For instance, a Thai person who was born and raised in Thailand and has been learning English (and informally Korean through an interest in Korean Pop) might not identify him/herself as 'fully' belonging to Thai culture, but somewhat Thai, American and Korean, due to exposure to these foreign languages, as well as possibly American media or even Korean pop culture. Due to this fluidity and hybridity, cultural identity is constructed in a place which Kramsch (2011) called 'a third place'; yet for some language teachers and practitioners, the abstract concept of third place made it rather difficult to apply to professional practice. What can teachers do to help develop intercultural competence amongst foreign language students? For this reason, Kramsch (2010, 2011) later developed this concept of 'symbolic competence' which refers to 'the ability to read and interpret spoken and written discourse, identify the symbolic value of words and metaphors, grasp their social and historical significance, contrast them with metaphors in one's own language, and reframe one's interpretation of events' (Kramsch, 2010, p. 24). Moreover, Kramsch (2011, p. 365) also reiterated the significance of 'symbolic competence' in juxtaposition with intercultural competence:

> If intercultural competence is the ability to reflect critically or analytically on the symbolic systems we use to make meaning, we are led to reinterpret the learning of foreign languages as not gaining a mode of communication across cultures, but more as acquiring a symbolic mentality that

grants as much importance to subjectivity and the historicity of experience as to the social conventions and the cultural expectations of any one stable community of speakers.

As may be concluded, intercultural involves not only the ability to interact with people from other cultures but also the ability to construct meanings of what people say or write. Symbolic competence adds to our knowledge of IC, and ICC in understanding the intercultural, especially in today's globalised, transcultural society where the national culture framework may not be able to provide a full explanation to the intercultural.

The 'Intercultural' and the English Language: Language, Culture and English as a Lingua Franca (ELF)

For English language teachers, one key term in understanding the 'intercultural' is through 'language' or specifically 'the English language'. Risager (2005) recommended the notion of 'languaculture', also known as 'linguaculture', which she developed further from Agar's (1995) 'linguaculture' concept in order to explore the relationships between language and culture. Part of Risager's (2005) discussion was how individuals or language users carry with them 'languaculture' or 'culture in language' (Risager, 2005, p. 190). This linguaculture (or languaculture) involves the interconnections between language and culture in that the link between language and culture can be created in every new communicative event. For this reason, new cultural meanings can be constructed in these events, resulting in various linguacultures. In the case of the English language, for example, linguacultures are not necessarily tied with the cultures of native speakers of English (e.g. the British, or the American). This is because not all communicative events will involve these native speakers. As Risager (2007) emphasised in her later book *Language and Culture Pedagogy: From a National to a Transnational Paradigm*, individuals or language users have now become more mobile due to global mobility and migration, bringing about the cultural and linguistic flows which go beyond national boundaries, in other words, these flows are 'transnational'. The term 'trans' here raises questions concerning the relationships amongst national language, national culture and the intercultural, and how we may navigate ourselves amidst these elements.

Having noted that we may now carry with us a more fluid, hybrid 'lingua culture', the language here then does not necessarily refer to mother tongue or national language, but to any language that we use, including the English language which is considered an international language or a 'lingua franca'. The term 'lingua franca' has long been used when 'an intermediary or contact language' is required in international trade or contacts, being a language of commerce with a 'rather stable variety with little room for variation' (House, 2018). For today, English as a lingua franca or ELF is widely understood as a 'contact language' for communication across linguistic as well as cultural boundaries (Seidlhofer, 2001). Being a 'contact language' not owned by any national language or territory but rather used by individuals as a language of communication across the globe, ELF has developed to become a 'mixed contact language' which is 'more or less neutral' (House, 2018).

Despite these definitions, this view of ELF as a neutral construct is contested by scholars in the field. Baker (2015), for instance, pointed out that ELF is not neutral, but it carries with it the ideology, which contributes to language users' 'cultural identity and identification' (Holliday, 2011). Jenks's (2016) study of international students also suggested that students' discursive resources are derived from national identities and their interactions also contribute to the co-construction of the self and the other. As individuals use the language, they carry with them the lingua culture, and as they carry this lingua culture, it means that language is not neutral or free from cultural or ideological underpinnings (Risager, 2016). In other words, individuals have their own past and present experiences, as well as beliefs and values. When they use language in each communicative event, they also construct their own cultural meanings through the language used.

From these two perspectives where language is 'a contact language' (House, 2018) and where language is used in language users' 'cultural identity and identification' (Holliday, 2011), there appears the dichotomy where ELF is 'language as communication' and 'language as identification' (Edmondson & House, 2003; Fiedler, 2011). Whereas 'language as communication' is the use of language for practical communicative purposes without taking on cultural meanings of the language used, 'language for identification', on the other hand, can be referred to as language used in identifying oneself. When put into the context of ELF, this notion leaves room for interpretation and discussion revolving around the intercultural through the lens of ELF, language and culture.

In intercultural communication, ELF has become a framework to help us understand interactions amongst people from various cultures. Unlike the national cultural framework, however, ELF is more complex because of its contribution to each individual's lingua culture. Since an individual's lingua culture can be constructed in every new communicative event (Risager, 2005), ELF users may use ELF in each of these events differently, depending on their communication and/or identification purposes. In order to successfully communicate in the intercultural, ELF contexts, we may need to take into account other competence models, in addition to IC, ICC and symbolic competence.

Through the lens of ELF, Baker (2011, 2012, 2015) proposed the concept of intercultural awareness (ICA) as a model of the knowledge, skills and attitudes required in intercultural communication in diverse global settings. According to Baker (2011, p. 202), ICA is 'a conscious understanding of the role culturally based forms, practices and frames of reference can have in intercultural communication, and an ability to put these conceptions into practice in a flexible and context specific manner in real time communication'. In Baker's (2011, 2012, 2015) ICA model, there are 3 levels consisting of level 1 basic cultural awareness, level 2 advanced cultural awareness and level 3 intercultural awareness. Whereas level 1 focuses on the communicators' first culture or native culture (such as Thai and Malaysian) in comparison with others at a very general level, level 2 begins to shift away from fixed categories of national culture and focuses more on social groupings which can be fluid and dynamic based on various contexts. Level 3, on the other hand, does not look at the aspects of our culture or their culture, but rather the 'emerging' use of English as a global lingua franca in which language is not tied to one community.

The term 'emerging' is one key element in understanding the 'intercultural' through ELF. Due to the fluid, dynamic nature of ELF communication, we must view the intercultural in situated, specific, 'emerging' contexts (Baker, 2011). In the subsequent section I will discuss further how these notions are connected with the experiences of the undergraduate students studying in international undergraduate study programmes in Thailand and Malaysia.

The 'Intercultural' and 'Interculturality' in IHE in Thailand and Malaysia: Multiplicity of Nationality, Language and Identity

In this section I present examples of findings from my research project on international higher education in Thailand and Malaysia to illustrate how the notion of the 'intercultural' and 'interculturality' can be elaborated further in those contexts. Although we have previously discussed concepts concerning the 'intercultural' such as IC, ICC, ICA, it should be noted that those terms employ 'intercultural' as an adjective prior to nouns such as competence and awareness. 'Interculturality', however, is a term on its own, and in order to understand 'interculturality' we should be aware of its positioning amongst various notions related to the 'intercultural'.

Young and Sercombe (2010, p. 181) defined 'interculturality' as 'a dynamic process by which people draw on and use the resources and processes of cultures with which they are familiar but also those they may not typically be associated with in their interactions with others'. Certainly, as there is no single uniform of intercultural communication, the conceptualisation of interculturality must be context-based, and in this chapter I explore it using the research settings of IHE in Thailand and Malaysia. One main reason why I have chosen IHE for my investigation is because of the term 'international' which is often perceived as being 'intercultural'. Do peoples of various nationalities in the programme automatically make the setting intercultural? In terms of interculturality, how do participants draw on resources including cultural resources in the dynamic process of interdiscourse interactions? In addition, these international programmes promote themselves as being international due to their use of English as a medium of instruction (EMI). Being an English language instructor in this context myself, I also set out to investigate the roles of English, specifically English as a lingua franca, and its interplay with interculturality in these IHE contexts, and from this conceptualisation I would like to find out what implications it has on ELT practices.

In order to explore interculturality in the aforementioned settings, four focus group interviews were conducted amongst 24 undergraduate students in international study programmes from three universities, one Anglophone university in Malaysia, one public university in Thailand and one private university in Thailand. The programmes of study varied from business and law to education. Whilst it might be ideal to recruit participants of various nationalities in all settings, only the participants in Malaysia were international. The nationalities of eight research participants included Malaysian (Malay-Malay, Chinese-Malay), Maldivian, British, Indonesian and Sri Lankan. The 16 students from Thailand, on the other hand, were all Thai. Although it might raise questions in terms of the status of IHE, it should be noted that being international is not only about international students and staff. Rather it is also concerned with curriculum, and particularly in the studied contexts, the English language used in teaching and learning. In fact, we may consider that the number of Thai students in IHE represents the reality of IHE in the research settings, in that the majority of Thai universities are locally owned and use local brands, and thus attract mostly local, Thai students. The university in Malaysia, on the other hand, is a branch campus of an Anglophone university. With its name and status, it is not surprising that the appearance of the university will be 'international' attracting both Malaysian and international students from across Asia (as well as other parts of the world) to study with them.

Having discussed with the students in terms of their perceptions, specifically their expectations and understandings of the 'intercultural', I have found three key themes including nationality, language and identity, which explain interculturality in IHE. These three interrelated elements depict how students view their learning experience in

IHE. That is, as mainly non-native speakers of English (except one British student in the study), these undergraduate students not only learn content in English but also learn the English language itself. Many of them still have to take additional English language courses in order to fulfil the requirements of the university. It appears that they are not only subject learners but also English language learners. Their experience in English language learning in intercultural contexts of IHE is undeniably relevant to English language teachers.

Nationality and Identity as Multiple Resources in Interculturality

IHE is generally a site with participants from various countries, and thus portrayed as a context with peoples of different nationalities. One expectation especially from students who attend IHE is the opportunity to partake in intercultural communication. At the Anglophone university in Malaysia, students seem to generally believe that being in IHE can facilitate their intercultural learning by meeting peoples of various nations, learning about various cultures and languages. In fact, it was found that even though students defined themselves as a person from the UK, from Indonesia or from Malaysia, stories that they share in their discussions show their multiple cultural resources. Extract 1, for instance, illustrates multiple cultural resources of a British student who has lived and worked in Thailand and Malaysia.

Extract 1: Nationality and identity as multiple resources (Malaysian IHE)

S: *I'm from the UK. Actually the reason to study in Malaysia was from living in Thailand. Teaching in the south in Trang and I came to Malaysia quite often and went to Penang and I just fell in love with the country.*

Interestingly, this student introduces herself from her country of origin, but later on in the discussion, shares her knowledge about living and teaching Thailand as well as learning Bahasa with non-Malaysian friends in Malaysia. As can be seen, identity is not linked with one's nationality or country. In IHE settings, in particular, many participants have international experiences, and it has led to their identities which are tied with only one nationality. Their cultural and linguistic resources to draw upon in the process interculturality are evidently multiple.

Similar to Malaysian IHE, students who choose to study in an international academic programme in Thai IHE also expect IHE to provide them with more opportunities for international and intercultural communication. Extract 2 shows Thai students' views on multiple languages and nationalities as resources to engage in this process.

Extract 2: Multiple languages and nationalities as resources in interculturality (Thai IHE)

S1:   *Actually, international should involve many languages and many nationalities. This may be the case of the other campus, not this campus.*
T: *So you feel the other campus is more international?*
S1:   *Yes. Yes.*
S2:   *If we have people from more countries, more nationalities, that should be good. There'll be some 'broad' communication, connection, and then we'll know about their traditions. We will learn.*

If viewed through the essentialist view of national culture, we may interpret that Thai students face challenges in drawing on cultural resources in intercultural communication due to the low number of non-Thai students or staff. However, from a non-essentialist perspective, we must not conclude that the lack of various nationalities means a lack of interculturality. Whereas IHE in Malaysia consists of participants of various nationalities, the context of IHE in Thailand presents a more complex interaction site in terms of identifying culture with nationality. Due to the relatively small proportion of international staff and students in Thai IHE, the question lies in what resources the participants can draw upon in intercultural communication?

The English Language and Identity: Beyond National Cultural Framework

Many EMI university programmes (also known as international programmes) in non-English speaking countries such as Thailand attract mostly home students. The reason could be partly linked with the preference for native English education, resulting in their choice of studying in English-speaking countries such as the UK, the US or even in an Anglophone university locating in non-English speaking countries such as Singapore or Malaysia. Despite the lack of varieties of peoples participating in these contexts of IHE, it does not necessarily refer to the lack of intercultural communication. If we wish to shift away from the stereotypical concept of national culture, we need to explore what else, apart from nationality, can be considered as a resource for participants to draw upon in the process of interculturality or in intercultural communication.

IHE is an intriguing setting where not only nationality but also a foreign language has a significant role in intercultural communication. Due to today's ideological underpinning of EMI in IHE's formal academic discourse (Jenkins, 2017), the English language becomes a symbol of internationalisation (Duong & Chua, 2016). Whilst English is used in intercultural communication by speakers of different mother tongues, English can also interestingly play a role in 'intercultural' communication of speakers of the 'same mother tongue' or the 'same nationality'.

In Thai IHE, for instance, intercultural communication is derived from the English use of Thai students who are socially defined as 'inter kids' and 'non-inter kids' (or 'Thai kids'). The 'inter kids' are those who have studied abroad or at an international school or a school where English is used as a medium of instruction, whereas 'non-inter kids' are Thai students who attend Thai language medium schools following the curriculum of Thailand's Ministry of Education. Due to this school experience tied with the English language, it is often the case that these 'non-inter kids' feel that their English is not as fluent as the 'inter kids', and thus identify themselves as being different from the 'inter kids'.

Below is an extract of 'Thai kids' discussing the 'inter kids' use of English in their IHE context.

Extract 3: The intercultural in Thai IHE: English use between inter kids and non-inter kids

S1: *It's instilled since they were young. They've been learning it and they have to speak English all the time. They're probably used to it.*
S2: *Can rarely speak Thai.*
S1: *Like when they type Thai they use karaoke Thai [English letters to pronounce Thai words].*
S2: *some can't even speak Thai.*
S3: *I think it's a bit much. They can't even write Thai.*

Extract 3 above offers us another perspective of understanding the 'intercultural' that it does not necessarily involve only 'nationality'. Rather, the intercultural can occur through the identification process of students from various sociocultural backgrounds. Their education and family upbringing, for instance, can result in their multilinguistic resources which are beyond their national language culture. Thai students in Thai IHE, for instance, use English differently and these different uses of English require their negotiation for successful intercultural communication. In fact, intercultural communication does not only take place in English-medium classrooms or study programmes. Some Thai students mentioned an identity struggle in two situations. Firstly, when they, as 'non-inter kids' from IHE, socialised with their peers who study in Thai programmes, and secondly when they, as students from Thai IHE, had to communicate with others in the workplace, as shown in Extract 4.

Extract 4: The use of English in social identification (Thai IHE)

S1: *After being in this program for a while, we simply speak one word in English one word in Thai, without realising it.*
S2: *This is a disadvantage.*
S1: *Sometimes we talk to others who study in Thai programs when we go out, we will say 'actually' (instead of using the Thai word which means actually).*

S2:   *Yes. It's like we can't think of a Thai word because we use English too much. Something like that.*

S1:   *Actually, I think it has both pros and cons. The con is sometimes if we apply for a job and if the organisation has a Thai style, I feel that it doesn't look good if you use one word in English one word in Thai. So when applying for a job, I have to think a lot, whether to go for English totally or can I use one word in English one word in Thai. I have to think a lot.*

S2:   *Most international companies with foreigners will not care that much anyway, but for Thais, they will be like .... What?*

As can be seen, Extracts 3 as well as 4 exemplify how each individual carries with him/her a 'language' element of culture, or a lingua culture, which contributes to their culture as well as social identity. As an English language teacher, social groups such as these provide certain implications on how we may interpret interculturality in IHE. In international study programmes with mostly local students, especially, interculturality could be understood through the view of 'interdiscourse interactions' (Kramsch, 2011). Although students in these programmes may share the same nationality, this does not mean their linguistic and cultural resources are similar. Especially in today's global, mobile world, the 'lingua' component of lingua culture is no longer homogeneous, but diversely heterogeneous. Part of the lingua culture which English language users (or students in IHE) carry is English. In the contexts of IHE, participants, regardless of being native or non-native speakers of English, employ the English language in cultural identity formation.

English and Interculturality in IHE: A Lingua Franca or a Cultural Franca

Further to the previous sections which discuss the multiplicity of nationality and identity, followed by how the English language challenges the national cultural framework in identity construction and in interculturality, this section will take the argument further, specifically to the roles of the English language in interculturality in IHE, whether it is a lingua franca or a cultural franca. First and foremost, it is rather obvious that English has played a dominant part in IHE. It is a lingua franca in formal academic discourse where English is used in instruction and classroom communication. For non-formal or social discourse, likewise, it is English which helps international students to communicate with others who have different mother tongues. This is particularly true in the Malaysian IHE context as mentioned by one Malaysian student in Extract 5.

Extract 5: The use of English as a lingua franca in social communication (Malaysian IHE)

S: *I think if we are dealing with students from different countries so English as a medium is an excellent medium because we understand. There's no barrier to communicate to other students who come from different countries.*

Whilst being an academic as well as a social lingua franca, English can be perceived and used differently due to users' lingua culture. In this sense, it could be said that English or English as a lingua (ELF) is contextual and mutually understood amongst participants in its own intercultural contexts. If we are to propose that English is a 'true' lingua franca in IHE contexts, we need to explore ELF in IHE through the lens of both 'language as communication' and 'language as identification' (Edmondson & House, 2003; Fiedler, 2011). With regard to interculturality in particular, we must investigate 'co-constructed common ground elements that rely both on relatively definable cultural models and norms as well as situationally evolving features' (Kecskes, 2015, p. 179). How can ELF be employed as linguistic and cultural resources for ELF users to draw upon so that 'common ground' can be 'co-constructed'?

Since interculturality is a complex, dynamic process whereby both familiar and unfamiliar resources are drawn upon by interactants (Young & Sercombe, 2010), a 'detailed awareness of common ground between specific cultures' as well as 'an awareness of possibilities of mismatch and miscommunication between specific cultures' are required by intercultural speakers, before moving onto becoming an advanced intercultural speaker who is able to 'negotiate and mediate between different emergent culturally and contextually grounded communication modes and frame of references' (Baker, 2012). Extract 6 below is a statement given by a Thai student who studied with native English-speaking lecturers and lecturers who graduated from English-speaking countries. In her statement, she explained that some of the English expressions used in class by these lecturers, or slang, as she defined it, could cause misunderstandings in classroom interactions.

Extract 6: Misunderstandings through the use of English slang (Thai IHE)

S1:   Some instructors are native or graduated from abroad. They are used to using slang, but we don't want them to use slang in class. They will look less professional. ..... we want language to be something easy to understand and clear in itself and doesn't need a lot of translation or interpretation.

In Extract 6, the use of slang shows that the lecturers carry with them the 'linguaculture' (Risager, 2005), but more importantly they seem to bring in 'native' English culture with their English. When the lecturers use slang based on native cultural norms which the students are not familiar with, 'common ground' cannot be established and successfully negotiated. Whereas the students interpret slang as non-professional and inappropriate for lecturers to use in class, the lecturers themselves do not share the same meaning of slang. Whilst the lecturers use English slang as language to identify themselves, they are unable to use ELF for successful communication in the IHE setting. In such ELF communication, what can be an explanation for this difficulty?

Jenkins (2005) maintains that the use of native-speaker idiomatic language, despite normally being regarded as demonstrating a high level of L2 proficiency, can be a particular threat to intelligibility in ELF communication. This has led to a question of how ELF should be approached in interculturality in order to reach the 'co-constructed common ground' (Kecskes, 2015). Perhaps, English is not only a 'lingua franca', but also a 'cultural franca' or in Sussex and Curtis's (2018, p. 2) word a 'cultura franca' which is:

> a broadly common set of practices and values ranging from ad hoc, almost pidgin, practices negotiated real time and in situ for interpersonal communication, all the way to elaborate codes of values and interaction.

Although Sussex and Curtis (2018) introduced this notion of English as a cultural franca merely as an initial proposal for further empirical investigation, it is very much in line with ELF and interculturality, in terms of intelligibility concerning ELF pronunciation (Jenkins, 2005, 2007), lexicogrammar (Meierkord, 2004) and L1 idioms (Prodromou, 2007). For intercultural communicators to get their message across and understand one another there requires mutuality and intelligibility through the use of English, not only as a lingua franca, but also a cultural franca. IHE exemplifies a complex interaction site for interlocutors to negotiate their identity through English as language in communication and identification. Whether they are lecturers or students, English is expected to be deployed by them, but there is somehow common ground between them. Being on an 'international' academic discourse, English has been given a symbolic form of language of IHE, but with intercultural participants of diverse nationalities, languages and cultural frame of references this common ground is contextually co-constructed.

As English language teachers in IHE, what are the consequent implications of this varied English use? More importantly, what can we do to facilitate interculturality in our classrooms?

Expectations and Realities of ELF and Interculturalities in IHE: Pedagogical Practices and Implications for ELT

Our discussion throughout the chapter has shown that interculturality is a dynamic process where students and lecturers draw upon their linguistic and cultural resources to interact with others in IHE settings. In other words, their lingua culture (Risager, 2005) can influence their intercultural communication, and so can their perceptions towards the lingua culture of other intercultural speakers they communicate with. The term 'international' in IHE has resulted in IHE ideology as an educational setting with peoples of various nationalities and languages participating in intercultural communication where English is used as a medium of instruction as well as social interactions, in other words English as a lingua franca. In reality, however, this is not always the case. International students and staff are usually common in Anglophone countries and Anglophone branch campuses, but not in many other IHE settings. For many locally owned international study programmes and EMI programmes, the majority of students are local. The opportunity for these home students to communicate with peoples from various countries is slight to moderate when compared with Anglophone settings. Yet it appears that each student has his/her own lingua culture, part of which is the English language which he/she employs as a resource throughout the process of interculturality. In intercultural communication, in such settings, intercultural speakers use English as a lingua franca for communication and identification (Edmondson & House, 2003; Fiedler, 2011), and in order to co-construct 'common ground' (Kecskes, 2015), I propose that English may be used and taught not as only a lingua franca but also as a cultural franca (Sussex & Curtis, 2018).

The question now is how can we teach English as a lingua franca as well as a cultural franca and embed interculturality in our teaching? In higher education contexts in general, English language instructors teach English to non-native speakers mostly in the form of English for specific purposes (ESP) courses. These range from English for academic purposes (EAP) courses as pre-course entry requirements, remedial courses, and elective modules, to English for Occupational Purposes (EOP) courses which focus on English skills for future professions such as English for aviation, English for tourism, English for economists and English for engineers. Since a number of these courses focus on improving students' target language skills of listening, speaking, reading and writing, the assessment of learner success is very much based on fluency and accuracy within the native English paradigm. There are attempts in bringing in Global Englishes language teaching (Galloway, 2017; Galloway & Rose, 2018); however, in many non-Anglophone settings learners and teachers are not always exposed to varieties of English. Many English language teachers as well as pre-service teachers which I have worked with, for instance, have never been or studied abroad. The English that they know and learn is mostly from the media and ELT textbooks which are often American English or British English. This is considered the English understood by English language teachers and learners, regardless of their nationalities and mother tongues. Whilst it might be ideal to embrace fluidity and hybridity of language use, we can still make use of native English as 'a broadly common set of practices and values' or 'a cultural franca' (Sussex & Curtis, 2018) in our classroom teaching.

By teaching English as a 'cultural franca' I mean that we can still teach English grammar and pronunciation, following a native-speaker phonological or grammatical model. This idea of using native English as a starting point (Kuo, 2006) does not necessarily mean that we want our students to write or speak 'exactly' like a native speaker. Instead, we can view these grammatical sentence structures or sound systems as a set of rules broadly understood by English speakers, whether native or non-native. In ensuring the shared understandings, teachers must become more aware of not enforcing the lingua culture of native speakers which are not intelligible amongst teachers and students. Being aware, however, is a rather ambiguous term. Some of us who are already teaching or are practising to be English language teachers may wonder if we should exclude the use of slang and idiomatic expressions.

Despite the critique of the irrelevance of native English idioms in ELF communication (Jenkins, 2000), idiomatic expressions can be co-created by ELF users, regardless of native English speaker norms (Seidlhofer

& Widdowson, 2009). My interpretation of this phenomenon is very much related to the lingua culture of students and teachers. In other words, teachers and students use idioms, slang or other forms of formulaic language they know in social interactions, and it is through this use of language classroom participants can participate in the process of interculturality. In practice, language teachers should allow themselves and their students to use idiomatic expressions and words derived from their mother tongues or lingua cultures, provided that these can be co-constructed. By being co-constructed, I refer to the user's ability to explain the meaning of the word used, as well as the listener's ability to understand it, but not necessarily use it. For instance, before I finish my class, I sometimes say 'Shall we call it a day?' Although this expression might be viewed as a native speakers' expression, it should be allowed as long as the user/speaker provides space for negotiation during communication. In my case, after saying this expression, I provide further explanations so that my Thai, Nepali, Chinese and Fillipino students understand the meaning, but at the same time, I also allow them to ask me questions and discuss further how they will phrase this expression in a similar situation. Their intercultural experiences and 'emerging' use of ELF may result in various expressions in various situations which are not only tied to one nation (Baker, 2011, 2012, 2015). In this sense, I encourage my students to be aware of the fluidity and hybridity of intercultural communication via ELF. In English language classrooms, this similar conversation can also easily take place with teachers' facilitation. By integrating group discussions and collaborative projects, students can socially participate and negotiate in intercultural environments. At the same time, teachers will also have to act as facilitators to help resolve conflicts and misunderstandings which may occur during these tasks.

Despite the above recommendation, some English language teachers who teach in an almost monocultural classroom containing students of mostly the same nationality or mother tongue, may wonder how interculturality can be implemented. In fact, if we take the example of 'inter kids' and 'non-inter kids' we can see that nationality or mother tongue language does not always refer to the homogeneity of culture. English has been part of these kids' lingua cultures and it can contribute to the intercultural in classroom. In English language classrooms, I propose that English may be viewed as big 'E' and small 'e'. The big 'E' can refer to the phonological or grammatical model whereas the small 'e' is the actual use of English adopted by speakers with various sociocultural and historical experiences. Whilst the big 'E' is the usual focus of teaching English, the small 'e' can often be neglected. To take into account this small 'e', English language teachers can assign group tasks which allow students to be more creative with their English, instead of restricting themselves to standardised language patterns and grammatical models. Speaking tasks, for example, should allow students to bring in their own experience and not only restrict it to the native English contexts. However, talking about the UK or the US should not be a taboo, either. For some language classrooms, it might turn out that it is the teacher's responsibility to help students to develop intercultural awareness, either by providing them with comprehensible language input consisting of English from non-Anglophone as well as Anglophone resources. For example, listening tasks can contain different accents and lexical resources, which help to develop linguistic tolerance amongst ELF users. In IHE, in particular, this linguistic tolerance is an important issue, especially when students graduate from university and embark their work journey in an English-speaking environment.

Conclusion

This chapter aims to discuss interculturality through the 'intercultural' and English as a lingua franca (ELF) in IHE in Thailand and Malaysia. Initially, we have explored the concepts revolving around the intercultural in the studied contexts. Through our discussion, the intercultural appears to be the interplay amongst the multiplicity of nationality, language and identity. Today's globalised world presents the intercultural as a hybrid and fluid process in nature. Although we *may* somehow categorise cultural groups based on their nationality, it can be seen that national culture provides a restricted framework to understand interculturality.

In IHE, the English language has become a lingua franca or ELF which people from different cultures (e.g. nations, social groups) use in not only communicating but also identifying themselves from one another. Whilst being a useful resource for participants to draw on in the process of interculturality, ELF can be interpreted differently by each participant. It requires a common ground amongst participants for successful intercultural communication. In this chapter, I propose considering English as a 'cultural franca' (Sussex & Curtis, 2018) in intercultural communication. Perhaps, English is not only a lingua franca, but also a cultural franca where peoples across the world share 'something' in common. In English language teaching, ELF appears to the reality of how English is used globally in intercultural communication, yet the ELF pedagogy still appears unclear. Whilst there are attempts to shift away from the native-speaker paradigm, I propose that certain principles such as the grammatical rules and sound systems can still act as a starting point, a shared common ground in teaching or learning English. Nonetheless, as English in communication and identification can vary due to its users' lingua culture, English language teachers have a role to implement interculturality and help develop intercultural awareness so that common ground can be successfully co-created. Whilst facilitating social understanding and harmony, embracing cultural differences is what we can do to tackle realities and make them achievable.

Engagement Priorities

1. Identify what 'interculturality' is in your own context. What are the contributing factors to interculturality, e.g. nationality, language, educational background and social interests?
2. Is the English language a contributing factor to social grouping in your context?
3. How can English (or English as a lingua franca) cause cultural or intercultural misunderstandings in your context? How can you use English or teach English to resolve these issues?
4. Do you consider English as a cultural franca in your context? Why or why not?

Recommended Texts

Baker, W. (2015). *Culture and identity through English as a lingua franca: Rethinking concepts and goals in intercultural communication*. Berlin: De Gruyter Mouton.

In his book, Baker offers a postmodern view into understanding language, culture and identity in intercultural communication through the lens of English as a lingua franca or ELF. The proposed model of intercultural awareness (ICA) provides an alternative to building communicative competence in English language teaching, leading to debate and discussions in terms of teaching intercultural communication and the English language in the ELF paradigm.

Risager, K. (2007). *Language and culture pedagogy: From a national to a transnational paradigm*. Clevedon: Multilingual Matters.

Shifting away from the national-culture national-language paradigm, Risager conceptualises 'linguaculture' in the transnational paradigm, and suggests transnational language and culture pedagogy in culture and language. This historical perspective and the development of pedagogical approaches in this book stimulate its readers to explore the various contexts and contacts of language and culture in today's globalised world.

Curtis, A., & Sussex, R. (2018) (Eds). *Intercultural Communication in Asia: Education, Language and Values*. Cham: Springer.

This edited volume offers an insight into the Asian contexts of intercultural communication, part of which discusses language and culture from various perspectives including English as a lingua franca. Grounded in the studies in the book chapters, English as a cultura franca is proposed as an alternative to the widely known notion of English as a lingua franca. Further conceptualisation of the cultura franca notion presents a ground-breaking research agenda for those in related fields.

References

Agar, M. (1995). *Language shock: Understanding the culture of conversation.* William Morrow.

Aguilar, M. (2015). Engineering lecturers' views on CLIL and EMI. *International Journal of Bilingual Education and Bilingualism, 20*(6), 722–735.

Baker, W. (2011). Intercultural awareness: Modelling an understanding of cultures in intercultural communication through English as a lingua franca. *Language and Intercultural Communication, 11*(3), 197–214.

Baker, W. (2012). From cultural awareness to intercultural awareness: Culture in ELT. *ELT Journal, 66*(1), 62–70.

Baker, W. (2015). *Culture and identity through English as a lingua franca: Rethinking concepts and goals in intercultural communication.* De Gruyter Mouton.

Baker, W., & Hüttner, J. (2017). English and more: A multisite study of roles and conceptualisations of language in English medium multilingual universities from Europe to Asia. *Journal of Multilingual and Multicultural Development, 38*(6), 501–516.

British Council. (2018). *The shape of global higher education: Understanding the ASEAN Region.* Available at: https://www.britishcouncil.org/sites/default/files/h233_the_shape_of_asean_higher_education_report_final_v2_web_1.pdf. Accessed 11 Oct 2018.

Byram, M. (1997). *Teaching and assessing intercultural communicative competence.* Multilingual Matters.

Byram, M., Rybakova, B., & Starkey, H. (2002). *Developing the intercultural dimension in language teaching: A practical introduction for teachers.* Council of Europe.

D'Andrade, R. (1990). Some propositions about the relations between culture and human cognition. In J. W. Stigler, R. A. Shweder, & G. Herdt (Eds.), *Cultural psychology: Essays on comparative human development* (pp. 65–129). Cambridge University Press.

Deardorff, D. K. (2006). The identification and assessment of intercultural competence as a student outcome of internationalization at institutions of higher education in the United States. *Journal of Studies in International Education, 10,* 241–266.

Doiz, A., Lasagabaster, D., & Sierra, J. (2013). Globalisation, internationalisation, multilingualism and linguistic strains in higher education. *Studies in Higher Education, 38*(9), 1407–1421.

Duong, V. A., & Chua, C. S. (2016). English as a symbol of internationalization in higher education: A case study of Vietnam. *Higher Education Research & Development, 35*(4), 669–683.

Edmondson, W., & House, J. (2003). English in the world and English in the school. In H. Cuyckens, T. Berg, R. Dirven, & K. Panther (Eds.), *Motivation in language: Studies in Honor of Günther Raddan* (pp. 321–345). John Benjamins.

Fiedler, S. (2011). English as a lingua franca—A native- culture-free code? Language of communication vs. language of identification. *Journal of Applied Language Studies, 5*(3), 79–97.

Galloway, N. (2017). *Global Englishes and change in English language teaching: Attitudes and impact*. Routledge.

Galloway, N., Kriukow, J., & Numajiri, T. (2017). *Internationalisation, higher education and the growing demand for English: An investigation into the English Medium of Instruction (EMI) Movement in China and Japan*. British Council.

Galloway, N., & Rose, H. (2018). Incorporating global Englishes into the ELT classroom. *ELT Journal, 72*(1), 3–14.

Geertz, C. (1973). *The interpretation of cultures*. Basic Books.

Gregersen-Hermans, J. (2016). *The impact of an international university environment on students' intercultural competence development*. Unpublished Doctoral Thesis. Centre for Higher Education Internationalisation. Universita Cattolica del Sacro Cuore, Milan.

Hofstede, G. (1997). *Culture and organizations: Software and the mind*. McGraw-Hill Companies.

Holliday, A. (2011). *Intercultural communication and ideology*. Sage.

House, J. (2018). The impact of English as a global lingua franca on intercultural communication. In A. Curtis & R. Sussex (Eds.), *Intercultural communication in Asia: Education, language and values* (pp. 97–114). Springer.

Hu, G., & Lei, J. (2014). English-medium instruction in Chinese higher education: A case study. *Higher Education, 67*(5), 551–567.

Jenkins, J. (2000). *The phonology of English as an international language*. Oxford University Press.

Jenkins, J. (2005). Teaching pronunciation for English as a lingua franca: A sociopolitical perspective. In C. Gnutzmann & F. Intemann (Eds.), *The globalisation of English and the English language classroom* (pp. 145–158). Günter Narr.

Jenkins, J. (2007). *English as a lingua franca: Attitude and identity*. Oxford University Press.

Jenkins, J. (2015). Repositioning English and multilingualism in English as a lingua franca. *English in Practice, 2*(3), 49–85.

Jenkins, J. (2017). Mobility and English language policies and practices in higher education. In S. Canagarajah (Ed.), *The Routledge handbook of migration and language* (pp. 502–518). Routledge.

Jenks, C. J. (2016). Talking national identities into being in ELF interactions: An investigation of international postgraduate students in the UK. In P. Holmes & F. Dervin (Eds.), *The cultural and intercultural dimensions of English as a lingua franca* (pp. 93–113). Multilingual Matters.

Kecskes, I. (2015). Intracultural communication and intercultural communication: Are they different? *International Review of Pragmatics, 7*(2), 171–194.

Kohn, K. (2015). A pedagogical space for ELF in the English classroom. In Y. Bayyurt & S. Akcan (Eds.), *Current perspectives on pedagogy for ELF* (pp. 51–67). De Gruyter Mouton.

Kramsch, C. (1993). *Context and culture in language teaching*. Oxford University Press.

Kramsch, C. (2010). Theorizing translingual/transcultural competence. In G. Levine & A. Phipps (Eds.), *Critical and intercultural theory and language pedagogy* (pp. 15–31). Heinle.

Kramsch, C. (2011). The symbolic dimensions of the intercultural. *Language Teaching, 44*(3), 354–367.

Kuo, I. C. (2006). Addressing the issue of teaching English as a lingua franca. *ELT Journal, 60*(3), 213–221.

Meierkord, C. (2004). Syntactic variation in interactions across international Englishes. *English World-Wide, 25*(1), 109–132.

Odağ, O., Wallin, H. R., & Kedzior, K. K. (2015). Definition of intercultural competence according to undergraduate students at an international university in Germany. *Journal of Studies in International Education, 20*(2), 118–139.

Otten, M. (2003). Intercultural learning and diversity in higher education. *Journal of Studies in International Education, 7*(1), 12–26.

Prodromou, L. (2007). Bumping into creative idiomaticity. *English Today, 23*(1), 14–25.

Risager, K. (2005). Languaculture as a key concept in language and culture teaching. In B. Priesler, K. Kjaerbeck, & K. Risager (Eds.), *The consequences of mobility* (pp. 185–196). Roskile University.

Risager, K. (2007). *Language and culture pedagogy: From a national to a transnational paradigm.* Multilingual Matters.

Risager, K. (2016). Lingua francas in a world of migration. In P. Holmes & F. Dervin (Eds.), *The cultural and intercultural dimensions of English as a lingua franca* (pp. 33–49). Multilingual Matters.

Seidlhofer, B. (2001). Closing a conceptual gap: The case for a description of English as a lingua franca. *International Journal of Applied Linguistics, 11*(2), 134–158.

Seidlhofer, B., & Widdowson, H. G. (2009). Conformity and creativity in ELF and learner English. In M. Albl-Mikasa, S. Braun, & S. Kalina (Eds.), *Dimensionen der Zweitsprachenforschung* [Dimensions of second language research] (Festschrift for Kurt Kohn) (pp. 93–107). Narr Verlag.

Street, B. (1993). Culture is a verb: Anthropological aspects of language and cultural process. In D. Graddol, L. Thompson & M. Byram (Eds.), *Language and Culture* (pp. 23–43). British Association for Applied Linguistics in association with Multilingual Matters.

Sussex, R., & Curtis, A. (2018). Introduction. In A. Curtis & R. Sussex (Eds.), *Intercultural communication in Asia: Education, language and values* (pp. 1–20). Springer.

Wikan, U. (2002). *Generous betrayal: Politics of culture in the new Europe.* University of Chicago Press.

Young, T. J., & Sachdev, I. (2011). Intercultural communicative competence: Exploring English language teachers' beliefs and practices. *Language Awareness, 20*(2), 81–98.

Young, T., & Sercombe, P. (2010). Communication, discourses and interculturality. *Language and Intercultural Communication, 10*(3), 181–188.

Zhou, Y., Jindal-Snape, D., Topping, K., & Todman, J. (2008). Theoretical models of culture shock and adaptation in international students in higher education. *Studies in Higher Education, 33*(1), 63–75.

9

Moving from Cultural Ethnocentrism to Enthnorelativism Through the Affordance of English Language Learning Experience

Zia Tajeddin and Minoo Alemi

List of Abbreviations and Acronyms

CEFR   Common European Framework of Reference
DMIS   Developmental Model of Intercultural Sensitivity
EFL   English as a foreign language
EIL   English as an international language
GENE   Generalized Ethnocentrism
ICC   Intercultural communicative competence
LS   Language students
NLS   Non-language students

Z. Tajeddin (✉)
Tarbiat Modares University, Tehran, Iran

M. Alemi
Islamic Azad University, West Tehran Branch, Tehran, Iran

© The Author(s), under exclusive license to Springer Nature
Switzerland AG 2021
M. Victoria and C. Sangiamchit (eds.), *Interculturality and the English Language Classroom*, https://doi.org/10.1007/978-3-030-76757-0_9

233

Introduction

With the rise of English as an international language (EIL), the scope of language education has expanded to address the need of learners for effective communication in intercultural encounters. The exigency of intercultural competence has been reflected in the recent models of communicative competence (Alptekin, 2002; Byram, 1997; Deardorff, 2008; Kramsch, 1993; Liddicoat & Scarino, 2013) in which intercultural competence functions as a critical component of communicative language ability. L2 speakers' movement from L1 culturality to interculturality to become 'intercultural speakers' (House, 2007) requires their development in the zone of interculturality from ethnocentric stages to ethnorelative stages (M. Bennett, 1993; Bennett et al., 2003). Ethnocentrism refers to attitudes about the centrality of one's own ethnic group and embodies denial, defense, and minimisation. Ethnorelativism is linked to the tolerance of different cultural standards and customs and the ability to adapt behaviour and judgements to various interpersonal contexts. It entails progression through acceptance, adaptation and integration.

This chapter begins with the definitions and models of intercultural competence and cultural ethnocentrism. It critically outlines the main body of research on ethnocentrism and the impact of learning experience on students' ethnorelativism (e.g. Baker, 2011, 2015; Dong, 2018; Durocher, 2007; Göncz, 2018; Knutson, 2006; Porto et al., 2018). The chapter proceeds with a report on a mixed-methods study which investigated the status of ethnocentrism and ethnorelativism among Iranian university students. The purpose of the study was to explore the impact of English learning experience on developing ethnorelativism. According to the non-essentialist perspective on culture (Holliday, 2011), this experience is assumed to afford opportunities for intercultural development. The English as a foreign language (EFL) students' field of university education was English language teaching and hence they had a rich background of language learning experience and used English as a medium of classroom communication. Conversely, non-EFL students were majoring in other subjects in which L1 Persian was the medium of communication and had no continued English learning experience. The findings showed that EFL learning experience can scaffold certain, rather than all, aspects of progression in the zone of enthnocentrism to ethnorelativism. From these findings, we can conclude that ethnorelativism is a multi-layered phenomenon. Some features of ethnocentrism, such as resistance to other nations' ethnic values, may be reconstructed through language education. Nevertheless, others features, such as resistance to interaction with other ethnic groups, may persist at the ethnocentric stage. This implies that the enhancement of ethnorelativism among students, including language students, requires awareness raising and intercultural instruction of different dimensions of ethnorelativism. Students should receive intercultural input, be mediated in their noticing of intercultural differences, and reflect on them. EFL contexts like Iran are interculturally limited in the sense that intercultural contacts between language students and interlocutors with different national, religious, L1, and ethnic backgrounds within this context are rarely practiced. To compensate for this interculturally limited context, in which cultural knowledge is mainly constructed through ELT textbooks, online communication and social networking are likely to benefit students' movement to ethnorelativism. Finally, the chapter brings to light the nature of interculturality as a complex phenomenon in which movement from ethnocentrism to ethnorelativism does not progress along a constantly linear trajectory. It follows that intercultural education, including language education as a mediator for boosting openness to other cultures, should constantly address various aspects of ethnocentrism and the development of intercultural competence needed to boost inclusive transition towards ethnorelativism.

Intercultural Competence and Ethnocentrism

Intercultural competence and its aligned concepts, such as cultural sensitivity, cultural knowledge and cultural tolerance, have been defined by numerous intercultural researchers. Thomas (2003) defined intercultural competence as the ability 'to (help) shape the process of intercultural interaction in a way that avoids or contextualises misunderstandings, while creating opportunities for cooperative problem solving in a way

that is acceptable and productive for all involved' (p. 141). Schönhuth (2005, as cited in Rathje, 2007) drew on different definitions of
intercultural competence to define it as the ability 'to establish contact
in an appropriate way and to establish conditions that are acceptable for the free expression and effective exchange of all involved'
(p. 102). Bringing to light the importance of non-verbal communication, Lustig and Koester (2006) accentuated both verbal and non-verbal
aspects of intercultural competence. They described it as a composite of
knowledge, motivation and skills in verbal and non-verbal communication and appropriate and effective behaviours. An improvement in the
conceptualisation of intercultural competence was made in Hiller and
Woźniak's (2009) multi-dimensional perspective. They ascribed cognitive, emotional/attitudinal, and behavioural dimensions to intercultural
competence which are reflected in individuals' tolerance for ambiguity,
behavioural flexibility, communicative awareness, knowledge discovery,
respect for others, and empathy.

In line with these definitions, intercultural competence has been
portrayed in different models. Deardorff (2006) structured her model
based on four main components which include specific attributes, skills,
and behaviours that constitute intercultural competence. The components consist of (a) attitude, which refers to respect for other cultures,
openness needed to withhold judgement, and curiosity and discovery
entailing tolerance of ambiguity; (b) knowledge and skills, including
cultural self-awareness, deep cultural knowledge, and sociolinguistic
awareness; (c) desired internal outcome, which requires adaptability, flexibility, an ethnorelative view, and empathy; and (d) desired external
outcome, requiring 'appropriate communication and behaviour in an
intercultural situation' (Deardorff, 2006, p. 256).

Among these models, Byram's (1997) model of intercultural communicative competence (ICC) is pedagogical by nature and well applicable
in instructed language learning contexts. The model consists of five
distinct but intertwined principles: (a) attitudes, (b) knowledge, (c) skills
of discovery and interaction, and (d) skills of interpreting and relating.
The interplay of the first four principles may lead to the fifth, namely
critical cultural awareness. The first principle in Byram's ICC model

is attitudes. Byram posited that successful intercultural communication hinges on establishing and maintaining good social relationships; accordingly, attitudes of curiosity and openness are prerequisites for and outcomes of intercultural learning. Intercultural communication with members of other cultures entails both declarative and procedural knowledge, which constitutes the second principle. As to skills of discovery and interaction, namely the third principle, Byram defined them as 'the ability to recognize significant phenomena in a foreign environment and to elicit their meanings and connotations, and their relationship to other phenomena' (p. 38). Byram defined the fourth principle, which is based on the skills of interpreting and relating, as the 'ability to interpret a document or event from another culture, to explain it and relate it to documents from one's own' (p. 52). The interplay of the first four principles ideally should lead to the fifth, namely critical cultural awareness or an evaluative orientation towards the examination of difference, where learners' evaluative points of reference are explicit and where the new evaluative orientation towards difference enhances a readiness for political engagement. The ICC model foregrounds evaluative, relativising intercultural criticality ('*Savoir s'engager*') for developing intercultural competence in foreign language education. This conceptualisation abandons the notion of 'native speaker'. Rather, it aims to adopt an intercultural approach to promote the 'intercultural speaker'. In Byram's ICC model, foreign language teachers are tasked with guiding learners in acquiring intercultural competencies in attitudes, knowledge, and skills in the process of using the L2.

As the preceding conceptions indicate, intercultural competence is intertwined with the concept of ethnocentrism. As Zotzmann (2015) rightly argued, intercultural incompetency, that is being unaware of other perspectives, might easily lead to ethnocentrism and prejudice. It follows that fostering intercultural competence creates the space for reducing 'ethnocentric attitudes, such as the ability to reflect upon taken-for-granted assumptions and the willingness to acknowledge difference' (Zotzmann, 2015, p. 168), which is the aim of contemporary foreign language teaching. The study reported in this chapter was founded on M. Bennett's (1993) developmental model of intercultural sensitivity, which regards moving from ethnocentrism to ethnorelativism as the main mani-festation of this sensitivity. In this model, M. Bennett (1986, 1993) conceptualised intercultural sensitivity as a developmental phenomenon, the core of which is intercultural sensitivity to cultural differences and the capability to accommodate cultural differences. The model subsumes a continuum of six stages of intercultural sensitivity: (a) denial, (b) defense, (c) minimisation, (d) acceptance, (e) adaptation, and (f) integration. The ethnocentric stages in M. Bennett's model include denial, defense, and minimisation. With the development of intercultural sensitivity, L2 users move from ethnocentrism to ethnorelativism. The ethnorelative stages are acceptance, adaptation, and integration.

The first stage in M. Bennett's (1993) model is denial. An indi-vidual denies the existence of cultural differences. This position is mainly observed among individuals who do not have regular interactions with interlocutors from culturally diverse groups. In the second stage of ethno-centrism, namely defense, an individual notices cultural differences but is defensive against the differences as they consider them as threat-ening to their own reality and self. The third stage is minimisation, in which cultural differences are acknowledged but minimised because an individual reasons that human similarities outweigh cultural differences.

After the first three stages of ethnocentrism in M. Bennett's (1993) model, an individual may experience stages four through six, which constitute ethnorelativism. The fourth stage, acceptance, moves an indi-vidual from the zone of ethnocentrism to that of ethnorelativism. In this stage, an individual acknowledges and respects cross-cultural differences in behaviour and values but withholds evaluating them as positive or negative. In the fifth stage, adaptation, an individual is able to look at the world through different eyes, thereby improving key skills for commu-nicating with people of other cultures. The final stage in M. Bennett's model is integration. It allows an individual to value both a variety of other cultures and their own identity vis-a-vis other cultures and to inte-grate aspects of their own home cultural perspectives with those of other cultures.

M. Bennett's (1993) development model, including J. Bennett and M. Bennett's (2004a, 2004b) specification of the cognitive, affective, and behavioural realisation of each intercultural stage, is of great value for pedagogical purposes because it informs different types of culture learning activities and different approaches to teaching these for each intercultural stage in L2 classrooms. The defining assumption in the J. Bennett and M. Bennett paradigm is the need for intercultural programmes. M. Bennett (1993) strongly argued that intercultural sensitivity is not a natural developmental process but requires education in intercultural communication to change learners' behaviour and to aid them in transcending from traditional ethnocentrism to explore new relationships across cultural boundaries. Intercultural competence is not considered a naturally occurring phenomenon since people tend to be ethnocentric and prefer contact with those with whom they are culturally similar. It is only through the process of awareness and understanding of cultural differences through education and experience that people begin to view cultural differences as being positive, interesting, and desirable (Paige et al., 2002).

In this chapter, we assume that English language learners' and users' movement from ethnocentrism to ethnorelativism entails and is facilitated by the development of intercultural competence. Ethnocentrism, as a barrier to ethnorelativism, can be reduced as a result of increasing intercultural competence. Intercultural competence affords English language learners and users the ability to engage in the process of communication in a globalising society, and, in turn, to develop sensitivity to other cultures and respect cultural differences for intercultural enjoyment as a sign of ethnorelativism. Accordingly, in line with many studies on the positive relationship between intercultural competence and ethnorelativism and negative ties between ethnocentrism and intercultural competence (e.g. Chen, 2010; Wrench et al., 2006), we assume that intercultural competence functions as a necessary element for the journey to ethnorelativism. Against this backdrop and the conceptualisation that intercultural competence typically affords effective and appropriate engagement with cultural differences required for ethnorelativism, we will examine these two concepts below as two interrelated variables.

The above review of the conceptualisations of intercultural competence and ethnocentrism suggests that the development of intercultural competence plays a role in the second language learners' and users' movement from ethnocentrism to ethnorelativism. The result of this ethnorelativism journey is the promotion of 'intercultural speakers' who have more inclusive minds towards the world and become capable of intercultural citizenship (Fang & Baker, 2018; Porto et al., 2018). The phrase *intercultural speaker* was coined by Byram and Zarate (1997) and refers to someone who has developed intercultural communicative competence and who has the ability to interact with people of other languages and cultures in their own country or elsewhere (Byram, 1997). An intercultural speaker can simply be regarded as someone who has, to some extent, acquired some or all of the five *savoirs* of intercultural competence. Byram (1997) thus emphasised that an intercultural speaker has the ability to engage critically and reflectively with other L2 speakers from their own culture and those from other cultures and is able to interpret familiar and unfamiliar cultural concepts. As such, an intercultural speaker has both sufficient intercultural competence and ethnorelative orientation to be able to fulfill the functions depicted by Byram. Similarly, Kramsch (1998) characterised an intercultural speaker as an intercultural mediator or someone who is a 'broker between cultures of all kinds' (p. 30), capable of communicating or mediating across languages and presumably cultural borders, and has the 'responsibility' to remain open to 'the other' (MacDonald & O'Regan, 2007, p. 275). While the former capability is mainly dependent on intercultural competence, the latter capability and responsibility require the manifestation of ethnorelativism by an intercultural speaker. This conceptualisation of intercultural speaker by Byram and Kramsch emphasises the element of 'intercultural' rather than 'bicultural' and consequently is inclusive of ESL and EFL learners. In particular, it applies to EFL contexts which require continued intercultural instruction to create spaces for language learners to become intercultural speakers. As such, an intercultural speaker 'may or may not be bicultural but, crucially, has the skills to understand and present the values, beliefs, and behaviours of his/her own and other groups and their cultures, and the differences and similarities among them' (Wagner & Byram, 2017, p. 2).

Being an intercultural speaker requires moving from ethnocentrism to ethnorelativism although this journey may not follow a linear trajectory. Many variables are implicated in progression from ethnocentrism to ethnorelativism. Among these variables, particular attention has been paid to the impact of study abroad, multilingualism, and language learning experience on lowering the possibility of ethnocentric behaviours and perceptions towards other peoples. Below we outline studies which were devoted to the impact of language learning on ethnocentrism.

A body of research has dealt with ethnocentrism as related to language learning (e.g. Dong, 2018; Göncz, 2018; Hosseini Fatemi et al., 2016; Lett, 1976; Lu & Hsu, 2008; Putnam, 2011; Shiri, 2015). In an early study, Lett (1976) stated that the more cross-cultural understanding there is, the less ethnocentric behaviour there will be. Therefore, learning a foreign language might well result in a better and deeper understanding of cultural differences. She added that it is possible for such understanding to be transferred to the learners by their teachers and/or well-designed teaching materials. The study by Lu and Hsu (2008) demonstrated that language learners can be introduced to L2 norms and cultures through learning the L2, which might, in turn, decrease the ethnocentrism levels among them. In the same vein, Putnam (2011) showed that learners' intercultural misunderstanding and levels of ethnocentrism are dramatically affected by their knowledge of a second or foreign language. She is also of the opinion that 'language students will find their eyes and minds opened to a new world of perspective, behavior, and culture' (p. 55) provided that the connection between culture and language is acknowledged. Shiri (2015) drew on the 2007 draft of the Culture Proficiency Guidelines to survey how intercultural communicative competence (ICC) was developed and maintained among American learners of Arabic who completed their study-abroad summer language programmes in five Arab countries. The survey was also aimed at investigating those components of the programmes which fostered the development of particular components of ICC. Data indicated that the completion of daily activities aided students in developing their ICC at the intermediate level. Despite this, they also progressed into higher levels in many respects by, inter alia, identifying, comparing, and contrasting traditions, history, and politics or by participating in low-frequency social events. Interestingly, Shiri found that the students' developing levels of ICC were sustained upon their return to the United States, as evidenced by their ability to shift perspectives and their sensitivity to stereotyping. Overall, this trend of research evidenced the positive role of learning experience in the ethnorelative orientation of language learners.

The Study Method for Measuring University Students' Ethnocentrism

Successful development of intercultural competence depends on a wide range of variables, such as nature of the academic field, degree of cultural preparation, length of stay, degree of language proficiency, type of intercultural experience, and many more (Grandin & Hedderich, 2009). These may influence the outcome of individuals' intercultural competence. However, as Fantini (2009) noted, language learning experience and target language proficiency are frequently ignored or not clearly delineated in many models of intercultural competence, including M. Bennett's (1993) model. It is assumed that language learning experience may bring about awareness and understanding of cultural differences which can enable individuals, including learners, to view cultural differences as positive, interesting, and desirable (Paige et al., 2002). In many EFL contexts where the learner is not in the host cultural context and/or where the development of intercultural competence is mainly confined to the exposure inside the classroom, it is of utmost value to investigate how the six stages of moving from ethnocentrism to ethnorelativism are experienced by EFL learners. To this end, the study reported below, part of a large-scale study conducted by Tajeddin et al. (2018), set out to investigate the degree of ethnocentrism among Iranian language and non-language students at university. To this end, it addressed the following question: To what extent does second language education affect the degree of ethnocentrism and ethnorelativism among language students compared with non-language students?

The participants included 200 M.A. students or graduates who took part in this study on a voluntary basis. Half of them were majoring in the English language and the rest were from non-English-language fields of study. The two groups are henceforth referred to as language students (LS) and non-language students (NLS). They did not have any experiences of living abroad and included both male ($n = 88$) and female ($n = 112$) students. Thirty out of 200 participants filling out the questionnaire voluntarily accepted to take part in the interview phase of the study. They were provided with sufficient information regarding the purpose of the study and every participant was assured that their personal information would remain confidential.

To evaluate the language learners' ethnocentric attitudes, an adapted version of ethnocentrism scale originally designed by Neuliep and McCroskey (1997) was used. The items in Neuliep and McCroskey's Generalized Ethnocentrism (GENE) scale are designed to reflect a conceptualisation of ethnocentrism that can be experienced by anyone. In a study using the GENE scale, Neuliep and McCroskey reported that reliability for the scale, as determined by Cronbach's alpha, was .92. They also found that the GENE scale demonstrated predictive validity for a number of conceptually related constructs such as cross-cultural contact. The scale, henceforth referred to as the questionnaire, used in the current study included 15 items on a five-point Likert scale ranging from 1 (strongly disagree) to 5 (strongly agree). In addition to the GENE scale, participants were asked to provide demographic data about their age, gender, education, and experience of living abroad. The English version of the questionnaire was translated into Persian, the participants' native language, to facilitate the understanding of both groups.

To elicit more in-depth data about the level of ethnocentrism among Iranian university students, semi-structured interviews were conducted with 30 participants. The participants were interviewed individually in their native language. The interview questions were informed by the themes in the GENE scale. Each interview took 15–20 minutes. Data from the interviews were transcribed and analyzed through coding the data and extracting themes. In the next phase, to explore the stage of participants' ethnocentrism, M. Bennett's (1993) developmental model was applied. The model, as depicted in the previous section, consists of three stages of ethnocentrism and three stages of ethnorelativism. Ethnocentric stages consist of (a) denial, (b) defense, and (c) minimisation. Ethnorelative stages in this model include (d) acceptance, (e) adaptation, and (f) integration. The themes extracted from interview findings were subjected to this developmental model to investigate the participants' degree of ethnocentrism and ethnorelativism.

Effect of Language Education on Students' Ethnocentrism and Ethnorelativism

To investigate the differential effects of second language education on ethnocentrism among language students compared with non-language students, the questionnaire comprising 15 items on a five-point Likert scale was utilised. The two groups of students were compared on the means of their responses to each item and the total mean of the questionnaire. Table 9.1 presents the descriptive statistics of the two groups' ethnocentric attitudes. As the findings show, most of the students disagreed with many statements which included a sense of ethnocentrism. For instance, 70% of non-language students and 69% of language students disagreed with the statement that most cultures are backward compared with Iranian culture (Item #1). Also, 85% of the students from both groups disagreed that other cultures should try to be like Iranian culture (Item #15). As the content of the items shows, five items (Items #3, 7, 9, 13, 14) indicate an ethnorelative orientation whereas the other items measure the realisation of ethnocentrism. As we expected, language students manifested more ethnorelativism in all five items.

Ten items in the questionnaire measured the degree of ethnocentrism. The low means of these items manifest a low degree of ethnocentrism among both groups. The greatest amount of disagreement was found in Items #10 and #12. The low means (LS = 1.56; NLS = 1.58) and small agreement (LS = 3%; NLS = 3%) among both groups show that they tended to negate the statement that there is no need to cooperate with people who are different from Iranian culture (Item #10). Similarly, little acceptability was given to the statement about disliking interaction

Table 9.1 Descriptive statistics of students' performance on the ethnocentric attitudes questionnaire ($N = 200$)

	Items	Students	Means	1	2	3	4	5
1.	Most cultures are backward compared to Iranian culture	NLS	1.95	33	47	16	1	3
		LS	2.07	25	44	25	4	0
2.	Iranian culture should be the role model for other cultures	NLS	2.18	25	49	21	8	0
		LS	2.36	18	38	34	8	0
3.	People in Iranian culture could learn a lot from people in other cultures	NLS	3.22	0	3	6	55	34
		LS	2.27	1	1	3	60	35
4.	People from other cultures just do not know what is good for them	NLS	1.75	38	52	12	0	0
		LS	1.77	36	51	13	0	0
5.	People would be happier if they lived like people in Iranian culture	NLS	1.58	54	35	10	1	0
		LS	1.88	36	39	20	2	1
6.	People in Iranian culture have just about the best lifestyle of anywhere	NLS	1.71	46	43	9	1	1
		LS	1.84	34	51	8	5	0
7.	I respect the values and customs of other cultures	NLS	3.19	2	1	6	57	33
		LS	3.38	1	1	3	51	44
8.	I apply Iranian values when judging people who are different	NLS	2.48	16	42	19	21	2
		LS	2.09	19	50	16	6	1
9.	I have many friends from people of other cultures	NLS	2.39	4	18	22	40	13
		LS	2.48	5	18	14	49	14
10.	I do not cooperate with people who are different from Iranian culture	NLS	1.58	50	44	3	3	0
		LS	1.56	51	43	1	3	0

(continued)

Table 9.1 (continued)

Items		Students	Means	1	2	3	4	5
11.	I do not trust people who are from other cultures	NLS	1.66	41	52	5	1	0
		LS	1.67	42	48	9	0	0
12.	I dislike interacting with people from other cultures	NLS	1.59	52	37	7	1	1
		LS	1.54	52	45	0	3	0
13.	I change my behaviour when I interact with people from other cultures	NLS	1.83	5	39	30	19	6
		LS	2.17	5	15	44	24	10
14.	I accept the opinions of people from other cultures	NLS	2.64	2	12	26	37	22
		LS	2.99	1	2	19	53	25
15.	Other cultures should try to be like Iranian culture	NLS	1.73	45	40	12	1	1
		LS	1.71	44	41	12	0	0

with people of other cultures (Item #12). As to the other items focused on ethnocentrism, small to mid-range ethnocentrism was found among the two groups. However, contrary to our expectation, non-language students proved to be slightly less ethnocentric in five items, including Items #1, 2, 4, 5, 6.

To triangulate the findings, the participants were interviewed on their state of ethnocentrism and ethnorelativism. The findings from the interviews are described in terms of seven questions and themes related to each question. One point about the themes needs clarification. The percentage of each theme does not indicate the degree of agreement with that theme. Rather, it shows the percentage of interviewees who brought up an idea from which we extracted the theme. All extracted themes are described below.

Beliefs in the Values of Other Cultures: In question #1, the two groups were asked about their beliefs in the values of other cultures in relation to Iranian culture. Both groups referred to the following concepts:

- Respect for different cultures (LS: 80%; NLS: 53%)
- Historical background of Iranian culture (LS: 13%; NLS: 20%)

- Priority of Iranian culture (LS: 0%; NLS: 33%)
- Learning from a different culture (LS: 6%; NLS: 0%).

The highest frequency (80%) in this category refers to their belief in respecting different cultures, which was expressed by language students more than non-English students. One language student said, 'For sure I respect different cultures'. On the other hand, non-language students showed higher tendencies (33%) towards the priority of Iranian culture. As one non-language student stated, 'I respect Iranian culture more than other cultures'. The two groups' beliefs in all four areas of respect for other cultures clearly show the development of more ethnorelativism among English language students. These are in line with the findings obtained from the questionnaire.

Dependency on Home Culture as Immigrants: With regard to question #2, which elicited students' beliefs about dependency on their home culture if they migrate to another country, the following four themes emerged:

- Respect for different cultures (LS: 0%; NLS: 13%)
- Cultural conformity (LS: 26%; NLS: 33%)
- Cultural integration (LS: 40%; NLS: 33%)
- Common human identity (LS: 6%; NLS: 33%)
- Rich cultural values (LS: 6%; NLS: 0%)
- Avoidance of cultural prejudice (LS: 20%; NLS: 0%).

The highest rates highlight both groups' attitudes towards cultural conformity and integration. Cultural integration was supported, to different degrees, by language students (40%) and non-language students (33%). This excerpt from an interviewee indicates an ethnorelative tendency: 'They should integrate and adapt themselves with the culture of target countries that they immigrate'. As to cultural conformity, however, fewer language students confirmed it compared with non-English students (LS: 26%; NLS: 33%). This differential agreement with the two statements shows that language students valued ethnorelativism only on the edge of cultural integration rather than cultural conformity, which requires more detachment from home culture. Respect for different cultures was, to our surprise, absent from language students' stated beliefs while it was mentioned by 13% of non-English students. **Interaction with People of Different Cultures:** Question #3 in the interview was aimed to inquire about students' tendencies towards interaction with people of different cultures. From their responses, five relevant themes were extracted:

- Getting to know the modern world (LS: 6%; NLS: 6%)
- Necessity of worldwide communication (LS: 26%; NLS: 0%)
- Indifference to other cultures (LS: 6%; NLS: 6%)
- Willingness to learn about other cultures (LS: 60%; NLS: 20%)
- Tendency towards knowing one's own culture (LS: 6%; NLS: 13%).

Willingness to learn about other cultures (60%) and necessity of worldwide communication (26%) were found more in language students' accounts than those of non-language students. Their answers show their willingness to interact with speakers of other languages because they see it as a way for worldwide communication and a tool for learning from different cultures. By contrast, getting to know the modern world and indifference to other cultures showed the same recurrency among the students of both groups. Overall, these findings indicate that language students manifested more ethnorelative orientation in three of the five areas.

Being Neighbours with People of Different Cultures: Tendencies of students of both groups towards being neighbours and coexisting with people of different cultures were investigated in question #4. The interview responses yielded the results outlined below:

- Willingness to coexist with other cultures (LS: 80%; NLS: 73%)
- Preference of one's own culture (LS: 0%; NLS: 13%)
- Getting to know the modern world (LS: 13%; NLS: 13%)
- Learning from a different culture (LS: 6%; NLS: 0%).

The findings revealed that the majority in both groups (LS; 80%; NLS: 73%) were willing to live with people of different cultures. This strong ethnorelativism is reflected in a statement by one of the students: 'I eagerly accept to be neighbor with people of different culture and that's really interesting'. The idea of getting to know the modern world (LS; 13%; NLS: 13%) received the same attention from both groups. The last theme in this category was the tendency to learn from other cultures, which was stated by a small number of the language students (6%) and none of the non-language students.

Education in International Schools: Students' willingness to send their kids, if they had or would have any opportunity, to mixed-cultures international schools was elicited through question #5. The analysis of the data elicited through the interviews resulted in the six themes below:

- Interaction with the opposite sex (LS: 13%; NLS: 0%)
- Opportunity for international communication (LS: 26%; NLS: 0%)
- Opportunity for learning more about Iranian culture (LS: 33%; NLS: 33%)
- Priority for instructional quality (LS: 13%; NLS: 6%)
- Learning a foreign language (LS: 33%; NLS: 6%)
- Compatibility with differences (LS: 26%; NLS: 6%).

Their kids' interaction with people of the opposite sex, which is probable in international schools rather than local single-gender schools in Iran, and also opportunity for international communication were emphasised by 13% and 26% of language students, respectively, while the frequencies for non-language students were zero. Also, in line with a more ethnorelative orientation, compatibility with differences featured more in language students' statements (26%) rather than in what the other group stated (6%). To sum up, language students were more detached from ethnocentrism with regard to the acceptability of mixed-cultures international schools.

Interest in Other Cultures: Question #6 was asked to explore students' interest in knowing other cultures. The list below presents the themes extracted from both groups' interviews about this interest:

- Getting to know the modern world (LS: 13%; NLS: 66%)
- Helping enrich one's own private life (LS: 0%; NLS: 6%)
- Priority in knowing Iranian culture (LS: 6%; NLS: 6%)

- Tendency towards knowing other cultures (LS: 40%; NLS: 53%)
- Learning from a different culture (LS: 20%; NLS: 6%)
- Indifference to knowing other cultures (LS: 0%; NLS: 13%).

On this topic, the non-language students (66%) manifested far more willingness than the language students (13%) to know the modern world, to enrich their own private life (LS: 0%; NLS: 6%), to know other cultures (LS: 40%; NLS: 53%), and to be indifferent to other cultures (LS: 0%; NLS: 13%). Equal importance was attached to giving priority to knowing Iranian culture by both groups. The only theme which was observed more frequently among language students was learning from another culture (LS: 20%; NLS: 6%). Their belief in learning from another culture is evident in one student's words, '… learning more and more would be a positive aspect in this regard'. As these findings indicate, interest in knowing other cultures was largely more prevalent among non-language students.

Dependency on Iranian Culture: Responses to question #7 indicated the students' levels of dependency on Iranian culture. The analysis of their statements yielded the themes below:

- Rich cultural values (LS: 13%; NLS: 0%)
- Personal identity (LS: 6%; NLS: 6%)
- Cultural habits (LS: 40%; NLS: 13%)
- Interest in Iranian culture (LS: 13%; NLS: 46%)
- Flexibility in accepting Iranian culture (LS: 26%; NLS: 33%).

Interest in Iranian culture was found more frequently among the non-language students (46%). As one of them maintained, 'I grew up with Iranian culture so I have extreme dependency to it'. However, the theme of cultural habits, namely being used to Iranian culture, showed more recurrence among language students (40%). As one stated, 'It's inhibited in my personality and I'm highly used to it'. As these findings show, there was a varied pattern of dependence on Iranian culture, indicating that neither group was more ethnocentric in all respects.

We classified all the preceding thematic categories elicited from interviews according to M. Bennett's (1993) model, which we described early in this chapter. This model includes two orientations of ethnocentrism and ethnorelativism. Ethnocentrism is divided into three stages of denial, defense, and minimisation. In our findings, three categories revealed our participants' orientation to some degree of denial: human identity, cultural habits, and dependency on Iranian culture. The second stage of ethnocentrism is defense, whereby an individual shows resistance to cultural differences. At this stage, people experience cultural differences as more real than do people at the denial stage. At this stage, non-language students showed stronger defense against other cultures according to the five themes within the defense category. However, language students were more defensive with regard to esteeming Iranian 'rich cultural values' and 'indifference to other cultures'. Through minimisation, i.e. the third ethnocentric stage, people acknowledge cultural differences but minimise them. The beliefs held by the participants in our study show that minimisation was slightly higher among the non-language students.

Besides ethnocentrism, our study sheds light on the ethnorelative orientation of the participants, including acceptance, adaptation, and integration. Acceptance, as the first stage of ethnorelativism, indicates that people consider their own culture as one of a number of equally complex worldviews and that people with this worldview are able to experience others as different from themselves, but equally human. Learners improve a perception of their own cultural context and hence can accept the existence of various cultural contexts. As to the acceptance of other cultures, language students in our study manifested the acceptance orientation at a far more rate. Beliefs in 'learning from different cultures' and 'respect for different cultures' were more strongly held by language students. Adaptation is the second stage of ethnorelativism. In our study, adaptation was generally higher among language students, particularly in relation to 'compatibility with differences', which enables students to shift their cultural frame of reference and consciously adopt understandings of other cultural groups. The last stage of ethnorelativism is integration, which requires that people extend their ability to perceive events in an intercultural context. In our study, language students proved to be far more ethnorelative than non-language students. In particular, they expressed greater orientation for engaging in 'international communication'. Also, language students were found to be more willing to avoid cultural prejudice. As to co-existence with other cultures, both language and non-language students agreed on the need for co-existence.

Implications for Intercultural Pedagogy

The variable selected in our study was language learning experience. As the findings revealed, this experience aids in reshaping certain dimensions of ethnocentrism among language students, as compared with non-language students, but falls short of creating spaces for the inclusive and continuous moving of language students from ethnocentrism to ethnorelativism. Language students seemed to have a rather underdeveloped ethnorelative perspective with regard to very few manifestations of ethnocentrism such as their tendency to apply Iranian values when judging people who are from other cultures. However, compared with non-language students, they expressed greater tendency to get engaged in international communication. This bumpy route of success or failure in ethnorelativism indicates that the impact of learning experience should not be idealised because intercultural instruction does not receive sufficient attention in many language classes. As Baker (2015) contended, although the importance of cultural and intercultural features is recognised in language teaching, they typically remain low on the teachers' priorities list because of the pressures and constraints teachers face. This low priority may be due to a lack of the intercultural component in teacher education programmes, contributing to poor ICC uptake (Young & Sachdev, 2011). Besides the teacher variable, many textbooks, as Baker added, represent the Common European Framework of Reference (CEFR) 'native speaker' norms, expectations, and proficiency which are more aligned with the restricted understandings of communication and communicative competence. Most importantly, the development of intercultural sensitivity and hence increased ethnorelativism necessitate that higher education develop mechanisms to prepare students for intercultural encounters (Krajewski, 2011). In lack of these encounters, as suggested by Byram et al. (2002), there are surrogate activities including online social networking mediums as well as simulations and role plays to activate students' schemata and background knowledge about other countries and cultures. This kind of simulated or online experiential learning is powerful in developing ethnorelativism among students through raising their self-awareness and improving their interpretation and evaluation of other cultures.

The progression of language learners towards ethnorelativism indicates a complicated, chaotic trajectory. Although they demonstrated numerous features of ethnorelativism compared with their non-language peers, they preserved a greater tendency for some aspects of the three stages of ethnocentrism. As Krajewski (2011) posited, intercultural competence does not develop along a linear, orderly trajectory but is influenced by numerous personal and circumstantial factors. There are possible reasons for this developmentally complex picture. The first is that language proficiency is not the only factor in constructing university students' ethnocentric-ethnorelative orientation. In addition to exposure to L2 culture through a language education programme, students receive intercultural understanding and awareness in other ways like travelling abroad, watching TV programmes on English-speaking channels, and reading texts on the Internet. It follows that language-education-mediated programmes and, in turn, the development of English language proficiency provide one window, among many others, to ethnorelativism and the state of being intercultural speakers. A far more important reason may relate to the stage-model depiction of ethnocentrism proposed by M. Bennett (1993). In the model, as the name of each stage indicates, movement towards ethnorelativism from the initial ethnocentrism is implied to be linear. As the model dictates, an individual is expected to linearly progress through the three stages of ethnocentrism and afterwards the three stages of ethnorelativism. Our findings, however, clearly provide evidence against this assumed linearity. The reason is that the construct of ethnocentrism-ethnorelativism is not monolithic and unidimensional. Individuals may move from denial, that is the first stage of ethnocentrism, to minimisation, as the last stage of ethnocentrism, with regard to some aspects of the dimensions constituting each stage but not the others. The same applies to progression throughout the three stages of ethnorelativism.

This shows that an individual cannot be placed at one particular stage of ethnocentrism-ethnorelativism, as revealed by our data. While some aspects of ethnocentrism may be reshaped as a result of language education, other aspects may persist. This chaotic, complex progression can be termed 'hybrid ethnocentrism-ethnorelativism' although it may seem to be paradoxical. From these findings, we can conclude that ethnocentrism is a multi-layered phenomenon. While some features are reconstructed through language education, others may persist at the ethnocentric stage of denial, defense, or minimisation. This implies that the enhancement of ethnorelativism among students, including language students, requires awareness raising and intercultural instruction of different dimensions of ethnorelativism. Depending on the degree of affinity between L1 and L2 cultures, cultural contacts with target culture people, general attitudes towards other cultures, and degree of multiculturality of a society, the individuals' journey towards ethnorelativism is variedly shaped.

Our survey of ethnorelativism and the findings from the study reported in this chapter have numerous implications for intercultural education in language classrooms. First, language teachers should plan their teaching to include materials and tasks that develop the specific elements of intercultural competence. The specification of competencies encapsulated in Byram's (1997) notion of ICC includes (a) attitudes, (b) knowledge, (c) skills of discovery and interaction, (d) skills of interpreting and relating, and (e) critical cultural awareness. These competencies should inform classroom instruction and be translated into pedagogical activities applicable in most EFL contexts like Iran, where instructed, rather than informal and naturalistic, language learning is predominant. Second, to pave the ground for this interculturally oriented language education, language teachers need professional development through pre-service and in-service teacher education programmes to become aware that both linguistic and intercultural education are needed to make learners competent intercultural speakers. Therefore, language teachers should enhance their intercultural competence and the skills of instructing it. Third, unlike countries like Thailand, China, Japan, and Malaysia, some other EFL contexts such as Iran are characterised by poor intercultural input and limited opportunities for authentic intercultural interactions. In these contexts, teachers should plan online and social-networked activities to help learners engage in intercultural communication in the process of ethnorelativism. Fourth, as our findings indicate, moving from ethnocentrism to ethnorelativism is no linear progression. Language learners may become ethnorelative in certain aspects of the three stages proposed by M. Bennett (1986, 1993) but be persistent in other aspects of their ethnocentric orientation. This non-linear pathway to ethnorelativism implies that learners need awareness raising by their teachers to ensure that all aspects of ethnocentrism are overcome as a precondition for becoming intercultural speakers. Finally, our study shows that the experience of language learning per se falls short of improving ethnorelativism as language education may focus on purely linguistics competence. Thus, learning experience may not create spaces for the acquisition of intercultural competence when the focus on linguistic aspects impedes the development of ethnorelativism among learners. It follows that syllabus designers and teachers should develop or select teaching materials which embody texts and tasks loaded with intercultural concepts and activities.

Conclusion

In this chapter, we defined the concept of intercultural competence and outlined models of intercultural competence. In particular, we described M. Bennett's (1993) model, which is focused on moving from ethnocentrism to ethnorelativism through six stages. We then reported on a study about the degree of ethnocentrism and ethnorelativism among language and non-language university students. While language students are more resistant to progress to the ethnorelative stage in a few areas, they are likely to approximate an ethnorelative orientation in many other aspects as a result of language exposure. Three conclusions can be drawn from these findings. First, the findings revealed that progression from ethnocentrism to ethnorelativism does not progress along a constantly linear, predetermined trajectory. As such, unlike M. Bennett's assumption, intercultural learning cannot be idealised as a linear process of staged development. Second, inconclusive findings about the role of being a language or non-language student in the development of intercultural sensitivity indicate that there are other learner and socio-cultural variables that could mediate or cause tensions in fostering the development of this sensitivity. Third, intercultural learning is afforded through language learning experience. However, interpreted within a non-essentialist framework, intercultural learning is a complex process in which the role of learning experience depends on not only the opportunities for language learning but also on language use in terms of the extent of intercultural contacts, types of contacts and contact contexts, interlocutors, and intercultural topics being discussed. In our study, language learners had limited opportunities for intercultural language use and hence remained ethnocentric in some respects. In view of this, language teachers can locate those aspects of students' ethnocentric prejudices that manifest an entrenched resistance to change and engage students in different intercultural awareness-raising activities to lower their ethnocentrism. These activities include, inter alia, online intercultural exchange, artifact exploration, intercultural role plays, and cultural comparison activities.

Although this study shed light on the developmental aspect of ethnocentrism, it was limited to the university context and an EFL setting which is not regarded to be highly intercultural. Moreover, the variable implicated in the ethnorelativism of the students was their state of being language or non-language students, which relates to language exposure. However, ethnorelativism should be improved by considering other variables. Policymakers and teachers should consider how the interaction among different variables, such as language learning experience, study abroad, exposure to English-mediated satellite programmes, learner age, and learner gender, impacts ethnocentrism. These variables could be considered in isolation or in combination with each other. Aligned with this, various scales, including M. Bennett's (1993) Developmental Model of Intercultural Sensitivity (DMIS), can be used to compare ethnocentrism of learners from expanding circle countries (e.g. Iran, Egypt, and Japan) and outer circle countries (e.g. India, Bangladesh, and Malaysia). The findings from these comparisons can be beneficial for more interculturally informed teaching materials and instructional activities to help the development of ethnorelativism among language learners.

Engagement Priorities

Language learners in many EFL contexts find their use of English limited to classroom interactions and hence have little, if any, opportunity for authentic intercultural communication with users of English from other cultural backgrounds. This may function as a barrier to the acquisition of intercultural competence and, in turn, impede ethnorelativism. In view of this, what intercultural activities create authentic learning spaces for learners in EFL contexts?

The study reported in this chapter showed that some aspects of university students' ethnorelativism were impacted by the state of being English-major or non-English-major students. However, length of learning experience, i.e. being elementary learners vs. advanced learners of English, might also contribute to the reconstruction of learners' ethnocentrism. How can learning experience contribute to ethnorelativism?

Intercultural competence gained in the process of language learning can facilitate intercultural engagement and hence create better venues for English language learners' and users' approximation to ethnorelativism. Nevertheless, it seems that strong L1 identity and source culture identity could impede this shifting process. What other learner variables might be implicated in this process?

Recommended Texts

Bizumic, B. (2019). *Ethnocentrism: Integrated Perspectives*. Abingdon: Routledge.

(This book adopts a broad, multidisciplinary approach to ethnocentrism by integrating literature from disciplines such as psychology, sociology, and anthropology. It reorganises the existing literature on ethnocentrism, its origins, and its outcomes.)

Liddicoat, A. J., & Scarino, A. (2013). *Intercultural Language Teaching and Learning*. Hoboken, NJ: Wiley-Blackwell.

(This book surveys wide-ranging concepts in intercultural language teaching and learning and covers theoretical issues regarding language, culture, and communication as well as pedagogical issues such as intercultural classroom interactions, programs, and assessment.)

Wagner, M., Cardetti, F., & Byram, M. (2019). *Teaching Intercultural Citizenship Across the Curriculum: The Role of Language Education*. Alexandria, VA: American Council on the Teaching of Foreign Languages.

(This book introduces theory and practice in teaching and assessing intercultural communication and citizenship. Also, it helps gain a better understanding of how to design language curricula for intercultural citizenship.)

References

Alptekin, C. (2002). Towards intercultural communicative competence in ELT. *ELT Journal, 56*(1), 57–64.

Baker, W. (2011). From cultural awareness to intercultural awareness: Culture in ELT. *ELT Journal, 66*(1), 62–70.

Baker, W. (2015). Research into practice: Cultural and intercultural awareness. *Language Teaching, 48*(1), 130–141.

Bennett, M. (1986). A developmental approach to training for intercultural sensitivity. *International Journal of Intercultural Relations, 10,* 179–196.

Bennett, M. (1993). Towards ethnorelativism: A developmental model of intercultural sensitivity (revised). In R. M. Paige (Ed.), *Education for the intercultural experience* (pp. 21–71). Intercultural Press.

Bennett, J., Bennett, M., & Allen, W. (2003). Developing intercultural competence in the language classroom. In D. L. Lange & R. M. Paige (Eds.), *Intercultural communicative language culture at the core: Perspectives on culture in teaching (ICLT): Implications for effective teaching second language learning* (pp. 237–270). Information Age Publishing.

Bennett, J., & Bennett, M. (2004a). *Developing intercultural competence: A reader.* The Intercultural Communication Institute.

Bennett, J., & Bennett, M. (2004b). Developing intercultural sensitivity: An integrative approach to global and domestic diversity. In D. Landis, J. Bennett, & M. Bennett (Eds.), *Handbook of intercultural training* (3rd ed., pp. 147–165). Sage.

Byram, M. (1997). *Teaching and assessing intercultural communicative competence*. Multilingual Matters.

Byram, M., Gribkova, B., & Starkey, H. (2002). *Developing the intercultural dimension in language teaching: A practical introduction for teachers*. Council of Europe.

Byram, M., & Zarate, G. (1997). Defining and assessing intercultural competence: Some principles and proposals for the European context. *Language Teaching, 29*, 14–18.

Chen, G. M. (2010). The impact of intercultural sensitivity on ethnocentrism and intercultural communication apprehension. *Intercultural Communication Studies, 19*(1), 1–9.

Deardorff, D. K. (2006). Identification and assessment of intercultural competence as a student outcome of internationalization. *Journal of Studies in International Education, 10*(3), 241–266.

Deardorff, D. K. (2008). Intercultural competence: A definition, model, and implications for education abroad. In V. Savicki (Ed.), *Developing intercultural competence and transformation: Theory, research, and application in international education* (pp. 32–52). Stylus.

Dong, Y. (2018). *The impact of English language study on intercultural sensitivity, ethnocentrism, and intercultural communication apprehension among Chinese students*. Master of Arts in Communication. Paper 3. Available at https://digitalcommons.bryant.edu/macomm/3. Accessed 20 Jan 2019.

Durocher, D. O. (2007). Teaching sensitivity to cultural difference in the first-year foreign language classroom. *Foreign Language Annals, 40*(1), 143–160.

Fang, F., & Baker, W. (2018). A more inclusive mind towards the world': English language teaching and study abroad in China from intercultural citizenship and English as a lingua franca perspectives. *Language Teaching Research, 22*(5), 608–624.

Fantini, A. E. (2009). Assessing intercultural competence: Issues and tools. In D. K. Deardorff (Ed.), *The SAGE handbook of intercultural competence* (pp. 456–467). Sage.

Göncz, L. (2018). Generalised ethnocentrism among high-school students in a multicultural setting: The role of the degree of multilingualism. *Journal of Multilingual and Multicultural Development, 39*(3), 224–239.

Grandin, J. M., & Hedderich, N. (2009). Intercultural competence in engineering global competence for engineers. In D. K. Deardorff (Ed.), *The SAGE handbook of intercultural competence* (pp. 362–373). Sage.

Hiller, G. G., & Woźniak, M. (2009). Developing an intercultural competence programme at an international cross-border university. *Intercultural Education, 20*(4), 113–124.

Holliday, A. (2011). *Intercultural communication and ideology.* Sage.

Hosseini Fatemi, A., Khajavy, G. H., & Choi, C. W. (2016). Testing a model of intercultural willingness to communicate based on ethnocentrism, ambiguity tolerance and sensation seeking: The role of learning English in Iran. *Journal of Intercultural Communication Research, 45*(4), 1–15.

House, J. (2007). What is an 'intercultural speaker'? In E. Alcón Soler & M. P. Safont Jordà (Eds.), *Intercultural language use and language learning* (pp. 7–21). Springer.

Knutson, E. M. (2006). Cross-cultural awareness for second/foreign language learners. *Canadian Modern Language Review, 62*(4), 591–610.

Krajewski, S. (2011). Developing intercultural competence in multilingual and multicultural student groups. *Journal of Research in International Education, 10*(2), 137–153.

Kramsch, C. (1993). *Context and culture in language teaching.* Oxford University Press.

Kramsch, C. (1998). The privilege of the intercultural speaker. In M. Byram & M. Fleming (Eds.), *Language learning in intercultural perspective: Approaches through drama and ethnography* (pp. 16–31). Cambridge University Press.

Lett, J. A. (1976). *The relationship of foreign language study to close-mindedness and ethnocentrism among selected secondary school students.* Doctoral dissertation. Available at https://etd.ohiolink.edu/rws_etd/document/get/osu134 5748959/inline. Accessed 5 Jan 2019.

Liddicoat, A. J., & Scarino, A. (2013). *Intercultural language teaching and learning.* Wiley-Blackwell.

Lu, Y., & Hsu, C.-F. (2008). Willingness to communicate in intercultural interactions between Chinese and Americans. *Journal of Intercultural Communication Research, 37*(2), 75–88.

Lustig, M. W., & Koester, J. (2006). *Intercultural competence: Interpersonal communication across culture* (5th ed.). Pearson.

MacDonald, M. N., & O'Regan, J. P. (2007). Cultural relativism and the discourse of intercultural communication: Aporias of praxis in the intercultural public sphere. *Language and Intercultural Communication, 7*(4), 267–278.

Neuliep, J. W., & McCroskey, J. C. (1997). The development of intercultural and interethnic communication apprehension scales. *Communication Research Reports, 14*(2), 145–156.

Paige, R. M., Cohen, A. D., Kappler, B., Chi, J., & Lassegard, J. (2002). *Maximizing study abroad: A student's guide to strategies for language and culture learning and use.* University of Minnesota.

Porto, M., Houghton, S. A., & Byram, M. (2018). Guest editorial special issue: Intercultural citizenship in the (foreign) language classroom. *Language Teaching Research, 22*(5), 484–498.

Putnam, W. (2011). A sociocultural approach to ESL for adult learners. Master's thesis. Available at http://digitalcommons.usu.edu/gradreports/12. Accessed 15 Oct 2018.

Rathje, S. (2007). Intercultural competence: The status and future of a controversial concept. *Language and Intercultural Communication, 7*(4), 254–266.

Schönhuth, M. (2005). *Glossar Kultur und Entwicklung: Ein Vademecum durch den Kulturdschungel.* Trierer Materialien zur Ethnologie.

Shiri, S. (2015). Intercultural communicative competence development during and after language study abroad: Insights from Arabic. *Foreign Language Annals, 48*(4), 541–569.

Tajeddin, Z., Alemi, M., & Ghadiri, S. (2018). *Ethnocentrism among Iranian university students: The impact of English language learning.* Unpublished manuscript, Islamic Azad University, West Tehran Branch, Tehran, Iran.

Thomas, A. (2003). Interkulturelle Kompetenz: Grundlagen, Probleme und Konzepte. *Erwa¨gen, Wissen, Ethik, 14*(1), 137–221.

Wagner, M., & Byram, M. (2017). Intercultural citizenship. In Y. Y. Kim (Ed.), *The international encyclopedia of intercultural communication.* Wiley. Available at https://doi.org/10.1002/9781118783665.ieicc0043. Accessed 20 Dec 2019.

Wrench, J. S., Corrigan, M. W., McCroskey, J. C., & Punyanunt-Carter, N. M. (2006). Religious fundamentalism and intercultural communication: The relationships among ethnocentrism, intercultural communication apprehension, religious fundamentalism, homonegativity, and tolerance for religious disagreements. *Journal of Intercultural Communication Research, 35*(1), 23–44.

Young, T. J., & Sachdev, I. (2011). Intercultural communicative competence: Exploring English language teachers' beliefs and practices. *Language Awareness, 20*(2), 81–98.

Zotzmann, K. (2015). The impossibility of defining and measuring inter-cultural competencies. In D. J. Rivers (Ed.), *Resistance to the known* (pp. 168–191). Palgrave Macmillan.

10

Using 'Interculturality' to Increase the Value of ELT in Academic Contexts

Nick Pilcher and Kendall Richards

Introduction

In this chapter we argue three interconnected points in relation to how the practice and approach to ELT in Academic Contexts can be seen as analogous to a culture, and how interculturality can play a role in how this culture can adapt and modify its approach. These points are made with the goal of increasing the value of ELT as it is used in Academic contexts to help students with their subject degree assignments, and are as follows. One: the ELT branch of EAP that many students follow is communicated by teachers through a practice and approach (culture) that is grounded exclusively in written text analysis and production techniques such as Systemic Functional Linguistics, Genre Analysis and

N. Pilcher (✉) · K. Richards
Edinburgh Napier University, Edinburgh, UK
e-mail: N.Pilcher@napier.ac.uk

K. Richards
e-mail: K.Richards@napier.ac.uk

© The Author(s), under exclusive license to Springer Nature
Switzerland AG 2021
M. Victoria and C. Sangiamchit (eds.), *Interculturality and the English Language Classroom*, https://doi.org/10.1007/978-3-030-76757-0_10

Corpus Linguistics. Two: the subject degrees that students follow are often approached through a practice and process (culture) that involves the communication (and understanding) of academic messages through media that require knowledge and usage of other non-text based media such as visual or mathematical language. Three: using 'interculturality', and in particular, Deardorff's pyramid model of intercultural competence, EAP teachers can learn from lecturers and students when the different approaches are needed by students. We now argue these points in three sections here, drawing on theory and data from previous projects (Richards & Pilcher, 2013, 2014, 2016, 2018, 2019, 2020a, 2020b; In Press; Pilcher & Richards, 2014, 2016, 2017, 2018; Tseng et al., 2018, 2020) were pertinent.

One: Current ELT Approaches to EAP Are Grounded in Key Linguistics Theories

As outlined above, the first point we argue is that the ELT branch of EAP that many students are taught in when they study on pre-sessional or in-sessional preparation and support courses is approached through a process (culture) grounded exclusively in written text analysis and production techniques such as Systemic Functional Linguistics, Genre Analysis and Corpus Linguistics. Before making this point it is perhaps necessary to answer a question that previous reviewers of this chapter have rightly intimated, and thus that many readers may ask. This question is: Surely EAP is an inanimate object, whereas culture is animate, and so how is it possible to see the ELT branch of EAP as being a culture? While it would be perhaps a get out of jail free card approach to argue in line with Jahoda (2012) that culture has many definitions and can be seen as many things, we nevertheless argue that EAP and the approach to it is a cultural one. Those teachers who deliver EAP are invariably from a background of ELT and then do further training, often in Applied Linguistics, where they learn many techniques of text analysis such as those based in the Systemic Functional Linguistics (Halliday et al., 2014) school, the Genre Analysis school (Swales, 1990) and in processes ostensibly identifying key lexis that students need that will be grounded in Corpus Linguistics (McEnery & Hardie, 2012). This, then, informs key pedagogical processes for teachers such as: how they approach analysing written assignments, points made by lecturers, and also how they approach teaching students how to produce their assignments.

The evidence for this comes from the fact that many teacher development materials (e.g. Alexander et al., 2008; Swales & Feak, 2004) are grounded in how such linguistics theories help and are applied to written texts, and in turn how these then can be taught to students to help them produce assignments themselves. These in turn cascade to key textbooks such as Access EAP, Robert Jordan's Academic Writing (2003) and Swales and Feak's Academic Writing for Graduate Students (2004). This then is both the key components of the subject, but also the basis on which the subject is approached by teachers. We authors, as practising EAP teachers ourselves, were schooled in such techniques and worked with others who also followed such techniques, and attended many events such as those of BALEAP (the British Association of Lecturers in English for Academic Purposes) where such techniques were used and continue to be used, in research and pedagogy. The approach, and the culture of the approach as defined by its key processes and their components was therefore one whereby the techniques studied, the techniques applied and the techniques used to inform materials were those of written textual analysis, on the (not necessarily false) assumption that this is what students studying in Further or Higher Education need if they come from a background where English is not their first language.

We argue this is a 'culture' as such from a number of possible views and perspectives. If we are to view culture as a reified and solid entity defined by national boundaries, in line with how those such as Hofstede (1984); Trompenaars and Hampden Turner (2011), Minkov (2012) and many others have been said to see culture (by, for example Holliday, 2019), then EAP would only be seen as a culture if similar types of reified elements are considered. However, if in contrast, EAP is seen as continually emerging from the ground up from a non-essentialist small culture perspective (cf. Holliday, 2019) then arguably, approaches to how EAP is taught are indeed, we argue, a culture. Analogously, the culture and practice of how EAP is approached is structured through what Giddens

(1984) terms the 'duality of structure' whereby practices exist and are determined both by the parameters and key aspects which define them; and also by the behaviours and actions of individuals who follow these parameters and key aspects. In other words, the culture of how EAP is approached is, we argue, defined by its grounding in the theories of Systemic Functional Linguistics, Genre Analysis and Corpus Linguistics and by EAP tutors being trained in these key aspects and following them in practice. This culture is very much grounded in the written text, in an approach that has deeply entrenched roots back to the very father of linguistics, Ferdinand De Saussure, for whom language was concrete and could be taken away for analysis and teaching (1959).

And what then of this culture? Is it bad? Is it unhelpful? After all, most assignments students need to produce use written text and students' degrees are awarded on these. Furthermore, much of the input that students on degrees study is in the form of written text. Surely it is the case that EAP can approach these tasks through the use of tools teachers are schooled in that is helpful to the students and that they can convey to the students. To reiterate what many of the texts such as Jordan and Swales and Feak do and in terms of the linguistics techniques they draw upon, students can be taught how to analyse readings and example assignments themselves. In this way they can be shown how to be aware of numerous highly useful text-related aspects such as: the vocabulary that is used most frequently in academic writing (McCarthy & O'Dell, 2016—Corpus Linguistics), how to express key functions such as 'cause and effect' or 'problem and solution' (Jordan, 2003—Systemic Functional Linguistics) to study the purposes of particular sentences and to create research gaps (Swales & Feak, 2004—Genre analysis) and approach analysing texts for reproduction.

And, indeed, we do to a large extent agree. We entirely agree such aspects can be useful, and that this approach, or as we describe it, this culture of the key tenets and approaches to teaching EAP has its merits. First and foremost we see it as having merits for those delivering the subject in that it can quickly allow the person who is teaching the EAP subject to quickly see the function of a particular sentence or paragraph, and the sorts of terms used. Further, we agree that in many cases this is also helpful to students to know. In fact, we ourselves draw on and use these techniques and also teach students about them. Nevertheless, what we have also discovered in studies we have undertaken,[1] some of which we cite from below by way of illustration, is that students often require more than simply having such techniques at their disposal, and that they need to be proficient in literacies that are non-text and visual based, emotionally based, or consist of communicating in mathematics. In other words, we have learned that the approaches and aspects of EAP that we ourselves have been schooled in and use can be made far more effective and helpful if put alongside the approaches and aspects that students in different subjects may need that are not text based, and it is this we wish to communicate in the remainder of the chapter. In the next section we want to show students often require these other media of communication in their subjects, and then finally to suggest how the lens of interculturality, and in particular Darla Deardorff's (2006, 2009) pyramid of intercultural competence, despite recognising critiques of its neo-essentialist pitfalls (Ferri, 2014, 2016), can be drawn upon by EAP teachers to help focus and tailor what they do for students.

Two: Students Often Require Media That Necessitate Knowledge and Usage of Non-Text Based Visual or Mathematical Language

The second point we now want to argue, following on from the first one above, is that students study subjects that are often approached through a process (culture) that involves the communication (and understanding) of academic messages through media that are visual, emotional or mathematical. Indeed, this is what we now do ourselves more, and explain to students that what they are required to do for their subjects may

---

[1] We do not go into detail here about the methodology we have used for these studies. We note however that the methodologies have been broadly qualitative, commonly consisting of interviews or focus groups, and that all details of the methodologies can be found in the studies cited through their full journal or chapter references in the end of text reference list.

be unique to those subjects; and that text analysis can guide with some elements, but they also need to be focused on others as wel.

Similarly, as with the above section however, we feel a need to justify why we see these approaches to subjects as being cultural. What is it, in other words, that would make the subject of engineering describable as a culture, or of nursing, design, history, any other subject, of being a culture? Much work has been done into how entities establish themselves as subjects. This has been written about in terms of different subjects as distinct entities having their own tribes and territories (Becher, 1989) and by us as them having their own unique psychological and ideological elements (Pilcher & Richards, 2016, 2017; Richards & Pilcher, 2014, 2016, 2018, 2020b). More recently, Legitimation Code Theory is also emerging as a way to see subjects as having their own semantic depths (Maton, 2014) whereby they appropriate and express terms in a particular way. In terms of how they become established, subjects have been described as needing to define their own territories as being distinct from others, to establish themselves through academic journals and texts and research and to become cemented through inclusion in examination systems (Goodson, 1993).

Thus, subjects do not simply appear and exist, but they emerge and establish key aspects and tenets that define them. They then continue to develop and change, partly again through a process of structuration whereby their aspects exist for those coming to the subject, but as people follow these aspects they are reinforced (Giddens, 1984). In this way, we argue, firstly, they can indeed be seen as cultures (which also emerge, have their own aspects and tenets and change), but, secondly, and we note this for what comes later, this is also identical to how EAP has emerged.

What then, are the other media of communication that students' need that may not be text based? Firstly, many students study subjects that are taught and are assessed through media that are non-written text based and often do not need any accurate writing to be successful. Rather, the visual aspects are key and what students are assessed on, to the extent that for Computing, students could submit in Mandarin as 'we don't care what the actual [verbal or written lexica] language… is, we want to know the visual communication' (Interactive Media Design [Computing] Lecturer, cited in Pilcher & Richards, 2016, p. 7). As another lecturer in Design itself said 'the students can prepare boards with their design work which may be fantastic.... full of spelling mistakes... grammar mistakes... doesn't make sense at all you know... but designers are not terribly concerned with that' (cited in Pilcher & Richards, 2016, p. 7).

Further, the idea of an emotional literacy is key to the approaches and cultures of some subjects, for example in Nursing, as one lecturer we spoke to noted, 'we very much aim to...teach compassion as part of our curriculum, that's actually a code of core element of the curriculum and increasingly so across all of nursing' (Nursing Lecturer cited in Richards & Pilcher, 2018, p. 8). Often, this emotional type literacy would require a knowledge of active listening, and the skilful use of compassionate non-verbal communication, to the extent where English was not so important. As one Learning Disability Nursing lecturer we have spoken to noted in relation to people they were working with as Learning Disability nurses: 'for some of our people...even the English itself probably isn't that important. The tone and the empathy and the warmth you could probably almost speak gobbledygook and it wouldn't matter as long as a tone is engaging you are still communicating something' (Learning Disability lecturer cited in Richards & Pilcher, 2018, p. 9).

At this point, we expect many readers may be asking the question, or that the question will at least be springing to mind, along the lines of the following: this is all very good and well, but isn't it rather obvious that these subjects would need these things? Moreover, surely these are elements that the students would learn on their subject degrees, not the responsibility or area of the EAP tutor? And, indeed, in answer we do not disagree, we ourselves are the first to admit we are not experts in Design or Nursing or many of the subjects the students we are working with study. However, we note two key points of relevance here: firstly that the written 'English' is not cleavable from the other media but rather it is melded with them, and secondly, it is not necessary to have subject proficiency, but rather, it is helpful to have an awareness and curiosity about other subjects.

In terms of the first point that the written 'English' works with other media of communication, it is perhaps key to note, and something that is alluded to above, is that in these subjects the two ideas of 'English' and the 'Subject' are not necessarily discrete. As the Designers note, the focus can be on the visual to the expense of grammatical accuracy, and for Nurses the communication can be focused on the emotional to the extent whereby any 'English' uttered may as well be 'gobbledygook'. Significantly, we also note that many lecturers we have spoken to talk about how the 'English' operates not so much alongside and separate to the other media of communication in a subject, but rather, is merged and connected with it. For example, one lecturer in Computing we spoke to commented on how students would need to 'wrap' around local vocabulary with the subject, as follows: 'you're talking about the theory of databases… about set theory… statistics and physics of games and so on now that is mathematical and that is something students would have to be familiar with to be able to… to wrap the local vocabulary around it' (Computing lecturer, cited in Richards & Pilcher, 2016, p. A135). Similarly, an Accounting lecturer commented on how words were important in their subject but that for the students the mathematics was also extremely integral to the words used in that they could 'tie' their words into it, as follows: 'not every question's numerical… we aren't totally numeric driven… it probably only makes up 25% maybe… obviously the numbers can help the students… they can actually, sort of, then, sort of, tie their words into it' (Accounting lecturer, cited in Richards & Pilcher, 2016, p. A135). Thus, different subjects require their students to communicate using media that are not text based, but also require them to 'wrap' around and 'tie' in the text they know with these other media (Pilcher & Richards, 2016; Richards & Pilcher, 2016, 2018).

In relation to the second point of awareness and curiosity, we argue that although it is not in any way essential (nor should it be) to be aware of all the complexities and subtleties of the subjects students will go on to study, but that what is important is an awareness and curiosity in relation to these different elements. In the same way, having this awareness and curiosity is akin to having an awareness and curiosity in relation to any culture, and akin to being aware that the approach taken in one particular culture (EAP) may be relative to that culture, and that learning about other cultures (other subjects) can help both with understanding and with communication. It is here that we argue interculturality can help, and now turn to our third point outlined above.

Three: Using 'Interculturality', and in Particular, Deardorff's Pyramid Model of Intercultural Competence, EAP Teachers Can Learn from Lecturers and Students When the Different Approaches Are Needed by Students

Interculturality is possessed of emerging and dynamic qualities and of the ability to change and adapt, and, critically, to illustrate how practices and communications are continually evolving, changing and emerging. Interculturality has qualities of being a 'dynamic process' (Young & Sercombe, 2010, p. 181), of being an 'emerging paradigm' (Zhu, 2015, p. 10) and of representing a 'way of being in the world' (Lavanchy et al., 2011, p. 12). As such, interculturality helps people understand and operate in continually changing and evolving worlds, yet at the same time it retains a sense of purpose and original identity. In terms of how interculturality is approached, or done, it has been considered to be 'transcending barriers of communication based on different ways of seeing, feeling, and understanding the world' (Parry, 2003, p. 101), and to address 'encounters between multifaceted individuals' (Lavanchy et al., 2011, p. 12). Notably, in interactions in interculturality, individuals can draw on a wide range of identities that they possess, and not 'all the identities' may be 'salient or relevant in the same way at a given point in an interaction' (Zhu, 2015, p.10). Importantly, in such interactions, individuals may 'draw on and use the resources and processes of cultures with which they are familiar but also those they may not typically be associated with in their interactions with others' (Young & Sercombe, 2010, p. 181).

We argue that by following these principles of interculturality, and seeing EAP as being a 'dynamic process', as an 'emerging paradigm' and of representing a way of being in the world', then individuals working in EAP will see it as simply one culture of approaching the communication of academic knowledge. Further, if teachers approach EAP in the way that interculturality suggests, as 'transcending barriers' of communication occurring between 'multifaceted' individuals possessing different identities, then they can learn about other media of communication needed in subjects and see when and where students need to know about written text analysis, and where they need to prioritise other aspects.

As a possible focus and exemplar for how this interculturality could be framed, we draw on Deardorff's (2006, 2009) pyramid model of intercultural competence (cited in Fig.\10.1) to outline an approach we believe can help EAP students with their subjects through drawing on its own approaches and resources and also to find out about others. We highlight any key terms from the model in bold font for prominence. Deardorff's model of intercultural competence is based on the foundations of the three key tenets: **respect** for other cultures; **openness** to learning from them; and **curiosity and discovery**. This then allows an individual to build **cultural self-awareness**, a **deep understanding** of what the culture consists of, and to gather **culture specific information** through using the skills of **listening, observing, interpreting** and to **analyse, evaluate** and **relate** these to what is key. In turn, for the next stage this leads to a **desired internal outcome** of **adaptability** to **different styles and behaviours**, of being **flexible to understanding different** cognitive elements and their role, and of having **empathy** for other cultures, and then at the top of the pyramid this all leads to the **desired external outcome** of **behaving and communicating effectively and appropriately to achieve one's goals**.

Deardorff's work has been critiqued (along with other similar competency based models) as erroneously assuming that the idea of 'competence' can be accurately and objectively interpreted by an individual using it (see Ferri, 2014, 2016). As such it has been rightly critiqued as being somewhat neo-essentialist in its underpinning foundations, and, as suggested by Ferri (2014), as holding the danger of creating and establishing a divide between 'self' and 'other'. Analogously, the idea of there being a third space has been rightly critiqued by Holliday (2019) as being essentialist in nature given its assumption of there being a 'first' and a 'second' space. As a way out of this impasse, Ferri (2016, pp. 98–99) suggests that, rather than assuming an objective understanding of what

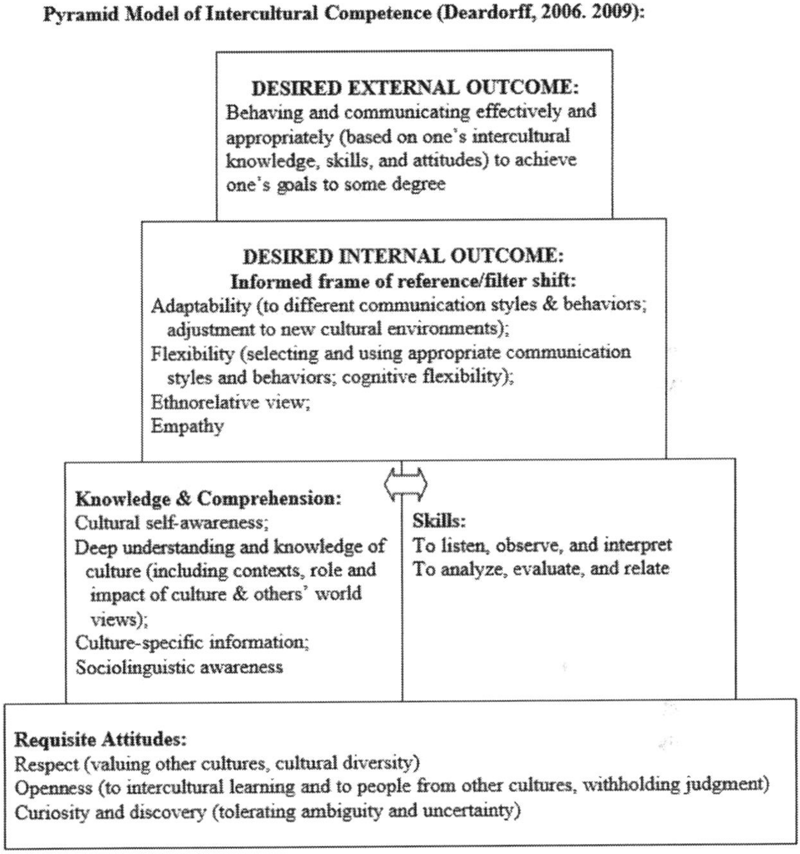

Pyramid Model of Intercultural Competence (Deardorff, 2006. 2009):

DESIRED EXTERNAL OUTCOME:
Behaving and communicating effectively and appropriately (based on one's intercultural knowledge, skills, and attitudes) to achieve one's goals to some degree

DESIRED INTERNAL OUTCOME:
Informed frame of reference/filter shift:
Adaptability (to different communication styles & behaviors; adjustment to new cultural environments);
Flexibility (selecting and using appropriate communication styles and behaviors; cognitive flexibility);
Ethnorelative view;
Empathy

Knowledge & Comprehension:
Cultural self-awareness;
Deep understanding and knowledge of culture (including contexts, role and impact of culture & others' world views);
Culture-specific information;
Sociolinguistic awareness

Skills:
To listen, observe, and interpret
To analyze, evaluate, and relate

Requisite Attitudes:
Respect (valuing other cultures, cultural diversity)
Openness (to intercultural learning and to people from other cultures, withholding judgment)
Curiosity and discovery (tolerating ambiguity and uncertainty)

Fig. 10.1 Deardorff's model of intercultural competence (*Source* Deardorff, 2006, 2009)

'competence' is, intercultural communication be approached more with a 'deferred understanding' which involves a 'dialogic, ethical and open-ended understanding of communication'. We agree entirely with these critiques, but at the same time argue that Deardorff's pyramid model allows for a reflection and focus of a way to create dialogue between EAP approaches and other subject approaches, rather in the way that students can oscillate between essentialist and non-essentialist understandings of what culture is (cf. Zhou & Pilcher, 2018). In other words, while recognising the valid critiques of Deardorff's model, we argue it can still be used as a reflective base for dialogue to allow for participants to 'co-construct meaning' (Ferri, 2016, p. 99).

We envision individuals approaching EAP in a way whereby they operate interculturally to respect and value other cultures and cultural diversity, and work together to co-construct meaning (Ferri, 2016). Here, individuals working in EAP can help explain to students in their classes about the underlying approaches and key elements of the different subject areas and also of EAP itself. Teachers can explain that EAP itself has its own approach and key elements of helping students with written communication. However, in addition, and to show **Respect** and value other subject cultures, individuals teaching EAP can also explain that other subjects can consist of other communicative media for their academic messages (for example, the visual and philosophical for Design, the emotional and empathetic for Nursing and the mathematical for Accounting), and that these subjects will be underpinned by these elements, and that, crucially, the approaches taught in EAP may be useful at some times, and in particular ways (for example in ensuring written accuracy in visually designed written text in Design) but perhaps not appropriate at others (for example by prioritising grammar over empathy in Nursing). This in turn would be showing **Openness** to intercultural learning and the elements of other subject cultures. At the same time it would be withholding judgement on which elements were most appropriate for the different subjects and for students studying them. Finally, the whole aim of EAP would be one of **Curiosity** and **Discovery**, to find out more about other subjects and their cultures and underlying elements. Here, EAP specialists could focus on asking lecturers what was appropriate in their subjects. So, for example, rather than assume that a 'report' may consist of particular written text alphabet conventions, EAP specialists could investigate more about the purpose and function of a report in a particular subject area (cf. Richards & Pilcher, 2019; In Press). They may then see that in Design it will consist of visual elements, and that in Nursing it will be informed by cultural elements of emotion and empathy. Further, that its structure and length and purpose may well differ, as will the nature of sources it might require, or whether it would use the active or the passive.

This would be where those teaching EAP would be moving up to the next stage of Deardorff's pyramid, in that they would be acquiring more **knowledge** and **self-awareness** of how it is necessary to **listen, observe** and then **interpret** according to the different approaches in the subjects their students are studying. In a class it is possible that this may be one subject or a mixture and variety of subjects. The key thing we argue is that those teaching EAP would then be acquiring **socio-linguistic awareness** of each subject, for example, to see what different words and assessment formats meant and signified in how they are approached by different subjects. As noted above, we do not by any means envision here that those teaching EAP will (or should) become subject specialists. Rather, we envision that those teaching EAP continually increase their knowledge and comprehension of the approaches of other subjects through using their skills and through adopting and following an approach grounded in **Respect** for how other subjects approach their assessments, **Openness** to learning from them and **Curiosity** to find out more about them. It is in this approach to interculturality that we argue those teaching EAP can best help students following other subjects convey academic messages.

Moving then on to the next stage up of the pyramid, we see as being achieved through those teaching EAP achieving a **desired internal outcome** of becoming much greater in **adaptability** and seeing **the different communication styles and approaches** of other subjects and of **adjusting** to new environments of the different subjects. Those teaching EAP will in this way become more **ethnorelative**, focusing on the different approaches of other subjects rather than simply on the value of their own approaches. For example, rather than assuming immediately that written alphabet textual level tools and approaches will be helpful to all subjects, those teaching EAP specialists will instead be more open and aware of other approaches and media of communication, and be able to look upon and select from their own tools to help other students in their subjects, making some salient, and others less so. For example, those teaching EAP could prioritise the emotional element when helping students studying Nursing with written text, and prioritise how mathematical arguments can be helped with accompanying written text that ties around it in Accounting.

Ultimately, and looking at the final stage of the pyramid, we then see this as having the **desired external outcome** that those teaching EAP will behave and communicate effectively in order **to achieve their goals to some degree** of helping students in other subjects. In practical terms, we see those teaching EAP specialists as having expertise with the written text and an awareness that particular paragraphs will need to convey certain key points. Here, we see EAP specialists as looking towards the written text and asking questions such as 'How does this paragraph link to the question asked?' 'Is the paragraph clearly introduced?' 'Is it necessary to have visual elements to supplement the written text here?' 'Does it meet the empathy required to focus on person-centred care?' Here we cannot say for sure what such questions would be as we do not have to hand the specific context of the work those teaching EAP are helping students with, nor have knowledge of the subjects those students are following. However, what we do underline is that instead of trying to teach students that a 'report' should be framed in a particular way according to EAP texts and linguistic cultural approaches and elements, those teaching EAP could understand and appreciate that other subjects may have approaches that prioritise other aspects. As we outline above, for Design they are visual and philosophical, for Nursing they are emotional and empathetic and for Engineering they are mathematical and materials related. For other subjects they may be different. The key element is for those teaching EAP to operate by continually developing and adapting, asking lecturers about their subjects, and to sometimes make particular elements salient and to not impose others that may not be appropriate. As one lecturer we spoke to said, 'I'm teaching students a lot of stuff. Some of that they can acquire but you know what? They really, really need to know their subject' (Computing Lecturer, cited in Richards & Pilcher, 2019, p. 12; cf, Richards & Pilcher, 2020b). Thus, rather than assume its own approach is the one students need, it is to focus more on the approaches of other subjects and then see how students can be helped. In other words, rather than say to students that the EAP research shows a 'report' should be written in this particular way and that this is what they should themselves do, they could frame the presentation along the lines of, 'this is the way a report is written according to how EAP studies have found, but is it your experience of how a report in your subject is written?' or 'this is the way a report is written according to EAP studies, but maybe you could ask your lecturer if this is the case?' Furthermore, rather than trying to get students to follow specific patterns of genre analysis and linguistics in explaining to students what 'moves' (e.g. Swales & Feak, 2004) texts follow, it may be better to focus on whether the points students have made are clear and to the point and whether they are underpinned by the key elements of the subject culture.

Conclusion

In the above we argued three interconnected points in relation to how the practice and approach to ELT in Academic Contexts, i.e. EAP, can be seen as analogous to a culture. In turn, we outlined how we see interculturality as playing a role in how those teaching EAP can adapt and modify their approaches to be more encompassing of the different media (text, emotional literacy, mathematics) students need to communicate in their academic subjects. These points were made with the goal of increasing the value of how teachers deliver ELT as it is used in Academic contexts to help students with their subject degree assignments. Firstly, we argued that the ELT branch of EAP that many students follow is communicated by teachers through a practice and approach (culture) that is grounded exclusively in written text analysis and production techniques such as Systemic Functional Linguistics, Genre Analysis and Corpus Linguistics. We outlined how many of the key texts teachers are told how to approach EAP with students are grounded in these techniques (e.g. Alexander et al., 2008) and also how the many texts students are taught EAP from are grounded in such techniques (e.g. Jordan, 2003; Swales & Feak, 2004). Secondly we showed how the subject degrees that students follow are often approached through practices and processes (culture) that involve the communication (and understanding) of academic messages through media requiring knowledge and usage of other non-text based media such as visual or mathematical language. Here we gave a few examples from studies we have undertaken to show how some subjects value visual communication, others value emotional and others mathematical. We also showed how these subjects approached communication both by marrying these elements together with the English they used and also prioritised these elements over 'English' as such. Thirdly, while acknowledging the valid critiques of its approach (Ferri, 2014, 2016), we suggested the value of using 'interculturality', and in particular, Deardorff's (2006, 2009) pyramid model of intercultural competence, in order to help EAP teachers learn from different subject lecturers and students when other approaches are needed by students. Our own journey of discovery over more than a combined total of 60 years of teaching and of 40 years of teaching EAP has brought us to a place where we both draw on and choose from the written text based techniques and approaches we were originally schooled in as being 'the' approach to help students prepare for and produce their assignments, and also study and learn about the other approaches required along with or in priority over these techniques and approaches. It has been our aim in this chapter to suggest how others can draw on interculturality, and use Deardorff's pyramid as an exemplar, to modify and adapt their approach to teaching EAP and become more open and curious of the approaches to other subjects. Ultimately this has been done with the aim of suggesting ways for how those teachers who teach EAP can do so in a way that we consider to be more responsive to and considerate of the approaches to communicating the academic messages that students need to succeed in their subject degrees.

Recommended Texts

- Deardorff, D. K. (Ed.). (2009). *The SAGE Handbook of Intercultural Competence.* Thousand Oaks, CA: Sage Publications. This text is worth reading for its overview and introduction to intercultural competence and for its use of the pyramid model used here we hope readers can use to frame approaches.
- Richards, K., & Pilcher, N. (2020). Using Physical Objects as a Portal to Reveal Academic Subject Identity and Thought. *The Qualitative Report, 25*(1), 127–144. ISSN 1052—0147. This text is worth

reading to illustrate how we have used physical objects to understand how different subjects approach description and critique. We feel others can benefit doing similar with students and lecturers in order to understand the different approaches and 'cultures' adopted.

- Morris, P. (Ed). *The Bakhtin Reader. Selected Writings of Bakhtin, Medvedev, Voloshinov.* Edward Arnold. London, UK, pp. 160–173. This text is a very useful introduction to different ways of thinking about EAP and ELT we feel will help readers through its conceptualisations and approaches to language and dialogue.

Engagement Priorities

- Engage with learners on their courses about the role of different text types in their subject areas. Ask them questions such as 'How does mathematical language play a role in your subject?' 'What is the role of visual communication in your subject?' 'What are the key elements required for successful students in your subject?'
- Engage with learners to ask them if they can send you assessment tasks they are expected to do. Consider these in the light of how different approaches to teaching and prioritising key elements in the subject work.
- Engage with lecturers on the students' courses about the key features of assessment tasks. Ask them questions such as 'How should students organise the report?' 'What types of references and materials do students need to refer to?' 'How can students best structure an answer for their assessment?'
- Engage with your management if possible to ask them to build in time for you to go to students' lectures.

References

Alexander, O., Argent, S., & Spencer, J. (2008). *EAP essentials: A teacher's guide to principles and practice.* Garnet.

Becher, T. (1989). *Academic tribes and territories.* Open University Press.

De Saussure, F. (1959). *Course in general linguistics.* Philosophical Library.

Deardorff, D. K. (2006). Identification and assessment of intercultural competence as student outcome of internationalization. *Journal of Studies in Intercultural Education, 10,* 241–266. https://doi.org/10.1177/102831530 6287002.

Deardorff, D. K. (Ed.). (2009). *The SAGE handbook of intercultural competence.* Sage.

Ferri, G. (2014). Ethical communication and intercultural responsibility: A philosophical perspec-tive. *Language and Intercultural Communication, 14*(1), 7–23. https://doi.org/10.1080/14708477.2013.866121.

Ferri, G. (2016). Intercultural competence and the promise of understanding. In F. Dervin & Z. Gross (Eds.), *Intercultural competence in education: Alternative approaches to different times* (pp. 97–120). Palgrave Macmillan.

Giddens, A. (1984). *The constitution of society: Outline of the theory of structuration.* Polity Press.

Goodson, I. (1993). *School subjects and curriculum change.* Falmer Press.

Halliday, M. A. K., Matthiessen, C., & Halliday, M. (2014). *An introduction to functional grammar.* Routledge.

Hofstede, G. (1984). *Culture's consequences: International differences in work-related values* (Vol. 5). Sage.

Holliday, A. (2019). *Understanding intercultural communication: Negotiating a grammar of culture.* Routledge.

Jahoda, G. (2012). Critical reflections on some recent definitions of "culture". *Culture & Psychology, 18*(3), 289–303. https://doi.org/10.1177/1354067X1 2446229.

Jordan, R. R. (2003). *Academic writing course study skills in English.* Pearson Education.

Lavanchy, A., Gajardo, A., & Dervin, F. (2011). Interculturality at stake. In F. Dervin, A. Gajardo, & A. Lavanchy (Eds.), *Politics of interculturality* (pp. 1–29). Cambridge Scholars Publishing.

Maton, K. (2014). A TALL order? Legitimation code theory for academic language and learning. *Journal of Academic Language and Learning, 8*(3), A34–A48.

McCarthy, M., & O'Dell, F. (2016). *Academic vocabulary in use*. Edition with Answers. Cambridge University Press.

McEnery, T., & Hardie, A. (2012). *Corpus linguistics: Method, theory and practice*. Cambridge University Press.

Minkov, M. (2012). *Cross-cultural analysis: The science and art of comparing the world's modern societies and their cultures*. Sage.

Parry, M. (2003). Transcultured selves under scrutiny: W(h)ither languages? *Language and Intercultural Communication, 3*(2), 101–107. https://doi.org/10.1080/14708470308668093.

Pilcher, N., & Richards, K. (2014). Deconstructing 'Mono'-lingualism: Considerations of value for 'English' 'language' education in a global setting. In L. T. Wong & A. Dubey-Jhaveri (Eds.), *English language education in a global world: Practices, issues and challenges* (pp. 81–90). Nova Science Publishers.

Pilcher, N., & Richards, K. (2016). The paradigmatic hearts of subjects which their 'English' flows through. *Journal of Higher Education Research and Development, 35*(5), 997–1010. https://doi.org/10.1080/07294360.2016.1138455.

Pilcher, N., & Richards, K. (2017). Challenging the power invested in the International English Language Testing System (IELTS): Why determining 'English' preparedness needs to be undertaken within the subject context. *Power and Education, 9*(1), 3–17. https://doi.org/10.1177/1757743817691995.

Pilcher, N., & Richards, K. (2018). What is the 'academic purpose' of 'English' in 'English for acadmeic purposes'? In L. T. Wong & W. L. H. Wong (Eds.), *Teaching and learning English for academic purposes: Current research and practices* (pp. 3–20). Nova Science Publishers.

Richards, K., & Pilcher, N. (2013). 'Discuss, analyse, define…non-traditional students come to terms with cultures of learning in the UK. In L. Jin & M. Cortazzi (Eds.), *Researching intercultural learning: Investigations in language and education* (pp. 135–151). Palgrave Macmillan.

Richards, K., & Pilcher, N. (2014). Contextualizing higher education assessment task words with an '*anti*-glossary' approach. *International Journal of Qualitative Studies in Education, 27*(5), 604–625. https://doi.org/10.1080/09518398.2013.805443.

Richards, K., & Pilcher, N. (2016). An individual subjectivist critique of the use of Corpus linguistics to inform pedagogical materials. *Dialogic Pedagogy Journal, Volume 4*. https://doi.org/10.5195/dpj.2016.163.

Richards, K., & Pilcher, N. (2018). Academic literacies: The word is not enough. *Teaching in Higher Education, 23*(2), 162–177. https://doi.org/10. 1080/13562517.2017.1360270.

Richards, K., & Pilcher, N. (2019). How a view of language underpins approaches to supporting higher education students that facilitate neo-liberalism, and how to resist this. *Power and Education, 11*(1), 51–68. https://doi.org/10.1177/1757743818811801.

Richards, K., & Pilcher, N. (2020a). Study skills: Neoliberalism's perfect Tinkerbell. *Teaching in Higher Education*. https://doi.org/10.1080/135 62517.2020.1839745.

Richards, K., & Pilcher, N. (2020b). Using physical objects as a portal to reveal academic subject identity and thought. *The Qualitative Report, 25*(1), 127–144. ISSN 1052—0147.

Swales, J. (1990). *Genre analysis: English in academic and research settings*. Cambridge University Press.

Swales, J., & Feak, C. (2004). *Academic writing for graduate students: Essential tasks and skills*. University of Michigan Press.

Trompenaars, F., & Hampden-Turner, C. (2011). *Riding the waves of culture: Understanding diversity in global business*. Nicholas Brealey International.

Tseng, P., & Richards, K. (2020). Measuring the effectiveness of English medium shipping courses. *Maritime Business Review*, ahead of print. https://doi.org/10.1108/mabr-10-2019-0042.

Tseng, P. H., Richards, K., & Pilcher, N. (2018). Constructing English medium instruction indicators in the shipping courses of Taiwan's higher education. *Maritime Business Review, 3*(1), 20–35. https://doi.org/10.1108/MABR-07-2017-0020.

Young, T., & Sercombe, P. (2010). Communication, discourses and intercultur-ality. *Language and Intercultural Communication, 10*(3), 181–188. https://doi.org/10.1080/14708470903348523.

Zhou, V. X., & Pilcher, N. (2018). Intercultural competence as an inter-subjective process: A reply to essentialism. *Language and Intercultural Communication, 18*(1), 125–143. https://doi.org/10.1080/14708477.2017. 1400510.

Zhu, H. (2015). Negotiation as way of engagement in intercultural and Lingua Franca communication: Frames of reference and interculturality. *Journal of English as a Lingua Franca, 4*(1), 63–90. https://doi.org/10.1515/jelf-2015-0008.

11

Conclusion: Interculturality and the English Language Classroom—Intercultural Approaches and Moving Forward

Chittima Sangiamchit and Mabel Victoria

This volume highlights the role of interculturality in the English language classroom. Different approaches to interculturality in English language teaching and learning in various global contexts have been elaborated and thought-provoking questions have been raised in the nine chapters, for instance, 'Is it worth emphasizing the importance of the interculturality concept for language teacher education? If you teach global issues in your English language classes, which techniques and strategies do you think are appropriate for teaching global issues and skills? What challenges are there in implementing activities with a global citizenship orientation? What skills should pupils develop and in what areas of knowledge? Do current practices and materials foster an interculturality that will serve students in their educational goals? What changes

C. Sangiamchit (✉)
University of the Thai Chamber of Commerce (UTCC), Bangkok, Thailand
e-mail: chittima_san@utcc.ac.th

M. Victoria
Edinburgh Napier University, Edinburg, UK

© The Author(s), under exclusive license to Springer Nature Switzerland AG 2021
M. Victoria and C. Sangiamchit (eds.), *Interculturality and the English Language Classroom*, https://doi.org/10.1007/978-3-030-76757-0_11

283

in classroom practice could be made to better foster critical interculturality? What intercultural activities create authentic learning spaces for learners in EFL contexts?

The contributors of the volume grappled with these questions and offered their views based on their own local, specific praxis. What the readers of the collection take away will depend on their own contexts and the resources available to them.

In this concluding chapter, we offer our reflection on future directions with regards to policy, practices and research with a view to integrating interculturality in the English language classroom.

Major Challenges and Practical Approaches in Integrating Interculturality in English Language Teaching

Global connectivity due to a multitude of factors such as mobility, technological advancement and international education has highlighted the urgency of incorporating interculturality alongside English language fluency. In English medium instruction, it is a widely acknowledged fact that intercultural competence is important in order to enable students to interact successfully across multiple communities from the local to the global (Baker & Fang, 2019). When we started working on the volume, we were very aware that there is a lack of empirical studies that examine the applicability of interculturality in English language classrooms around the world. Most of the discussions have been at the theoretical level as pointed by Holmes and Dervin (2016), Byram et al. (2017), Fang and Baker (2018), Baker (2018) and Baker and Fang (2019). Therefore, as stated in the Introduction, the collected chapters have been written with this in mind. The contributors, drawing from their own situated knowledge and experiences have attempted to connect the rich theorizing in the field of the intercultural with the pedagogical. In other words, what the authors did was to ask themselves specific questions on how to enrich the praxis of English language teaching by transforming theories into practice.

After extracting the essence of each of the contributions, several themes come to the fore. One overarching issue is an orientation of national curricula towards the complexity and diversity in the use of the English language (see Chapters 2, 4 and 6). Svarstad in Chapter 2, for example, indicates that the new curriculum guidelines in Denmark have explicitly highlighted culture as complex and dynamic. Pfingsthorn, Czura, Kramer and Štefl in Chapter 4, points out that the cultural and linguistic diversity have been advocated in the Common European Framework of Reference for Languages (CEFR) which can illuminate role of interculturality towards foreign language teaching in the Polish, German and Czech contexts. This framework of the Council of Europe has been also mentioned by Abid in Chapter 5. However, Abid notes that intercultural citizenship and intercultural competence have not yet figured in the English language curriculum in the Tunisian context. The influence of CEFR is also visible in the Norwegian national curriculum in terms of intercultural competence development which aims to promote greater interaction, understanding and respect between interlocutors with different backgrounds (see Chapter 6 by Murray). Considering the evidence of how the intercultural has been given prominence in these ELT contexts, we suggest that there is indeed a growing awareness in many countries of the importance of interculturality. We see this as an important move in the right direction. The challenge then is for policy makers and governmental institutions to see it not as an end in itself but just a beginning. We argue that any changes in the curricula that combine intercultural and English language competence need to be accompanied by practical support in terms of resources and training for the practitioners—otherwise, it might be just 'lip service'. Requiring English teachers to embrace interculturality without equipping them with the right textbooks and materials will likely lead to confusion and impoverished pedagogical contexts.

Chapters 3, 5, 6 and 7 raise relevant issues related to teaching materials. In this regard, Abid in Chapter 5, for example, evaluates ELT's textbook "Skills for Life" for developing intercultural citizenship competences in Tunisian context. It is argued that the target culture, international cultures, the learners' own and global dimension should be part of textbooks in order to foster learners' awareness of these issues and develop global skills (Byram, 2008; Cates, 2000). As such, well-designed globally oriented textbooks should help connect learners to the rest of the world and develop their intercultural skills in the classroom (Byram, 2008; Cates, 2002). However, the textbook analyzed is found to present imbalanced different cultural representation, focusing more on native English varieties (e.g. American English and British English) but lacking the learners' cultures and limiting range of global issues. This reflects a lack of variety and inadequacy of contents and activities on textbooks which could limit learners' sufficient opportunities to acquire intercultural and/or global skills (Byram, 2008).

The influence of American culture has been found to exert a major influence in textbooks covering a range of topics, such as food, clothing, housing and wedding (see Chapter 7). The essentialist view of culture is depicted in the form of American culture in diverse situations. Interculturality is, therefore, still largely absent from adult ESOL scholarship and classrooms in the US. As stated in the Introduction, nation-based large culture approach can still be useful but it has to acknowledge other conceptualizations of culture. In Chapter 6 which explores the roles of EFL textbooks in intercultural competence development in Norwegian schools the author finds that teachers are somehow left on their own initiative to educate themselves regarding the different aspects of interculturality in textbooks. They have to assess which ones should be used in order to provide students' access to different thoughts, ideas and perspectives. While this is empowering, this might be demotivating for pre-service and new teachers who need more guidance on how to extend knowledge provided in textbooks.

Indeed, the contributors provide evidence to show that pedagogical materials do not correspond to the new and complex realities that students encounter in their every life as global users of English. The English language textbook is not quite related to the educational system and helpful for encouraging learners' intercultural competence due to the predominantly essentialist view of culture in the textbooks. To scaffold the learning, teachers need to supplement the essentialist view with non-essentialist notions of culture.

The limited intercultural knowledge of the student-teachers is another issue found in the study. As pointed out by Siqueira in Chapter 3, the student-teachers could not clearly articulate the term "interculturality". Despite their awareness of the global status of English and their teaching orientation to interculturality, their uncertainty of the intercultural concepts seem to restrict their competence in applying intercultural notions in their ELT.

Chapter 8 investigates the roles of English, specifically English as a Lingua Franca in interculturality in International Higher Education (IHE) of three universities in Thailand and Malaysia. Taylor underscores how interculturality interplays with nationality, language and identity. Despite the complex and fluid nature of interculturality, national culture is still used to categorize cultural groups. In IHE, English has played a crucial part as an important resource in interculturality. This chapter proposes it as a 'cultural franca' which is used as a useful resource of people from different cultures (e.g. nations, social groups) who share 'something' in common.

Ethnocentrism and ethnorelativism and their correlation with English learning experience were explored by Tajeddin and Alemi (see Chapter 9). They point out that the move from ethnocentrism to ethnorelativism is not linear. Rather, ethnorelativism requires intercultural input particularly in an interculturally limited EFL context like Iran. In other words, learning English does not equate with increased intercultural sensitivity. Interculturality comes with real live interaction with people from different lingua cultural backgrounds. Thus transition towards ethnorelativism can be encouraged through other supportive pedagogical resources, such as ELT textbooks, online communication and social networking in order to open students' eyes to diverse cultures and help develop their intercultural competence.

Students' learning experiences are further scrutinized in Chapter 10 by Pilcher and Richards. The contributors propose that EAP teaching needs to be ethnorelative and be able to accommodate different approaches for different subjects. In addition, they posit that other 'non-linguistic' approaches such as non-text visual or mathematical language, should yield students' understanding of their subject degrees and interculturality. Chapter 4 by Pfingsthorn, Czura, Kramer and Štefl investigated teachers' perspective towards the benefits of telecollaboration to interculturality. It questions if telecollaboration between EFL student and teachers in Germany, Poland and the Czech Republic is useful in enhancing their interculturality. The results show that interculturality is not perceived as an important marker of the student-teachers' professional identity; the teachers in the study did not fully embrace the intercultural benefits of telecollaborative exchanges.

Taking into consideration the issues and practical approaches to interculturality in different ELT contexts above, we outline our thinking in moving ELT forward in order to respond to the challenges of a highly interconnected, and linguistically/culturally diverse world. In the next section, we discuss implications with particular relevance to the teaching, learning and use of English.

Future Direction of Interculturality in the English Language Classroom

This section aims to propose future directions for policy, practices and research for helping both policy makers and practitioners to integrate interculturality in their ELT.

It is widely recognized that the notion of cultural and linguistic diversity has been importantly advocated in the field of European foreign language education (see Chapters 2, 4, 5 and 6) and intercultural competence has inevitably become an important element in ELT classroom. As Council of Europe (2001, p. 2) states, "the rich heritage of diverse languages and cultures in Europe is a valuable common resource to be protected and developed, and that a major educational effort is needed to convert that diversity from a barrier to communication into a source of mutual enrichment and understanding". With this in mind, educational policy makers in any contexts need to actively integrate 'interculturality' into ELT curriculum. Importantly, the notion should not only pay attention to the supranational level, such as in the CEFR, but also on national and institutional level (Chapter 4). Svarsad proposes this point in Chapter 2 emphasizing that the curriculum must be based on non-essentialist approaches for cultural learning in order to equip learners with broader understandings of interculturality. Curriculums need to be designed with a focus on the international and multicultural aspects

(Nault, 2006). Intercultural curriculum can provide a useful guideline to teachers about what skills should students develop, in what areas of knowledge and how to promote intercultural knowledge and competence in a classroom. In this way, intercultural curriculum can foster and develop both teachers' and learners' intercultural competence. In other words, there should be a stronger push to include non-essentialist notions of culture, culture that does not stop at borders.

In response to the development of the ELT curriculum, syllabus, textbooks and materials selection should be designed to meet the curriculum guidelines. Considering firstly at a syllabus design, it is important to cover broader understandings of interculturality and include components developing pedagogical skills for intercultural competence. That is to say, intercultural concepts in the syllabus should be made clear beforehand, framing what interculturality is and what intercultural themes and aspects should be focused on. Given the fact that there are a myriad of terms and concepts of interculturality (e.g. Baker, 2015; Dervin, 2016; Zhu, 2015), unclear guidelines in the syllabus could make tasks more difficult and confusing for teachers. Chapter 3 provides evidence regarding how uncertainty among practitioners, negatively impact on the pedagogy. Although the participants are aware of the importance of interculturality in teaching, they lack confidence in applying it. Therefore, we suggest a more detailed and conceptually clear ELT syllabus to provide clear guidance for teachers. An unambiguous ELT syllabus can also stimulate teachers' interest and commitment to developing students' intercultural competence. Curricular support and suitable textbook materials, for example (Young & Sachdev, 2011), need to be borne in mind in relation to syllabus design to promote students' engagement in intercultural themes. Svarstad suggests in Chapter 2 that students should be empowered to find intercultural topics of their interests. A syllabus design which is drawn on and cover critical intercultural communication has potential to foster engagement in complex understandings of intercultural communication and therefore meet the new curriculum demands.

Textbooks that are largely based on native English varieties favour an essentialist view of culture. It is not surprising because most textbooks are produced by a handful of publishers privileging American and

British publishers such as Cambridge, Oxford and Longman (Jindap-itak & Boonsuk, 2018) which potentially convey views, values, atti-tudes, knowledge and experiences of their own English-speaking society. Considering the current global realities of English use, the textbooks which present only a narrowly based view of native English cultures fall short of accurately presenting intercultural aspects and linguistic land-scapes of English communication among people from different lingua cultural background. We would argue that textbooks' contents and activ-ities play a critical role in developing learners' knowledge of global skills and raising their awareness about interculturality (Chapter 5). (Byram, 2008; Wagner & Byram, 2017), Teaching materials should embody texts and tasks loaded with intercultural concepts and activities. Well-designed and globally oriented textbooks should be therefore selected to provide learners a variety of global knowledge, connect them to the world and as consequence, develop their intercultural skills. An intercultural diversity-friendly textbook could advocate learners to explore, compare and reflect intercultural dimensions through what they learn. English learning mate-rials which represent cultural diversity could be alternative pedagogies with higher responsiveness for today's interculturality in ELT which are no longer about inner-circle convention and cultures but rather about effective multi-context intercultural communication (Rose & Galloway, 2019).

Apart from textbooks as a way to promote interculturality and achieve the goals of ELT syllabus and curriculum, online materials is another useful and accessible. Marcoccia claims that the Internet can be consid-ered as a medium of intercultural communication which fosters inter-cultural exchanges in foreign languages. It offers a broad multicultural arena of cultural diversity where people from different linguacultural backgrounds use English for intercultural communication and thus, they come into contact with a myriad of local languages and cultures. Online learning has been extensively used in intercultural education and effec-tively brought intercultural aspects into the classroom (Bueno-Alastuey & Kleban, 2016; Kohn & Hoffstaedter, 2017). Telecollaboration is one tool for enhancing interculturality and professional development (Chapter 4). Social media such as Facebook and Twitter can open up learners' opportunity in intercultural engagement. Online Video Conference, such as WebEx, Zoom and Google Meet alternatively support a discussion between teachers and students as well as among the students themselves, regardless of geographic location. To implement an interculturally oriented syllabus and curriculum in ELT through online channels in classroom activities, the teachers need to bring interesting global topics for the students' learning and discussion. This could present them with opportunities to not only explore new knowledge about global issues around the world, but also to develop their critical thinking skills and raise their intercultural awareness.

Intercultural language pedagogy and teacher professional development is another important point of reflection raised by the contributors in this volume. We suggest that in some contexts, unclear guidelines in ELT curriculum can present teachers a number of challenges going beyond cultural facts (Kearney, 2016) and other controversial issues related to cultural diversity. Teachers are often required to engage with new and challenging ideas about interculturality. However simply drawing from their own personal cultural knowledge and pedagogy are not enough to equip them to decide on suitable topics and contents for students. Instead, they need to become active learners and ready to change their conception to foster effective pedagogical practices as well as make students become competent intercultural speakers. Therefore, there is a strong need to provide a training and/or educational programmes for teachers to offer them a comprehensive instruction on both theoretical and practical aspects that help them design and implement concepts, techniques and strategies for teaching interculturality in their classroom. By supporting teachers through professional development programmes, they will hopefully feel more confident in applying the notions of interculturality in their teaching. This inevitably will help improve students' intercultural learning.

Conclusion and Moving Forward

A key message from all the contributions in this volume is that "interculturality is an important aspect of English communication and ELT practitioners have the difficult task of incorporating it in their praxis".

The authors argue for the importance of interculturality by focusing on different key issues in complex and diverse educational contexts. This volume provides readers with critical insights into the theoretical and practical approaches in global contexts.

To reiterate, we recommend the following actions should be made in order to effectively foster interculturality in ELT and equip learners'with knowledge and skills for their communication in the wider world. First, the development of ELT curriculum and a clear syllabus design are required to enable policy makers and administrators to identify explicit focus relevant to interculturality. Second, textbooks as interculturally based should incorporate non-essentialist views of culture and thus a move away from native English varieties but instead look at diverse and complex global cultures in order to prepare learners for effective multi-context intercultural communication. Third, online platforms should be another space for learners to further develop their interculturality in addition to textbooks. With the ubiquitous presence of social media and VDO conference platforms today, both teachers and students constantly expose to the media while there are many different global issues on these platforms, which could be useful for students' intercultural learning, and communicative channels among people from different first language and cultures. This electronic channel, therefore, could be additionally useful intercultural resources for the students' intercultural learning. Finally, teacher professional development is much needed to enhance up-to-date intercultural skills of the teachers themselves and improve their teaching quality.

We hope that the recommended all issues demonstrated in this volume will reflect ELT situations hitherto and help the readers examine their own contexts. We propose that ELT pedagogies should be reconceptualized, reworked and redesigned in a coherent process from the top (national educational policy, curriculum and syllabus) to the practical (teaching and learning). Teaching interculturality is a challenging task as it involves complex, diverse and fluid nature of myriad language and cultures. We do hope all the issues raised and recommended implications in this volume will be useful for ELT readers to adapt and apply in their local contexts. If you can answer some questions raised at the beginning of this chapter and also feel you can make a difference even just within the walls of your ELT classroom, after reflecting on the practices of the contributors in this volume, then the book will have achieved its purpose.

References

Baker, W. (2015). *Culture and identity through English as a Lingua Franca: Rethinking concepts and goals in intercultural communication.* De Gruyter Mouton.

Baker, W. (2018). English as a lingua franca and intercultural communication. In J. Jenkins, W. Baker, & M. Dewey (Eds.), *The Routledge handbook of English as a Lingua Franca* (pp. 25–36). Routledge.

Baker, W., & Fang, F. (Gabriel). (2019). *From English language learners to intercultural citizens: Chinese student sojourners' development of intercultural citizenship in ELT and EMI programmes.* ELT Research Paper. British Council.

Bueno-Alastuey, M. C., & Kleban, M. (2016). Matching linguistic and pedagogical objectives in a telecollaboration project: A case study. *Computer Assisted Language Learning, 29*(1), 148–166. https://doi.org/10.1080/095 88221.2014.904360

Byram, M. (2008). *From foreign language education to education for intercultural citizenship.* Multilingual Matters.

Byram, M., Golubeva, I., Han, H., & Wagner, M. (2017). *From principles to practice in education for intercultural citizenship. Bristol.* Multilingual Matters.

Cates, K. A. (2000). Entry for 'Global Education.' In M. Byram (Ed.), *The Routledge encyclopedia of language teaching and learning* (pp. 241–243). Routledge.

Cates, K. A. (2002). Teaching for a better world: Global issues and language education. *Human rights education in Asian schools* (pp. 41–50).

Council of Europe. (2001). *Common European framework of reference for languages: Learning, teaching, assessment.* Cambridge University Press.

Dervin, F. (2016). *Interculturality in education: A theoretical and methodological toolbox.* Palgrave Macmillan.

Fang, F. (Gabriel), & Baker, W. (2018). 'A More Inclusive Mind towards the World': English language teaching and study abroad in China from intercultural citizenship and English as a Lingua Franca perspectives. *Language Teaching Research, 22*(5), 608–624.

Holmes, P., & Dervin, F. (2016). Introduction—English as a lingua franca and interculturality: Beyond orthodoxies. In P. Holmes & F. Dervin (Eds.), *The cultural and intercultural dimensions of English as a Lingua Franca* (pp. 1–30). Multilingual Matters.

Jindapitak, N., & Boonsuk, Y. (2018). Authoritative discourse in a locally-published ELT textbook in Thailand. *Indonesian Journal of Applied Linguistics, 8*(2), 265–277.

Kearney, E. (2016). *Intercultural learning in modern language education: Expanding leaning making potentials.* Multilingual Matters.

Kohn, K., & Hoffstaedter, P. (2017). Learner agency and non-native speaker identity in pedagogical lingua franca conversations: Insights from intercultural telecollaboration in foreign language education. *Computer Assisted Language Learning, 30*(5), 351–367. http://10.0.4.56/09588221.2017.130 4966.

Nault, D. (2006). Going global: rethinking culture teaching in ELT contexts. *Language, Culture and Curriculum., 19*(3), 314–328.

Rose, H., & Galloway, N. (2019). *Global Englishes for language teaching.* Cambridge University Press.

Wagner, M., & Byram, M. (2017). Intercultural Citizenship. In Y. Y. Kim & K. L. McKay (Eds.), *The international encyclopaedia of intercultural communication* (pp. 1–6). Wiley-Blackwell.

Young, T. J., & Sachdev, I. (2011). Intercultural communicative competence: Exploring English language teachers' beliefs and practices. *Language Awareness, 20*(2), 81–98. https://doi.org/10.1080/09658416.2010.540328.

Zhu, H. (2015). Negotiation as a way of engagement in intercultural and Lingua Franca communication: Frames of reference and interculturality. *Journal of English as a Lingua Franca, 4*(1), 63–90.

Index